REFUGEES, CAPITALISM AND THE BRITISH STATE

Vickers has written a stimulating book, casting a Marxist lens on the policies with which the British state has sought to control and contain the demands of asylum seekers. Vickers' original research highlights the strengths and dignity within which asylum seekers and refugees seek to resist their subjugation as unpaid voluntary workers or marginalised low-paid labour and carve out a life in a society that cares little for them. Their capacity to look after each other stands in impressive contrast to the state's indifference. This is a book all anti-racist practitioners and students ought to read.

Lena Dominelli, The University of Durham, UK

Vickers' book makes an original, stimulating and thoughtful contribution, applying a familiar analysis in a new context. What marks this out from other literature regarding refugees and immigration more generally, is his use of Marxist theory to situate the discussion. Illuminated by rich local case material, this will be thought-provoking for a wide range of professional workers, not just advocates for refugees.

Gary Craig, Wilberforce Institute, UK

This is an informed and trenchant analysis of the role of the British state in shaping the experiences of refugees. Drawing on detailed new research and theoretical reflection it is indispensable reading for those interested in a deeper understanding of the changing position of refugees in contemporary societies.

John Solomos, City University London, UK

Dedicated to the lives and struggles of all those who are denied basic rights in Britain because of their country of birth or heritage.

Together we are stronger.

Refugees, Capitalism and the British State
Implications for Social Workers, Volunteers and Activists

TOM VICKERS
Durham University, UK

Routledge
Taylor & Francis Group

LONDON AND NEW YORK

First published 2012 by Ashgate Publishing

Published 2016 by Routledge
2 Park Square, Milton Park, Abingdon, Oxfordshire OX14 4RN
711 Third Avenue, New York, NY 10017, USA

First issued in paperback 2016

Routledge is an imprint of the Taylor & Francis Group, an informa business

British Library Cataloguing in Publication Data
Vickers, Tom.
  Refugees, capitalism and the British state : implications for social workers, volunteers and activists.
  1. Refugees – Government policy – Great Britain. 2. Refugees – Legal status, laws, etc. – Great Britain. 3. Racism – Political aspects – Great Britain. 4. Great Britain – Race relations. 5. Social capital (Sociology) – Great Britain. 6. Refugees – Services for – Great Britain. 7. Capitalism – Social aspects – Great Britain. 8. Communism and society.
  I. Title
  323.6'31'0941-dc23

Library of Congress Cataloging-in-Publication Data
Vickers, Tom, 1982–
  Refugees, capitalism and the British state : implications for social workers, volunteers and activists / by Tom Vickers.
    p. cm.
  Includes bibliographical references and index.
  ISBN 978-1-4094-4152-6 (hbk. : alk. paper)
  1. Refugees –Services for – Great Britain. 2. Immigrants – Services for – Great Britain. 3. Social service – Great Britain. I. Title.
  2012022752
  362.870941--dc23

                                                                                2012022752

ISBN 13: 978-1-138-27308-5 (pbk)
ISBN 13: 978-1-4094-4152-6 (hbk)

Contents

List of Tables

Acknowledgements

Many thanks to all the people who took part in the research that informs this book, for their time, energy and insights, and for sharing their experiences and perspectives. Thanks also to the organisations who helped to put me in touch with their volunteers and gave me access to their records; to Tyne and Wear Archives and Museums and Newcastle City Council for access to various documents; to my supervisors, Lena Dominelli and Sarah Banks, for giving me time amongst their hectic schedules and for their thoroughness and critical comments; to my wife, Annie, for her constant support; to my parents, Bob and Lyrrie, for their tireless enthusiasm; to Tina for her comments on dysconscious racism and Ann for her detailed comments on my draft; and to Carolyn, Lianne, Michael and all the other staff at Ashgate for their work in bringing the book to fruition. Last, but by no means least, I would like to thank my comrades and fellow activists, for sharing the work which has done so much to shape my understanding.

Chapter 1
Introduction

During the first years of the twenty-first century, refugees, as I define all those who seek asylum,[1] have arrived in Britain with backgrounds often including trauma, abuse and health problems. These have been compounded within Britain by factors, mostly driven by the British state, including destitution, periodic detention, and the constant psychological stress of threatened deportation to situations of extreme danger. According to the values considered by many to be fundamental to professions such as social work, community development and youth work, this should call for urgent intervention. However, at the same time workers have increasingly found opportunities to make such interventions being closed to them. The policy approach of recent Labour governments has been characterised as a split approach, combining strategies of forceful assimilation with punitive segregation. This includes, in the case of asylum seekers, removal of rights to many mainstream welfare services, a prohibition on paid work, and forced dispersal across Britain (Humphries 2004: 101; Prior 2006: 7). Despite enjoying greater formal freedom than statutory services, voluntary sector projects have also come under growing funding pressures in relation to work with asylum seekers (Fell 2004). It has been argued that social workers are not only providing inadequate support for migrants, but are increasingly playing 'a role of constriction and punishment' (Humphries 2004: 93–4), and acting as gatekeepers separating vulnerable people from vital resources (Hayes 2005: 191–2; also Briskman and Cemlyn 2005; Morris 2007; Valtonen 2008).

However, little has been done to analyse these conditions and demands in the wider context of contemporary British capitalism and the British state. Where the wider context has been considered with a critical eye, consideration has generally not moved any closer to the coalface of practice than evaluating national and international policy (e.g. Back et al. 2002; Craig 2007a; Hoogvelt 2007; a notable exception is the combination of practice case studies with broad structural considerations in Dominelli 1997). This leaves a large and significant hole in the literature. Whose interests does the British state represent? Why are refugees being treated so poorly, even when they have frequently brought skills

---

1   Due to the inherent mistrust and stigmatisation which has become implicit in the term 'asylum seeker' (Dummet 2001), instead of the official categories of 'refugee', 'asylum seeker' and 'refused asylum seeker', I use 'refugee' to encompass all those who have come to Britain seeking refuge, whatever the status currently accorded them by the British state (as does Williams 2006), and where relevant specify whether an individual is with or without 'status' in the sense of some form of leave to remain in Britain.

which are in short supply and in demand by the local economy? (a question raised by Dumper 2002, Phillimore and Goodson 2006 and Bloch 2007, among others). In what ways and to what extent do refugees consent to their treatment? What is the relationship between the interests of refugees and other groups of service users? These questions demand answers if social workers and other practitioners are to successfully navigate their role, and this book sets out to provide these through a Marxist analysis.

The Combination of Empirical Qualitative Data with a Marxist Analysis

Today, in a period of economic crisis, public sector cuts and escalating class struggle, Marxism remains largely forgotten, but offers important tools for social workers and service users to understand the structures of oppression they face and devise effective means of resistance. This book sets out to reclaim lost insights of Marxism and reinterpret them in the current context. It does this by focussing on one particular section of the international working class, refugees and asylum seekers in Britain. The analysis of this particular section demonstrates the more general utility of a Marxist approach, enabling an exploration of the interplay between state policies, how these are experienced by their subjects, and how conflicts are mediated. The approach taken owes much to Williams et al. (1979). The substantive focus of the book is twofold: to analyse the material basis of the oppression of refugees in Britain by the British state; and to examine the means by which the British state has 'managed' this oppression through the cultivation of a 'refugee relations industry', within a broader narrative of 'social capital building'. A central concern within this critique is the role played by those refugees and asylum seekers who perform key roles, often unpaid, within the refugee relations industry. The book weaves together theoretical insights from classical and contemporary Marxism, the recent history and literature on refugee flight and settlement in Britain, and empirical data which draws on research I conducted in Newcastle between 2005 and 2010. This included a mapping exercise of organisations active in Newcastle between 1962 and 2008 which explicitly related to migrants or ethnic minority people, of which three organisations were investigated in more detail as historical case studies, and five as contemporary case studies. A search of local archives was combined with in-depth qualitative interviews with 12 paid workers across these eight organisations and with eighteen refugees working as volunteers with four of the five contemporary case study organisations. This research enabled an exploration of the impacts, of the life histories, understandings and agency among those policies target, on the outcomes of policies and practices (a more detailed description of the methodology including descriptions of the case studies is included as an appendix).

The Wider Relevance of this Book

The questions raised above are not new; neither are they unique to refugees and those who seek to engage with them. Social workers and related practitioners have always had to struggle with the contradiction between a duty of care and a mission of social control (OU 1978b: 41). In many cases this has been particularly acutely felt where the same individual has been both a member of a target user group and fulfilling a practitioner role. For example, Ahmad (1993) recounts the pressures and expectations placed on black social workers, while Sawbridge and Spence (1991) discuss the issues faced by women in community and youth work roles. The loose collection of voluntary and community sector organisations which form the 'refugee sector' have been reliant on the work of refugees themselves for a long time, many in unpaid roles. As a part of the rapid expansion of the sector over the last decade, as refugees were 'dispersed' around Britain following policy changes in 1999, this has developed in new and sometimes unexpected ways. In the present context of economic crisis and wholesale cuts to both the public sector and voluntary and community funding, it seems likely that many other organisations will be forced to follow the same pattern, falling back on unpaid labour of community members as funding is withdrawn and unmet needs increase. While focussing on the position and experiences of refugees, this book therefore offers important lessons to much wider circles of practitioners and community activists. Likewise, while the book focuses on the distinctive approaches employed by Labour governments between 1997 and 2010 to manage refugees' oppression, I draw lines of continuity both backwards into the history of British welfare and its relationship to different forms of migration, and forwards to the Conservative–Liberal Democrat Coalition's concept of the 'Big Society'.

Distinctive features of Newcastle also need to be taken into account when considering the wider relevance of the research this book draws on. These include the city's relative physical isolation from other urban centres, with 'the Cheviot Hills to the north, Pennines to the west, North Sea to the east and a great swathe of farmland between the north east of England and Yorkshire' (Robinson 1988: 189), and longstanding deprivation relative to other parts of Britain (Robinson 1988: 194–6). Formerly a centre of shipbuilding and related industries, these industries have been in long-term decline, which accelerated in the 1960s and into the 1970s. It is an area commonly thought of as virtually 'monocultural' until very recently (e.g. Robinson 1988: 190), although this leaves out a history of migration stretching back hundreds of years (MacDermott 1977; Lawless 1995; Archive Mapping and Research Project 2007; Renton 2007). These features need to be considered when comparing the detailed accounts of Newcastle with other parts of Britain, and have required a moderate level of detail on the local situation in order to aid the reader in contextualising the accounts of refugees and others which are quoted in this book.

Forced Migration in Context: 'Capitalism *is* Crisis'

To understand the process by which people arrive in Britain as refugees, we need to consider the particular international context in which millions of people every year are forced to migrate, whether through 'crippling destitution, war or persecution' (Hayes 2005: 185). The remainder of this chapter outlines the key features of a Marxist analysis of the current international situation, including the division of the world into oppressed and oppressor nations, the impetus towards inter-imperialist rivalry and war, and the implications of this for migration to Britain, including gender dimensions. The functioning of an 'international reserve army of labour' is illustrated using historical and contemporary data at local and national levels, interwoven with theoretical reflections. As the receiving country under investigation, particular attention is paid here to Britain's relations to the situations refugees flee. This sets the context for the relation of interests between refugees and the British ruling class, and the state policies which follow from this, discussed in Chapter 2.

The Roots of the Capitalist Crisis

In recent years, the international crisis of capitalism, which has been building since the 1960s, has come to public prominence. Beginning with the subprime mortgage crisis in 2007, major banks wrote down debts by massive amounts, removing swathes of fictitious wealth from the global economy. This had knock-on effects throughout the international banking system, with mechanisms of commercial credit collapsing one after another (Palmer 2008: 3). This represented a serious failure of a key measure by which ruling classes had been able to put off or to mitigate capitalism's underlying tendencies to crisis since the period of post-war rebuilding in the 1940s and 1950s, with a seemingly endless extension of credit pursued by the most economically advanced capitalist countries. The credit system expanded to encompass an entire 'shadow banking' system including unregulated institutions such as hedge funds and private equity, and accounting for large parts of the international economy with what amounts to gambling on an international scale. By 2005 the US was spending 6.4 per cent of GDP more than it was earning, leading to a rising net debt to the rest of the world, estimated at $2.55 trillion at the end of 2005 (Yaffe 2006: 9). The series of 'bail-outs' since then – in other words massive injections of cash into the financial system by the state – did not resolve the crisis, but only postponed some of its worst consequences. The bail-outs will have massive and sustained consequences for large sections of the working and middle classes in many countries, including Britain, as the money paid out by the state is clawed back through significant reductions in the public sector, including cutting essential services and redundancies for tens of thousands of state employees (Yaffe 2009b; HM Treasury 2010a, 2010b). Meanwhile, the underlying problems in the capitalist system, which the expansion of credit played a role in covering over, remain, as evidenced by the ongoing debt crisis in the

Eurozone as of summer 2012, following further bail-outs of Ireland and Greece and devastating austerity programmes across Europe.

Well before the financial crisis of 2008, it was evident that capitalism was entering a crisis of serious proportions. Comparing the periods 1960–1980 and 1980–2000, world per capita income growth fell from an average of 3 per cent to 2 per cent, a significant fall given the numbers involved. In 54 out of 155 countries for which data is available, average incomes actually fell during the 1990s, and only thirty countries had annual income growth above the 3 per cent necessary to reduce poverty if inequality levels remained constant (Hoogvelt 2007: 24). By 2005, business investments in Britain were at the lowest level in relation to the rest of the economy since 1967, unemployment was at the highest level for three and half years, insolvencies were at record levels, mortgage repossessions at a thirteen-year high, and consumer debt stood at £1,160 billion, almost the size of Britain's GDP, and three times the level of the 1990s (Yaffe 2006: 10).

The crisis is fundamentally one of profitability. Marx identified that the rise in the organic composition of capital, that is fixed capital (the value of the means of production) relative to variable capital (the value of labour power), which results from technological development and capital accumulation, produces a *tendency* for the rate of profit to fall (Marx [1894] 2006). Strategies available to capitalists to counteract this tendency include increasing the total mass of profits, requiring new markets for the realisation of surplus value, and exporting capital from areas with a high organic composition of capital to those with a low composition (Kemp 1967: 27–8). It is therefore misleading to suggest, as Hoogvelt (2007: 19) does, that 'In the past, it was assumed not only by liberal economists but also those standing in the Marxist tradition, that the world market system (or capitalism) was inherently and *forever expansive* in character'. This characterisation of Marxist analysis ignores the understanding that, while perpetual growth is *necessary* for capitalism to avert crises, history demonstrates that this expansion is uneven in space and time, and periodically breaks down (Grossman [1929] 1992). This produces conditions of crisis in the system, which in the recent period has been expressed in the phenomena of 'globalisation' (Yaffe 2000).

A key feature of globalisation has been increasingly rapid international movements of capital in search of new sources of profit, which have facilitated the growth in size and power of multinational companies exerting monopoly power (UNCTAD 2007; Felices et al. 2008). Lenin ([1916] 1975) identified a tendency within capitalism, accentuated at times of crisis, for enterprises to both combine together (Lenin [1916] 1975: 18–20), and be bought up by large banks, resulting in an increased ability to compete with other firms through a monopoly position, and the distribution of profits over a smaller amount of capital (Lenin [1916] 1975: 52–3). This tendency was acutely expressed in the mergers and acquisitions boom of the late 1990s, where a large portion of the Foreign Direct Investment (FDI) investment between advanced capitalist countries represented the combination of existing capital rather than new 'greenfield' capital investment (UNCTAD 2001: xiii, 53). By 2002, in the automobile sector the top six multinational companies accounted for more than 75 per cent of the global market. In information technology hardware, the top three firms accounted for 71 per cent of the global supply of servers, two-fifths of the global sales of PCs and three-fifths of the global sales of mobile phones (Hoogvelt 2007: 23). This process has continued the tendency towards centralised ownership and control of capital in a handful of advanced capitalist countries, which, by dint of this, occupy an imperialist position within the wider system. Kundnani (2007) gives an articulate account of this process:

> ... under the auspices of 'globalisation' and the 'war on terror', multinational companies have assumed unfettered power over most of the world's national economies and Western governments have arrogated to themselves the right to openly intervene anywhere in the world. (Kundnani 2007: 2)

This is strikingly similar to the account provided by Lenin at the time of the First World War:

> A monopoly, once it is formed and controls thousands of millions, inevitably penetrates into every sphere of public life, regardless of the form of government and all other 'details'. (Lenin [1916] 1975: 55)

In 2008, five countries were together responsible for more than 50 per cent of accumulated outward stock of FDI, and ten countries were responsible for more than 70 per cent. Around 30 per cent of this stock was invested in materially underdeveloped countries (UNCTAD 2009: 251–4).

The increasing concentration of production has taken place together with the combination of banking and manufacturing capital into monopolistic 'finance capital', with banks controlling shares in many supposedly 'independent' companies, and interlocking with national governments (Lenin [1916] 1975: 44–8; Vincent 2005). Monopoly control of production by finance capitalists ensures monopoly returns on loans to other banks and companies, thus: 'With a stationary population, and stagnant industry, commerce and shipping, the [imperialist] "country" can grow rich by usury' (Lenin [1916] 1975: 51–2). Lenin observed that, while monopolies develop in response to capitalists' attempts to survive crises, their uneven development across different industries and countries increases the anarchy and tendency of the system towards crisis even further, in turn providing more pressure to combine into monopolies (Lenin [1916] 1975: 28–9). This has been evident over the last decade, where neo-liberal policies including deregulation of international movements of capital and finance have not only wrecked whole countries, but laid the foundations for the most severe crisis of the international financial system in a century (Yaffe 2009a). This crisis has contributed to a further destabilisation of the world, with increasingly aggressive attempts by the main imperialist states to advance their interests against their rivals in every corner of the world, squeezing oppressed countries ever tighter in their search for profits and increasingly resorting to direct military intervention: war. This has profound implications for the displacement of millions of people in oppressed countries.

Britain's Relation to Refugees' Countries of Origin: Capitalist Crisis and National Oppression

I use the concept of 'imperialism', not 'in the most general sense of the naked use of force to impose the will of major powers on smaller states' (Callinicos et al. 1994: 11), but rather to refer to a specific system, the current stage of capitalism. Within this system, states may employ a range of policies contingent on circumstances, of which the naked use of force is only one possible outcome. Some may argue against use of the term due to its politically-loaded character and prior assumptions. It may be responded that such objections merely serve to defend the interests and objectives of those people, processes and practices, which theories of imperialism seek to expose and critique, and therefore have no place blocking discussion (Kemp 1967: 1).

The establishment of capitalism in the nineteenth century required a massive accumulation of wealth in the capitalist centres, much of which was achieved through the extraction of wealth from areas such as India and the Caribbean through direct colonialism and uneven trade relations (Kemp 1967: 18–19). This was politically enforced through 'gun point diplomacy' and 'intellectually legitimised by racism' (Kyriakides and Virdee 2003: 285; also Kundnani 2007: 26–7). Under colonialism, uneven development and relationships of dependency between countries established an increasingly international division of labour. This expanded on British capitalism's earlier use of rural labourers forced off the land to work in the new industrial centres, to create an international reserve army of labour under constant pressure to move wherever capital had a use for them (Miles and Phizacklea 1987: 16–17, 142–3).

In the first decades of the twentieth century, Lenin ([1916] 1975: 16–17) observed the growth of industry and the concentration of production in ever-larger industries to be 'one of the most characteristic features of capitalism', tending towards increasingly uneven development between capital-intensive imperialist countries and underemployed oppressed countries, and constituting a distinct stage of capitalism as monopoly increasingly replaced free competition (Kemp 1967: 2). The fusion of banking and manufacturing capital into finance capital is a defining feature of the imperialist stage of capitalism. Imperialist finance capital is organised in companies whose operations are multinational but whose control and ownership remain concentrated in particular advanced capitalist countries, which become increasingly wealthy as a result of returns on capital invested in poor and less industrially-developed countries. This creates a situation that, at a high level of abstraction, can be characterised as a division of the world between imperialist, oppressor countries, where ownership and control of capital is concentrated, and oppressed, impoverished countries, whose economic development is held back and whose labour and resources are systematically plundered to the benefit of imperialist countries (Lenin [1916] 1975).

The characterisation of a division between imperialist and oppressed countries does not rule out the potential for oppressed countries to engage in antagonistic and oppressive relations with other oppressed countries, the movement of capital and labour to and from both oppressed and imperialist countries, or the existence of weaker and stronger imperialist countries. It does imply continuing relevance for the location of particular countries within the wider system, and a sustained division of the world into oppressed and oppressor nations. This involves relations of dependency between the two categories of countries on multiple levels, which set the context for modern patterns of migration, settlement, and the relation of refugees to the British state and to other sections of the working class in Britain.

In the last decades of the twentieth century, the imperialist character of capitalism intensified, taking on new and expansive forms. In many cases, the success of national liberation movements did not signal the end of oppression and exploitation on a national basis. While direct political control may have been conceded, control of economic resources was not. In many cases 'prime agricultural land, rights to mineral exploration and exploitation, and ownership of the mines remained firmly in the hands of large, multinational companies located in the West' (Kyriakides and Virdee 2003: 285). From the 1960s, rapid developments in technology and the organisation of communication and shipping combined with factors in many oppressed countries, such as freedom from environmental and planning controls, restrictions on union organisation, low wages, low health and safety standards, and lax controls on tax and repatriation of profits, to increase the profitability of international capital investment. This combination of factors contributed to a steady increase in capital outflows from Britain and other imperialist countries such as the United States (US) and Germany, towards oppressed countries (Cohen 2006: 155–7). In some areas, conditions for profitable investment were fostered through institutions such as the World Trade Organisation (WTO) and International Monetary Fund (IMF), in others through direct or indirect military intervention, in many cases operating alongside backing for authoritarian regimes, which were prepared and able to prevent resistance from disrupting production (Sivanandan 1991: 144–5), and the use of terrorism, assassination and destabilisation against 'uncooperative' states (Kundnani 2007).

Rates of return on investment in oppressed countries have played a crucial role in raising the average rate of profit and thereby generating the incentives to invest, which are necessary for continued capital circulation. Agreements by the governments of oppressed countries to allow the remittance of profits by investing multinationals has been observed as a key factor in decisions on where to invest. For example, of US$904.1 million earned from the Bauxite industry in Jamaica in 2004, only US$372.9 million was retained in Jamaica, the remainder going to the home countries of multinationals (Small 2007: 384). This represents a leaching of the national product from oppressed countries, the impact of which is accentuated by the differences in rates of return on investments in imperialist and oppressed countries. In 2005, Britain received an average rate of return of 5.0 per cent on investments in oppressed, materially underdeveloped countries, while countries investing in Britain received a rate of return of only 2.6 per cent. Similar differences appear for other imperialist countries. The difference in rates of return is such that Britain received a significant income from net debt in 2005; in other words, a greater amount of capital invested in Britain from abroad than Britain invested in other countries brought a net flow of profits into Britain (Whitaker 2006: 292–3). This represents super-exploitation, and a parasitic relationship, which is particularly pronounced for Britain. Between 1997 and 2007, Britain's overseas assets increased more than three times, reaching £6,357.9 billion in 2007, more than four and a half times Britain's GDP (Madden 2009: 17).

The parasitic nature of contemporary British capitalism becomes even clearer when we consider the changing division of labour between particular categories of productive and unproductive labour, with a massive restructuring of the economy away from manufacturing towards the service sector, and in particular the finance sector (Table 1.1).

Table 1.1   Change in numbers employed in Britain by sector, 1979–2005

Sector	% change in numbers employed
All sectors	+13.2%
Public services	+36.8%
Finance and business services	+111.0%
All services	+46.1%
Manufacturing	−52.3%

Source: Figures from Yaffe 2006: 9.

By 2008, Britain produced 2.9 per cent of world exports, following a steady decline which placed it ninth internationally (http://wto.org), and 3.1 per cent of global manufacturing output (UN Statistics Division). The British economy is now massively dependent on the international financial activities of the City of London, with financial and business services contributing a value added at basic prices of £397.9 billion in 2007, more than two and a half times that of British manufacturing. The contribution of distribution, hotels and catering also exceeds that of manufacturing (ONS 2009: 108–9). This massive wealth in the financial sector is not produced there, but flows through the sector from returns on loans and other investments. The wealth of the City of London is thus drawn to a significant extent from the mines of the Congo, the oil fields of Iraq and the sweatshops of Bangladesh, demonstrating the extent of Britain's imperialist parasitism on oppressed nations.

Added to the super-profits extracted from oppressed countries through direct and portfolio capital investments, additional profits are made by 'unofficial' means such as transfer pricing, unequal exchange, special tax regimes, fees, commissions and debt, channelled into Britain through the financial sector (Yaffe 2006). According to World Bank figures, the total external debt of 'low and middle income' countries increased by 67.8 per cent between 1999 and 2008, from $2,216 billion to $3,719 billion, despite these countries having paid back $4,293 billion over the same period (World dataBank). This shows how little debt cancellations under the Heavily Indebted Poor Countries and similar initiatives mean in practice, despite claims by imperialist governments suggesting these are acts of great benevolence. As a counterweight to the tendency of the rate of profit to fall as capital accumulates, the extraction of super-profits from oppressed countries is essential to capitalism's survival. That is, imperialism is not an option but a necessity for capital, and becomes increasingly so as the crisis worsens.

Inter-Imperialist Rivalries and War

The tendency for the rate of profit to fall contributes to intensified rivalries between imperialist countries, as they compete over increasingly important foreign sources of profit. Lenin's contemporary Karl Kautsky suggested that international cartels and other corporate amalgamations could be a force for peace, which followed logically from Kautsky's conception of imperialism as a mere policy. In response, Lenin pointeds to companies' tendency to turn to their own national governments for support in times of crisis and showed the cartels of his day to be transitory alliances based on a particular balance of forces, giving way as conditions changed to a renewed struggle along national lines (Kemp 1967: 73). Lenin ([1916] 1975: 79–82) describes the division and re-division of the world among the imperialist countries as fundamental to imperialism, driving both wars of colonial conquest and conflict between the imperialist powers themselves.

A hundred years after Kautsky and Lenin were writing, ownership and control of multinational companies continues to be concentrated overwhelmingly on a national basis, and they have their interests defended by their respective imperialist states. Pressures created by capitalist accumulation thus continue to necessitate competition on a national basis, ultimately leading to militarism and war (Kemp 1967: 58). Powerful economic interests have been linked to the invasions of Afghanistan in 2001 and Iraq in 2003, following which healthcare, water, electricity, oil, gas and mining in Afghanistan were all rapidly privatised and bought up by multinationals (Kundnani 2007: 102). Prior to the invasion of Iraq, its government had been making deals with China and Russia, and had begun to trade its oil in Euros. The jockeying that ensued between the major imperialist powers in the lead up to the war, rooted in strategic influence and opportunities for profit, underscored the continuing salience of inter-imperialist rivalries (Rayne 2003). In other cases, wars have not been carried out by imperialist states themselves, but by their proxies within oppressed countries. In the Democratic Republic of Congo

(DRC), a United Nations report in 2002 found that 'high level political, military and business networks are stealing the DRC's mineral resources, and by 2002, they had transferred at least $5 billion of assets from the state mining sector to private western companies, including 18 British firms such as Anglo American, DeBeers, Afrimex and Barclays Bank'. Under cover of the 'ethnic' conflict with Rwanda, exports of coltan, casserite, gold and diamonds increased five times, and fifteen flights a day were found to be leaving the DRC to transport these minerals to the European Union (EU) and US via Rwanda and South Africa (UN Security Council 2002; Kayembe 2006).

These contemporary rivalries are rooted in a fundamental shift in the relative economic strengths of the major imperialist powers, which has produced an imbalance between relative strengths in economic terms and in political and military terms (Table 1.2 gives a selection of indicators).

Table 1.2   Economic indicators for United States and European Union in 2008

	US	EU
% of Global GDP	23.4%	30.2%
% of Global Exports	9.3%	13.7%
% of Global FDI Accumulated Stock	19.5%	49.9%

Source: http://www.wto.org and UNCTAD 2009: 251.

The size of the EU economies present a clear challenge to US dominance, but these relative economic strengths have not yet been translated into a corresponding re-division of the world, and the US will do everything in its power to prevent such a re-division from happening. In the past, such re-divisions have only been achieved with horrific consequences for humanity. As Yaffe (2006: 9) says: 'It is important to remember that after the US replaced Britain as the strongest economic power, it took two world wars, the great depression and fascism before the US became the dominant global imperialist power'.

The crisis of the credit system, which has played a role in averting crises for the past 60 years, can only intensify these rivalries. On 23 January 2008, billionaire speculator George Soros predicted in the *Financial Times* (Asian edition) that the credit crisis would mark 'the end of an era of credit expansion based on the dollar as the international reserve currency', and have as its longer term consequences a:

> ... radical realignment of the global economy, with a relative decline of the US and the rise of China and other countries in the developing world. The danger is that the resulting political tensions, including US protectionism, may disrupt the global economy and plunge the world into recession or worse ... (cited in Palmer 2008: 3)

British Capitalism and the International Reserve Army of Labour

The first part of this chapter set the context within which migration to Britain takes place. We will now turn to the role of immigration itself within the imperialist system. Imperialism involves particular international divisions of labour, which both discriminate against and depend on the labour of workers from oppressed countries. In November 2009, then Prime Minister Gordon Brown announced plans to extend the period for which companies must advertise a post for British workers before offering it to migrants from two weeks to a month (Brown 2009). Even without such legal restrictions, in a survey across industries in the summer of 2009, 27 per cent of employers said they recruit migrants in order to fill jobs for which it is difficult to find British workers (CIPD 2009a: 10), suggesting a widespread preference for British workers. Yet this reduced preference for migrant labour in a period of crisis should not distract from its importance within imperialism at a systemic and historic level. Material underdevelopment of countries oppressed within imperialism has historically prevented these countries' domestic production from fulfilling their own populations' needs, thus simultaneously generating markets for imperialist exports, and maintaining a reserve army of labour for imperialist countries, which is necessary to allow for the fluctuations in demand for labour brought about by the contradictory tendencies of capitalism (Castells [1975] 2002; Miles 1987; Chinweizu and Jameson 2008).

It may be misleading to see a sharp distinction between refugees as 'forced migrants', and economic migrants as 'voluntary migrants'. We can speak of compulsion in migrant labour in the sense that 'the "sending" formation is characterised by structural unemployment and underemployment', which may leave some with economic migration as their only option for survival (Miles and Phizacklea 1980: 10). In many cases, foreign investment-driven development of export-oriented agriculture and manufacturing in materially underdeveloped countries has displaced rural workers from the land and at times has led to a restructuring of the labour force, by drawing more women into waged employment and creating rising unemployment among men even in periods of high growth, all contributing to the formation of an international labour pool of economically displaced people (Sassen 1988: 94–8). The collapse of socialism in Eastern Europe and the former Soviet Union massively increased the numbers and range of skills among this potential reserve army, with pressures to migrate including high unemployment, street homelessness, even among children, and an 'alarming rise in the rate of substance abuse, prostitution and criminality' (Hessle 2007: 356–7).

The economic underdevelopment of oppressed countries increases the importance of remittances by migrant workers as a source of foreign currency, further increasing the pressure on families to send members to work abroad, and for those abroad to send remittances, often putting up with worse conditions and sacrificing opportunities for advancement, such as longer term strategies of education or saving, in order to do so (Datta et al. 2007; Lindley 2009: 1326–8). These remittances, which in some cases exceed a country's foreign exchange earnings from merchandise exports, provide foreign currency to buy further imports, simultaneously maintaining the underdevelopment of domestic production in oppressed countries and the demand for exports from companies based in imperialist countries, reinforcing relations of dependency (Small 2007: 384–6). Attempts have recently been made to reconceptualise remittances by migrant workers, amounting to US$167 billion globally in 2005, as a means of supporting the development of sending countries, thus absolving more powerful parties from responsibility for development and poverty alleviation (Datta et al. 2007: 45–7). In the context of disparities in wealth between sending and receiving countries, remittances from low paid migrant workers may be understood as a subsidy to international capital: taking money from migrant workers' wages to help fund the maintenance of the labour power of family and friends in their country of origin, who are also members of the reserve army, whatever country they are employed in, and whether now or in the future.

While the above describes general trends, exact processes by which migration takes place in particular contexts are complex and various. For example, empirical investigation has suggested that major factors influencing Ethiopian migration to Europe since the 1970s have included the large increase in access to higher education in Ethiopia, which has not been accompanied by a similar increase in numbers of graduate jobs domestically, and the increasing integration of Ethiopia into the world economy, which has contributed to an increase in the idea of the superiority of European democracy and 'civilisation' (Tasse 2007: 344–5). The oppressed position of Ethiopia within the imperialist system has consequences for both of the causal factors highlighted above; facilitating a 'brain drain' of Ethiopia's graduates to imperialist countries' increasingly 'knowledge-based' workforces, and achieving the dominance of European values and prestige as a consequence of European imperialist countries' standards of living and multinational media apparatuses, which are possible on the basis of their dominant material position.

Within imperialist countries, the international reserve army of labour is used to undermine the bargaining power of the domestic working class even in situations of near full employment and cushion employers against shocks, while also enabling a higher rate of exploitation and profit through systematic discrimination, denial of rights and harassment of ethnic minority labour (Sivanandan 1974: 12; Castells [1975] 2002: 86–94; RCG 1979: 3). Migrant workers in low-skilled jobs frequently only have temporary rights to remain, insecure contractual arrangements, and experience exploitative practices including non-payment or underpayment of wages, unauthorised deductions, non-compliance with health and safety, long working hours and overcrowded, unsafe or otherwise unsuitable housing (Piper 2010: 111–12). The costs of the labour power of migrants to the ruling classes of imperialist countries is reduced by the subsidy to the costs of its reproduction paid by migrants' countries of origin, including in many cases the initial costs of training and education, and the costs of care during periods of non-productivity for capital in infancy and old age:

> They are not born: they are not brought up: they do not age: they do not get tired: they do not die. They have a single function – to work. All other functions of their lives are the responsibility of the country they come from. (Berger and Mohr 1975: 64)

In some cases, this translates into a direct wage difference, sometimes enacted through immigration controls. For example, in one West London food factory, workers reported a 70 pence difference in the hourly wage for those able to supply a national insurance number (Ahmad 2008: 864), while an independent audit of engineering construction work in the Midlands found migrants had been paid substantially below nationally agreed rates for the industry (GMB Press Release 2010). In addition to direct wages paid by an employer, compensation for labour under modern capitalism also consists of indirect or 'social' wages in the form of rights, protections, services, benefits, and so on, provided by the state. Importing labour with fewer rights of access to this 'social' part of the wage, who are also under pressure to accept lower monetary wages, both enables a faster rate of capital accumulation and relieves pressure to attack rights and wages of domestic workers, particularly where migrant labour can be secured on terms which allow migrants a temporary right to residence and few rights for dependents to join them (Freeman 1986: 55–6). On this point I concur with Freeman, but I differ when he goes on to argue that:

> Wide-spread migration has reduced the power of organized labor by dividing the working class into national and immigrant camps, by easing the tight labor market conditions that would have enhanced labor's strategic resources, and by provoking a resurgence of right-wing and nativist political movements. (Freeman 1986: 61)

The analysis Freeman presents here neglects the fact that workers are already divided by exploitation on a national basis, which is central to imperialism and lays the ground for chauvinist responses to migration by sections of the working class in imperialist countries.

It is not migration which divides workers and undermines the position of organised labour, but imperialism that creates a material split in the working class. Migration holds the potential to develop links between the workers of oppressed and imperialist countries, and in doing so to create the possibility of transforming the system. Workers from oppressed countries will only 'voluntarily' agree to play the role of super-exploited migrant labour while the material conditions of life available to most in their countries of origin are even poorer. The functioning of the international reserve army of labour is thus interdependent with the division of the world into oppressed and oppressor nations, and the two processes form mutually reinforcing elements of the wider system of imperialism. It is not inevitable that the response of workers in imperialist countries to migration will be a chauvinist, right-wing or 'nativist' one – they could instead make common cause with workers in oppressed countries and with migrants in their own, and throw themselves into overturning the system which divides and exploits them all. Whether this happens in a given situation is a political question, which will only be resolved in the course of struggle. This question will be returned to repeatedly through the rest of this book, in particular the element of state interventions which serve to impede such anti-capitalist unity from ever taking hold, as part of the management of oppression of the whole working class.

The Reserve Army and Immigration Controls

The 'post-nation state' view, put forward predominantly within a post-modernist framework and amply theorised by Hardt and Negri (2001), argues that developments in the last decades of the twentieth century, including successes of anti-colonial struggles and the collapse of the Soviet Union, together with technological advances, have resulted in a fundamentally new period, in which no state has genuine sovereignty, even within its own borders. Instead, they argue that we live in a globalised world ruled by 'a series of national and supranational organisms united under a single logic of rule', in which there are no oppressed or oppressor nations, but instead 'we continually find the First World in the Third, the Third in the First, and the Second almost nowhere at all' (Hardt and Negri 2001: xi–xiii). Within this view the speed of air travel and instantaneous electronic communications have compressed time and space, allowing an unprecedented movement and inter-permeation of people and cultures around the world: 'Once nearly impermeable borders are now open to cultural influences; people can migrate and/or engage in political protest, more than ever before' (Richmond 2002: 708). This view represents a clear class standpoint. It has been observed elsewhere that positions of power within social structures may enable certain individuals to move freely across boundaries between classed and racialised areas, viewing these categories as welcome 'diversity' rather than oppressive (Byrne 2002: 22–3). If this is true within a British city, it is even more so internationally.

Barber and Lem (2008: 4) point to the way in which borders in the current international context are marked by class and nation, with a freedom for capital to move across borders, while the movement of workers from oppressed countries continues to be heavily regulated. Privileged western academics may find borders 'porous' when they travel to give a lecture or join a protest in another country. For the majority of the world's people, however, this is not the reality they face. Instead the majority of migrants from oppressed countries face a very un-porous and expanding repressive apparatus of border police, reporting regimes, tagging, immigration prisons and mass deportations (Briskman and Cemlyn 2005; Kundnani 2007; Hobson et al. 2008; Gill 2009). Of the 15,040 people the UK Borders Agency reports deporting in the first quarter of 2010, nearly a third had been stopped at the 'border' as they attempted to enter the UK (Home Office 2010: 16).

Even for those who are forced to flee oppressed countries as refugees, often risking their lives hidden on trucks or crossing stretches of sea on rafts, it is predominantly more privileged members of oppressed nations who have the resources and contacts to leave the country, not for another oppressed country nearby, but for a wealthy imperialist country (Bloch 1999: 190–91). If doctors, professors and engineers from oppressed countries are forced to board a raft to cross borders, what impact does the speed of air travel have for the majority? Although Gilroy (2001: 108–9) argues that 'cultural processes', 'animated and encouraged' by technological developments, extend beyond those privileged sections that have direct access to them, for the most part, consciousness remains grounded in peoples' immediate material conditions, which include oppression on a national basis, as evidenced by the emergence of recent anti-imperialist struggles from Iraq to Nigeria (Chinweizu 2007; Harlan 2007). 'Our post-national future', which perspectives such as cosmopolitanism claim to look towards (Cohen 2006: 10–11), may be a long way off for the majority of humanity, and these elite perspectives cannot relate to struggles of the oppressed in the present period.

Simultaneous with creating conditions which put pressure on workers to move to areas of greatest demand for labour, legislation is brought in to strictly regulate their movement, strengthening national boundaries and the state. States of a certain kind in oppressed countries play a vital role in maintaining those countries' incorporation in the imperialist system, without the need for direct occupation by the armies of imperialist states. It is telling that a leading theoretician of neo-liberalism like Fukuyama (2004) should argue that problems encountered in the course of neo-liberal reforms have frequently been rooted in 'a basic conceptual failure to unpack the different dimensions of stateness and to understand how they related to economic development' (Fukuyama 2004: 5). Essentially, Fukuyama argues that interventions by the US government and agencies such as the IMF and World Bank need to include not only privatisation of profitable areas, but also the development of certain areas of the state, which, judging from the attention Fukuyama devotes to international security and terrorism, would include a significant investment in the military and other apparatus of state repression. This is a tendency which has been seen in many oppressed countries in recent years, from Colombia (Petras 2001; Isacson and Poe 2009), to the Palestinian Authority (Frisch and Hofnung 1997; Zanotti 2010), to US policy more broadly (e.g. Commission on Weak States and US National Security 2004). This contemporary history of state building as a central part of imperialist strategy runs directly counter to Hardt's and Negri's claims.

The Reserve Army in Practice

A survey of historical trends demonstrates the functioning of the international reserve army of labour in practice. International dynamics of development/ underdevelopment and oppression create a space within which experiences of racism, incorporation and resistance are played out at a local level, as discussed in more detail in later chapters. This is not new. For example, in the North East, regular visits of seasonal agricultural workers from Ireland, Britain's oldest colony, took place from at least the mid-eighteenth century, increasing noticeably during the Napoleonic wars and with the advent of the cross-channel steamship, which began regular services in 1818. These seasonal migrant workers were joined in significant numbers from 1823 by more permanent migrants coming to work in the expanding urban centres, where demand for labour was high and far higher wages were available than in Ireland (MacDermott 1977: 154–9). Yet, while international movement of labour continues to be driven by such economic needs and conditions, wage differentials in themselves have often proved inadequate to facilitate the migration needed by capital, and have frequently required backing up with direct recruitment by companies and states (Tasse 2007: 339–41). For example, in order to provide labour for the National Health Service (NHS) and other newly established institutions in the 1950s, workers were actively recruited from areas such as the Caribbean (Williams 1992: 164). In common with other parts of Britain, nursing student registers for Newcastle General Hospital show recruitment from Africa, the Caribbean and South East Asia between 1940 and 1962 (Newcastle General Hospital 1940–1962).

Patterns of Migration and Settlement in Post-War Newcastle
As well as demand for labour to work in the expanding state welfare services, migration to Britain in the 1950s and 1960s was influenced by the expansion of the service and light manufacturing sectors, which called for an increased workforce for unskilled jobs, and rising international competition, which increased pressure to find workers who would work for lower pay and in worsening working conditions in older sectors of production such as textiles and metal manufacture (Miles and Brown 2003: 118, 131). Many workers came from South Asia during this period, to cities including Newcastle, although in relatively small numbers compared to many other cities. The 1961 Census shows that out of a quarter of a million Newcastle residents, around 5,500 were born outside Britain, of whom 832 were described as Indian, 370 Pakistani, and 160 Caribbean. For all three groups, this represented more than double the population a decade earlier (Atkinson 1972: 129–30), and community leaders suggested actual figures were considerably higher (Telang 1967: 6–7). The largest source of migration to Newcastle from Pakistan and India between 1947 and the 1960s was the Punjab region, where migration was driven by a combination of factors in the aftermath of colonialism. This included political and religious conflict following partition, which led to the migration of eight to ten million people, many of them forced to become refugees on one side or the other of the new border, and economic factors in rural areas characterised by unemployment, pressure on the land and fragmentation of holdings. Another contributing factor to this particular period of migration may have been the impending 1962 Commonwealth Immigrants Act, which forced a decision for many between leaving Britain permanently, or having their families join them in Britain (Atkinson 1972: 130–35). The class position of immigrants

played a significant role in influencing opportunities for family reunification, with those coming to Newcastle for more highly qualified jobs or as graduate students having greater resources to bring their families during initial migration, while those on lower incomes were often forced to work and save in Britain for a period before they could afford for their families to join them (Telang 1967: 8).

Migrants from South Asia during this period were concentrated predominantly in working class occupations. Just under a quarter of Indian and Pakistani heads of household surveyed in the West end of Newcastle in 1968 worked in public transport as drivers and conductors, with Newcastle Corporation recruiting immigrants as conductors from 1950 but only later allowing promotion to driver. Trade union concentration was particularly high among immigrants working on the buses, with an estimated 81 per cent of immigrant conductors and drivers unionised in 1968, accounting for 64 per cent of all immigrant trade unionists in the city (Atkinson 1972: 163). Most of those working in the private sector worked in factories (Atkinson 1972: 157), with forty to fifty working or training as draughtsmen, clerks or technicians at one factory to the east of Newcastle, and fifteen to eighteen Pakistani women employed at a sewing factory in the West end of Newcastle, on the requirement that they speak English (Telang 1967: 13). A 1968 survey found a very small minority of first generation migrant women from Pakistan and India in paid employment, but far higher proportions of their adult women offspring, working as nurses, teachers, secretaries, clerical assistants, computer operators and machinists (Atkinson 1972: 163–4). Out of 88 families surveyed, four Indian and one Pakistani resident owned their own shop, and several others made their living as travelling salesmen, mainly in the drapery business (Atkinson 1972: 158). A professional I interviewed, who was a long term resident of Newcastle's East end, remembered the reception given to one such travelling salesman when he was a child:

> I can remember one guy coming around ... in the '60s, coming round with yer suitcase full of wares, selling, and I can remember my dad getting a hold of him and throwing him across the street, and his suitcase after him, you know: 'you black bastard, fuck off' and all the rest of it. (Interview, 2005)

Such hostile reception was not uniform, however; in particular, Renton (2007) suggests that the region's pit villages (organised around coal mining) provided an important and relatively unprejudiced market for South Asian salesmen at this time (Renton 2007: 131).

Only four heads of households in the 1968 survey (5.7 per cent) were unemployed, three of them for reasons of ill-health, despite living in areas of high overall unemployment (Atkinson 1972: 160). Alongside such high levels of employment, the experience of immigrants to Newcastle in the 1950s and 1960s seems to fit the broader national pattern, pointed to by Small (2007: 378), of significant job downgrading compared to occupations in migrants' countries of origin, particularly for qualified professionals. The 1968 survey found no professional or managerial workers, and a tendency for lower-skilled work than might be expected given levels of experience and qualifications, with two respondents with university degrees working in Newcastle as a bus conductor and a travelling salesman (Atkinson 1972: 160–61). Many migrants during this period were concentrated in the West end, with high levels of multi-occupied, overcrowded, run-down and derelict properties, and frequent movement in and out of the area (Atkinson 1972: 110–11). The majority of migrants from India and Pakistan living in Newcastle at that time were owner-occupiers, having bought a house through long hours of overtime, and only one family out of 88 reported being on the council's housing list (Atkinson 1972: 142–9). Estate agents in Newcastle at the time denied discrimination against immigrants in granting mortgages, but admitted taking higher deposits, on the basis that they viewed immigrants as 'here today, gone tomorrow', and believed immigrants to 'prefer older properties' (Telang 1967: 15). Migrants during this period thus faced direct and indirect racism, even as the state and British capital made active use of their labour.

The double standards inherent in the treatment of migrants to Britain is further underlined by the contrast between Vietnamese and Japanese migrants to Newcastle during the 1980s. At the end of January 1985 there were 25 Vietnamese families living in Newcastle, totalling around 100 people. Serious problems were reported in housing conditions, and at the start of 1985, only twelve of the 42 people of working age were employed, six as cleaners, two in takeaways, one a hairdresser, one as a school caretaker and two in factories. Others were reported to have skills but no opportunities to use them (Newcastle City Council 1985: 1–3). In stark contrast were the approximately 400 Japanese migrants living in the North East by the late 1980s, many connected to the recently Nissan factory, and with a history of high level connections, diplomatic visits and migrations going back at least as far as 1862 (Conte-Helm 1989: 169). This illustrates a long-term trend, in which rights to entry and settlement have been granted on the condition of some benefit to British capital, either through investment, for those with capital, or through hard labour on low wages, for those with nothing to sell but their labour power.

Changing Patterns of Migrant Employment: Sweatshops and Domestic Bondage in Britain
From the 1980s, sweatshops and home-working developed in the shadow of the British textile industry, staffed predominantly by Asian women, and became increasingly important for profit margins in the industry as a whole (Kundnani 2007: 59). Other potential sources of reserve labour who have been drawn on at times to perform 'undesirable jobs' and raise the average rate of profit through super-exploitation, such as women in general, have higher values of labour power, which must be paid for by capital. In the case of women this arises from demands for the state to provide childcare, as it was forced to do during the Second World War, when employment of women rose dramatically (Miles and Phizacklea

1980: 12–13). The increasing mobility of capital since the 1980s has meant that where members of the international reserve army of labour have been employed within Britain, this has mostly been in types of work that are necessarily close to the point of consumption, such as food processing, catering, cleaning, nursing and personal services (Kundnani 2007: 58–9). This has contributed to a policy discourse of 'managed migration', with control prioritised over rights, and an increasing polarisation between professional and low-skilled groups of migrants (Piper 2010: 110). For example, employment of 'domestic help' in Britain rose significantly in the 1990s, with many migrants employed under the Home Office's domestic worker registration scheme. A survey in 2002 found that two thirds of respondents had experienced physical abuse from their employers, and 9 per cent sexual abuse. Passports were reported to be regularly withheld by employers and used to enforce harsh working conditions and low wages (Kundnani 2007: 60–61), with many workers forced to turn to employers for shelter from the state, even where they were abusive (Anderson 2010: 62–3).

Although the largest proportion of all migrants arriving in Britain between 2001 and 2008 was higher paid workers, the proportion of foreign-born employees within each occupation group increased across the board, the largest relative increases over the period being for: Elementary Occupations, those involving the most unskilled forms of work (an increase of 10.6 percentage points); Personal Service Occupations (an increase of 7.1 percentage points); and Process, Plant and Machine Operatives (an increase of 6.1 percentage points) (ONS 2008: 6–7). A survey of low paid migrant workers in London found 71 per cent sent money home, and 40 per cent had dependents outside the UK. On average, they remitted 20 to 30 per cent of their income, mostly as contributions to daily subsistence. Remittances took place most regularly among those from poorer backgrounds in African countries, and those with the highest levels of remittances were also those working the longest hours. Strategies to keep up payments included working in multiple jobs, sharing accommodation and minimising consumption, including eating as little as possible (Datta et al. 2007: 51–9).

The 'New Migration' from Eastern and Central Europe
2004 saw a significant development in freedom of movement and employment – though not necessarily access to state support in case of hardship – for citizens of the 'A8' countries in Eastern and Central Europe, with the further addition of the 'A2' countries, Romania and Bulgaria, in 2007. Datta et al. (2007) suggest A8 workers may have been a preferred source of labour, both for their 'whiteness' and on the understanding that they would be more likely to return to their country of origin than people who have travelled greater distances (Datta et al. 2007: 49). In 2007, there were an estimated 1.4 million registered migrant workers in the UK, around half of whom had arrived from the A8 and A2 countries since 2004, and somewhere between 300,000 and 800,000 unregistered migrant workers. Even for those who were registered, many worked in conditions so exploitative as to meet the international definition of 'forced labour' (Craig et al. 2007: 22; Ahmad 2008:

857). Between 2004 and 2009 there were high levels of A8 migration, with many remaining in Britain only for short periods, and registered as either self-employed, including many agency workers, or as part of the Workers Registration Scheme (WRS).[2] These migrants were concentrated in low-paid and unskilled jobs. The WRS was established, in the words of the Home Office, to provide 'transitional measures to regulate A8 nationals' access to the labour market ... and to restrict access to benefits.' In the first quarter of 2010, 71 per cent of requests by A8 workers for tax-funded, income-related benefits were refused (Home Office 2010: 23–4). Workers were required to remain on the WRS until they had been in continuous employment for at least 12 months, which, given the predominance of temporary and insecure contracts, was often difficult to achieve. While on the WRS, migrants had severely restricted access to unemployment, child and housing benefits. This gave these migrant workers a distinct relationship to capital, to the benefit of the ruling class, going some way to explain their preference for Eastern European workers over refugees, who, once they are granted refugee status, have far greater rights to remain in Britain and access state support (Chinweizu 2006).

As of the first quarter of 2008, the total number of workers in the UK who were born abroad, including those with British citizenship, was estimated at 3.7 million, or 12.5 per cent of the workforce. This represented an increase of 1.8 million since 1997, accounting for 55 per cent of the total increase in the UK workforce. The largest proportion of workers born abroad were from other European countries, with 0.7 million from the other pre-2004 EU countries, 0.5 million from A8 countries, and 0.2 million from other European countries (Clancy 2008: 19). Over this period, there was also a significant increase in the proportion of migrants from A8 countries in active employment, from 65.3 per cent in 1997 to 82.8 per cent in 2008, indicating the change in the nature of migration towards young, single people coming solely to work rather than bringing families to settle (Clancy 2008: 22). There were also significant increases in numbers in the UK from other parts of the world between 1997 and 2008, with numbers of UK residents born in Pakistan, Australia, New Zealand, and African countries excluding South Africa all nearly doubling, numbers from South Africa tripling, and numbers from the Americas and India increasing by a half (Clancy 2008: 30).

Super-Exploitation in British Agriculture
Since the 1990s, the low prices and 'just in time' methods of British supermarkets have depended on a flexible, low paid and disposable workforce, mostly made up of migrants. This workforce could be out of work at times and suddenly called upon to work seventy hour weeks at others, according to consumer demand, and were kept in their super-exploited position by dependency on gangmasters for food, work and board, together with threats and intimidation (Kundnani 2007: 59–60). In July 2009, the Unite union put forward a motion at Tesco's AGM, backed by the West Yorkshire Pension Fund, demanding action against the exploitation of

---

2   The WRS was abolished in April 2011.

migrant workers on temporary contracts in its meat and poultry supply chain, who the union said were being routinely paid less and treated worse than permanent staff, most of whom were British (Lawrence 2009). Without migrant labour, it has been argued that British agriculture could not continue in its present form (Craig 2007b: 34). The extent of British agriculture's dependency on migrant labour is indicated by reports in 2008 of farmers in parts of Britain being forced to leave produce to rot in the fields as a result of new restrictions on migrant workers from Eastern Europe (Surman 2008). 22 per cent of employers in the East of England, with large areas of agriculture, said they would be recruiting migrant workers in the third quarter of 2009 to meet seasonal demand for labour (CIPD 2009a: 8). Prior to 2004, much of this work was done by workers from Poland. With its inclusion as part of the A8, many Polish workers moved into marginally better-paid and more secure jobs, with their roles increasingly taken over by workers from the A2 countries, who had even more restricted labour rights than the A8. In the first quarter of 2010, 9,845 work cards were issued to A2 nationals under the Seasonal Agricultural Workers Scheme (SAWS) (Home Office 2010: 24). Thus, the international reserve army of labour has continued to play an important role, even as the countries from which currently employed migrants are drawn has shifted from Britain's former colonies to the ruins of former socialist countries.

Migrant Labour in Welfare Provision
State welfare in Britain also continues to be highly dependent on migrant labour. A 2009 study found that two in three NHS employers recruit from abroad, more often from outside the EU, and four in ten local government employers recruit overseas, with more than one in five employers in the education sector and NHS saying they would be recruiting migrant workers in the third quarter of 2009 (CIPD 2009a: 8). Numbers of work permits issued to healthcare staff from outside the EU rose 27 times between 1993 and 2003. 15,000 of the 20,000 nurses who joined the medical register in 2003–2004 came from overseas and one third of doctors on the register qualified abroad, more than double the proportion in the total British workforce (Jameson 2005; also Kyriakides and Virdee 2003). In the Philippines, where the government is forced to spend eight times as much on servicing its debt as it does on its health service, nurses and doctors are underpaid and under pressure to migrate. In Britain, they work in large numbers in positions well below their level of qualification, as exemplified in two hospitals in Glasgow, where some migrants were found to be working for effective wages of £8 a day after agency costs. In 2003, Filipinos working in Britain sent home $260 million in remittances (Kundnani 2007: 64–5).

Welbourne et al. (2007) describe how low levels of recruitment of social workers from within Britain and 'an exodus of experienced social workers from the profession' have been responded to in recent years by the recruitment of professionals from developing countries, with some coming on their own initiative, some recruited directly by local authorities in groups, and others recruited via agencies, with widely varying levels of support. Between 1990 and 2001, 10,000 social workers were issued with letters of verification allowing them to practice in the UK. In 2001–2002 overseas-trained social workers accounted for around a quarter of all new social work recruits, and between 2003 and 2004, there was an 82 per cent increase in numbers of trained social workers coming to the UK, with the largest number from outside the EU. Zimbabwe has lost half of its trained social workers to the UK, and is consequently experiencing severe shortages in welfare provision (Welbourne et al. 2007: 27–34). There is substantial involvement of migrant workers in delivering social care, with one study suggesting a fifth of all care workers looking after older people are migrant workers, and 28 per cent of those recruited in 2007, with many employed by agencies. The sector is outside the jurisdiction of the Gangmaster Licensing Authority and exploitation is rife, including excessive hours, rates of pay below the minimum wage, deception about expected wage levels, little to no holiday, and cases of debt-bondage (Wilkinson et al. 2009: 24–5).

The recruitment of welfare professionals is part of a significant 'brain drain' on oppressed countries, as even these countries' educational resources are plundered to the benefit of imperialist countries (Chinweizu and Jameson 2008). The Department of Health issued a code of practice to statutory employers in 2004, with a stated aim of restricting recruitment of healthcare professionals from over 150 'developing' countries. However, as of 2007, there was no requirement for private recruitment agencies to sign up to the code, and no sanction for non-compliance. This may, therefore, only serve to increase the predominance of private agencies in recruitment, operating largely on temporary contracts and offering fewer rights, such as access to training and promotion, than direct recruitment by local authorities (Welbourne et al. 2007: 34–5).

Migrant Workers and the Crisis
The global economic crisis has lead to a noticeable reduction in employment of migrant labour. In one survey, 39 per cent of UK employers with more than 500 workers said they had reduced numbers of migrant workers employed during 2009, and only 8 per cent of all employers surveyed said they planned to recruit migrant workers in the third quarter of 2009, compared to 27 per cent in a similar survey in autumn 2005 (CIPD 2009a: 8–10). Already in 2008, it was estimated that as many as 20 per cent of street homeless people in London were migrant workers from Eastern and Central Europe, who had lost their jobs and had neither funds to return home or access to state support (Homeless Link 2009: 5). This is the other side of the international reserve army of labour, to not only be available to work in a super-exploited position when needed, but to be the first to be cast off when demand for labour falls.

Gender and Migration

While it is beyond the scope of this book to deal with this question in detail, it is important to note that experiences of migration and settlement are powerfully gendered. The oppression of women under capitalism includes a disproportionate amount of unpaid work and inferior pay and conditions for paid work. This is enforced through discriminatory attitudes and violence, and interacts with oppression on the basis of country of origin and immigration status to produce particular situations facing women refugees which are more than simply 'gender plus racism'. Both are linked through the class struggle, not subsumed within a monolithic conception of the working class which is implicitly white, male, heterosexual and able-bodied, but as vital components of a Marxist understanding of class oppression and struggle.

The Oppression of Women under Capitalism

The central premises of the Marxist method, derived from empirical and historical study, are that people must produce in order to satisfy basic needs of survival, that the satisfaction of these need leads to further needs, that people act to reproduce not only themselves but also their species, and that all of this activity is organised socially depending on the means of production available (Marx and Engels [1845] 1991: 48–52). The social organisation of the family and its impact on gender relations is thus inseparable from the development of the forces of material production:

> According to the materialist conception, the determining factor of history is, in the final instance, the production and reproduction of immediate life. This, again, is of a twofold character: on the one side, the production of the means of existence, of food, clothing and shelter and the tools necessary for that production; on the other side, the production of human beings themselves, the propagation of the species. The social organisation under which the people of a particular historical epoch and a particular country live is determined by both kinds of production: by the stage of development of labour on the one hand and of the family on the other. (Engels [1884] 1981: 71–2)

The historical development of paternity took place following the development of production in male-dominated areas of animal husbandry and agriculture to the point where it became possible to accumulate wealth surplus to the needs of immediate subsistence (Engels [1884] 1981: 117–19). Paternity continues to play an important role within capitalism in its imperialist stage. Different forms of organisation may coexist at a particular point in time for different types of activity and different sections of society and this is the case for various forms of unwaged labour within the capitalist system, despite the all-pervasive appearance of the wage relation (Miles 1987). Under modern capitalism it is still predominantly women who are called on to perform unpaid domestic work in the home, in a form of private labour, while also at times being called on perform waged labour in the workplace, in a form of socialised labour (Adamson et al. 1976: 7; Kynaston 1996). The interdependence of these forms of organisation under capitalism has to be understood in the context of the dynamic needs of capital to obtain a healthy and compliant workforce at the lowest possible cost. Capital must attempt to transfer as much as possible of the costs of the reproduction of labour onto the working class, and this is intensified in periods of crisis, when falling profits call for cuts to state welfare spending (Adamson et al. 1976: 2–3).

Representations and Realities of Gender in Migration

Within recent popular typologies of migration to Britain, women have been largely invisible. The economic migrant is usually constructed as young, male and – the ideal for capital – highly mobile, either without a family or sending money to 'dependents' in their country of origin. Women are thus kept firmly off stage and in a passive role (Palmary 2010: 3–4). The asylum seeker has also often been presented as young and male, although in this case idle in unemployment, and frequently a sexual predator after young white women, who are also portrayed in a passive role as victims (for a discussion of related issues see Psaroudakis 2010). Gender violence has frequently been discounted as a legitimate grounds for asylum, ignoring the penetration of the state into domestic relationships and the way that state policies create the conditions for violence in both sending and receiving contexts (Chantler 2010; Kiwanuka 2010). Where women have featured as migrants in dominant discourses, it has often been in the context of racist fears of population growth of migrant communities, whether through 'family reunification' with migrant workers or refugee families who are depicted as a drain on welfare resources. In all of these roles, women who migrate from oppressed countries to Britain are portrayed as passive, dependent on either a male family member or the British state, and contributing nothing. Recently this has taken on a new form in the focus of governments, international organisations and the media on 'human trafficking', particularly the trafficking of 'women and children' for the purposes of prostitution (Gould 2010). Under conditions of increasingly limited grounds for legal migration to Britain from outside the EU, for many women crossing borders official designation as a 'trafficked woman' may be one of the only ways to gain access to state support, and central to fitting this definition is demonstrable helplessness, passivity and often naivety (Anderson 2010: 72).

In reality, women have migrated to and from Britain for centuries, with varying degrees of control over their lives, but always as political actors. Migrant women and their descendants have played leading roles in struggles across diverse public arenas, including the workplace, with the Grunwick strike from 1976–78 in Willesden, London, just one of the more famous (Davidson 2011), and the Gate Gourmet strike in 2005 at Heathrow Airport one of the more recent (Escovitchl 2005). They have faced particular forms of harassment and degrading treatment by the state, including the use of 'virginity tests' at Heathrow Airport in the 1970s (Smith and Marmo 2011). Before paid work was prohibited for all refugees without status in 2002, it had already been prohibited for many refugee women since 1996, on the basis that only a family's 'primary claimant' for asylum was entitled to work, and this was often a male member of the family (Dumper 2002: v). More recently, requirements have been imposed for women to pass English language tests in order to move to Britain to join family members, at the same time as changes to funding and charges for English for Speakers of Other Languages (ESOL) have reduced women's access to lessons. Women have also played an active role in refugee organisations of all kinds (WLRI 2005). For refugees with children in Britain, caring responsibilities often make the prospect of avoiding deportation by living 'underground' even more difficult; this may be a contributory factor to the high levels of participation of women refugees with young children in many public campaigns.

Conclusions and Outline of the Book

This chapter has provided a brief outline of the dominant, parasitic relationship between Britain and the oppressed countries from which the majority of refugees flee, including the historic role played by migrants from oppressed countries as workers employed by British capital, both in their countries of origin and within Britain. Impoverishment of oppressed countries, wars and racism, are not the result of arbitrary policy decisions or simply the random accumulation of individual actions. Although the forms they take and the timings of particular events will be historically determined and influenced by a multitude of factors, as general recurring features, they are necessary elements of the imperialist system. The smooth running of imperialism depends on the international division of the working class into a super-exploited majority, mostly located in oppressed countries, and a relatively privileged, and consequently docile, fraction within imperialist countries. The relation of British capitalist interests to driving factors of migration, including war, state repression and poverty, have been highlighted here for their complex and dialectical relationship with racism and refugee settlement in Britain, which will form the focus of the following chapters.

Chapter 2, 'Racism and the Political Economy of Refugee Reception', discusses the persistence of racism in Britain, with a complex relationship to the management of migration from oppressed countries and the super-exploitation of their inhabitants. The chapter presents an analysis of modern racism and its connection to nationalism and imperialism. This provides the context for a discussion of British state immigration policy and practice in relation to refugees, focusing on the asylum decision-making process, dispersal and the prohibition of paid work. The implementation and impacts of these policies since 2001 are analysed through a combination of individual refugee testimonies, local press reports, national policy evaluations and other literature.

Chapter 3, 'Refugees and the British State', begins by reflecting on the Marxist theory of the state in the light of the history of Britain's asylum policy. Literature on the state, imperialism and globalisation is used to reflect on refugees' personal accounts in the light of differences in the character of the state in oppressed and imperialist countries. This is followed by discussion of repressive and welfare aspects of the British state and their relation to immigration and asylum, alternating between the literature and refugees' accounts of their experiences and understandings in order to draw out complexities and contradictions. The chapter concludes by reflecting on changes in the British state currently underway and the implications for refugees.

Chapter 4, 'Introducing the Refugee Relations Industry', begins by sketching some key elements of the history of 'race relations' in Britain since the 1960s, drawing at times on Newcastle's particular history in order to better illustrate the fine detail of the tensions and contradictions inherent in this process, and to develop a picture of the local context on which more recent developments have built. The general line of development of the refugee sector under recent Labour governments is discussed, and local case studies are presented for two different models of organisation which the state has engaged with in different ways in its attempts to 'manage' refugees. The chapter concludes with reflections on the Coalition government's conception of the 'Big Society' in the light of the preceding discussion.

Chapter 5, 'Social Capital and the Management of Refugees' Oppression', focuses on the involvement of individual refugees in forms of organisation and activity fostered by the state through voluntary and community organisations in the refugee sector. Following discussion of Labour governments' interventions aimed at 'building social capital' since 1997, reported incentives for refugees to volunteer are explored and some of the outcomes of these interventions are considered. The chapter ends by considering the relevance of Labour's 'social capital building' to the Coalition's 'Big Society'.

Chapter 6 concludes with a discussion of implications for policy and practice, and considers the prospects for refugees under the current government.

Chapter 2

Racism and the Political Economy of Refugee Reception

Bowes et al. (2009) point to the continuing racialisation of asylum seeking, and the need to 'contextualise micro-level discussion within analysis of broader structures of inequality and exclusion, including those that draw on repertoires of racism' (Bowes et al. 2009: 24). The wider racialised context ensures that even where legislation is not itself explicitly discriminatory, the common understanding of problems within which it is implemented frequently leads to racist outcomes (Ben-Tovim et al. 1986: 20–21). This chapter discusses the persistence of racism in Britain, with a complex relationship to the management of migration from oppressed countries and the super-exploitation of their inhabitants. Following a short discussion of the position of black and migrant sections of the working class in Britain, including interfaces between racism and gender, the chapter presents a theoretical analysis of the material basis of modern racism and its relation to nationalism and imperialism. This provides the context for a discussion of key elements of state policy and practice which have influenced refugees' position, focusing on the asylum decision-making process, dispersal and the prohibition on paid work for refugees without status. The role of these policies in re-imposing labour discipline among workers from oppressed countries is analysed through a combination of national policy evaluations and other literature, local press reports and individual refugee testimonies. By providing a platform for members of an often marginalised and ignored section of society, who are directly subject to these policies, to speak, this aims to relate international and national systems, trends and policies to local and personal outcomes and experiences, in order to demonstrate some of the human consequences of the division and management of labour under imperialism.

Introduction

It has been argued that Britain has a history of constructing asylum policy in response to non-existent or false evidence (Schuster 2003: 7; also Crawley 2010), which forces us to question the real drivers behind policy. Recent approaches by Labour governments under the banners of combating exclusion and building social capital frequently failed to account for how geographical concentrations of deprivation and ethnic density do not occur 'naturally', 'but are themselves shaped by policy decisions and opportunity structures', and cannot therefore be taken as original cause for any related phenomenon (Platt 2009: 677). Similarly, what is frequently missing in discussion of integration is the context into which refugees are expected to integrate, and the positions available for them to occupy (Kostakopoulou 2010: 838). While the economic underdevelopment of countries occupying an oppressed position within imperialism has major significance for the causes of refugee creation, as discussed in Chapter 1, the dominant and parasitic relation of Britain to the countries refugees flee likewise has major significance for the nature of refugee reception.

Imperialist states have always been ready to acknowledge the positive value of immigration when it is under their control and benefits their labour markets, but when it is 'spontaneous', or out of their control, they express alarm (Borjas and Crisp 2005: 1). As demand for menial labour in the post-war period began to be satisfied, the state passed the 1962 Immigration Act, restricting entry to relatively skilled or qualified workers, or those with jobs waiting for them (Williams 1992: 164–5). Since then, there has been a succession of further acts, which have contributed to the shape of ethnic minority populations, with a decrease in primary immigration from Britain's former colonies and an increase in the proportion of population growth accounted for by family reunion and births in Britain. For example, whereas in 1951 there were around 30,000 people in Britain designated as West Indian, most of them born abroad, by 1991 there were over 550,000, of whom more than 300,000 had been born in Britain (Small 2007: 372–5). Taken together, over 50 per cent of people in Britain who define themselves as being of Indian, Pakistani, Bangladeshi, Black Caribbean or Black African origin were born in Britain (Ahmad and Bradby 2007: 799–800). The contemporary situation for many black people born in Britain has been described as 'integrated yet alienated', with weakening links to the countries members of their family might have migrated from and the highest rate of 'mixed race' marriages of any imperialist country, alongside rising levels of racism in areas such as the labour market (Williams 2007: 401). This exemplifies the contradiction within calls for refugees to integrate, when the terms of integration assign a subordinate position for the majority of black people. It is the role of the British state to 'manage' this contradiction, in order to maintain the smooth running of the imperialist system.

The Position of Black People in Britain Today

Discussion of migration, racism and anti-racism necessarily raises questions of the terms used to define people in a context where racialised categories are used to divide and oppress. Measures of the impact of racial discrimination need to address racism's multi-faceted nature, including spoken and unspoken, intentional and unintentional, individual, institutional and structural, and that individual instances of racism may impact on individuals beyond those directly experiencing them (Karlsen and Nazroo 2006: 31–3). Ethnic categories mean different things to different people and in different times and places, embodying shifting and complex combinations of language, religion, faith, culture, ancestry, nationality, histories of migration and a shared heritage (Vickers et al. 2012: 2). Despite their socially constructed nature, ethnic categories are an important means of assessing inequality and disadvantage. The use of 'colour-based terms', such as 'Black African', is contested in Britain, both amongst and outside the people these terms aim to refer to. Some state that their use is outdated, unnecessary and offensive, while others argue for their retention in order to capture experiences associated with racism and power, which may be lost in terms which privilege cultural differences (Aspinall and Chinouya 2008: 187–8). In the discussion that follows I use a variety of terms. I use the term 'black' to refer to people who face specific oppression due to more constantly identifiable features by which people are 'racialised' in a particular social and historical context, such as skin colour or cultural or religious styles of dress. I include within the category of 'ethnic minorities' not only black people, but also those with pale skin who experience racialised oppression based around factors such as immigration status, accent or religion, such as recent migrants from Eastern and Central Europe. Where possible and relevant, I use more specific categories, such as country of origin or religion. This flexibility is intended to enable a more adequate response to the shifting and contingent nature of racialisation, in which aspects of diversity amongst ethnic minorities may be more relevant in some situations, and shared features of oppression as black people more prominent in others. However, in many cases my reliance on secondary data sources forces me to use the categories of those sources.

As of 1994, 24.4 per cent of ethnic minority households in the UK lived below the poverty line, compared to 9.9 per cent of all households (Morrissens and Sainsbury 2005: 644). More recent data from the Family Resources Survey suggests such ethnic disparities in poverty rates persist (Platt 2007: 38–9). Black people in Britain are more likely than white people to be homeless, particularly for those aged 16 to 24, and financial institutions have been found to apply more rigid criteria in assessing the status of black people when applying for loans for private housing (Small 2007: 377). Butt (2006: 3–4) and Nazroo (2006: 12) survey data suggesting that ethnic minority groups in Britain have notably higher age-standardised rates of long-term limiting illness or disability that restrict daily activities, particularly for ethnic minority women, and also continuing discrimination against older members of ethnic minority groups, those with mental health problems, and families with children.

Diversity among ethnic minorities in Britain has rapidly increased in recent years, with new sources and patterns of migration and settlement, leading some to talk about 'super-diversity' (Vertovec 2007; Fanshawe and Sriskandarajah 2010). This leaves any single basis of categorisation inadequate, whether by self-defined ethnicity, country of birth, language group, or citizenship. For some groups, combinations of factors such as insecure and exploitative conditions of employment, migrant status, wide geographical dispersal, lack of recourse to public support, increased insecurity and competition as a result of recession, and racism, can render needs and experiences particularly 'invisible' to policy and the design of services (Manthorpe et al. 2008; Wilkinson et al. 2009).

Racism in Paid Employment

Inequalities and concentrations of disadvantage associated with membership of particular minority ethnic groups are apparent in aspects of people's lives including socio-economic status and types of employment (ONS 2006b; Clancy 2008; ONS 2008) and levels of unemployment (WLRI 2005; Heath and Cheung 2006; ONS 2006a). Concentration in less-skilled work is common among ethnic minorities and migrant groups, with indications that many migrants from oppressed countries experience de-skilling in the jobs they find in Britain, compared to their qualifications and experience in their countries of origin (Datta et al. 2007: 57). Roberts et al. (2008) report a range of case studies, which illustrate some of the ways racism functions in employment, despite race relations legislation, with a culture of implicit racial profiling in many companies. For example, they found Kurdish and Polish migrants in one company valued by management for their 'work ethic' and their availability during periods of rapid expansion, but considered incapable of planning or managing at a more senior level. Within manufacturing, distribution, and banking, ethnic minorities are substantially under-represented in professional and managerial jobs but are over-represented in semi-routine and routine work (Heath and Cheung 2006: 48). In 2004, 45 per cent of employed Bangladeshi men aged 22 or older earned less than the minimum wage, followed by 15 per cent of Pakistani men, and compared to only 4 per cent of white men (Heath and Cheung 2006: 18). Black people in Britain, therefore, continue to be disproportionately working class.

There are also racialised differences in access to any kind of paid work. In 2004, men from Black Caribbean, Black African, Bangladeshi and Mixed ethnic groups had unemployment rates around three times that of White British men (ONS 2006a). Using statistical analysis, it is possible to assess the level of disadvantage in employment associated with being from a particular ethnic group more reliably than simply looking at raw percentages. Ethnicity-associated disadvantage in employment, or the 'ethnic penalty', for Pakistani and Bangladeshi men and women, Indian men and women, and Caribbean men, has fluctuated since the 1970s, but all of these groups have remained in a consistently worse position than white people of the same gender (Berthoud and Blekesaune 2007: 27–8). Although unemployment rates for Chinese and Indian people are similar to those for white people, self-employment rates are relatively high among both these groups, as they are among Pakistanis, in some cases partly a response to difficulties experienced in trying to undertake waged work (Clark and Drinkwater 1998). Relatively low unemployment rates cannot, therefore, be taken as conclusive evidence that Indian and Chinese people do not experience ethnicity-related difficulties in the labour market (Heath and Cheung 2006: 13). When controlling for age, qualifications, marital status, year, and region, both men and women of all ethnic minorities except for Chinese experience a higher probability of unemployment associated with their ethnicity. This reveals, for example, that the relatively high levels of employment among people classified as Black African are only achieved as a result of their disproportionately higher levels of education, and that, when controlling for educational level, Black Africans actually experience more ethnic disadvantage as a group than other ethnic minorities. There is only evidence of a marginal change in this for the second generation compared to the first, despite greater access to English language and recognised qualifications and experience (Heath and Cheung 2006: 20–22). This suggests a continuing impact of racism, beyond its immediate role in the regulation of migrant labour.

There is thus ample evidence that racism continues to impact, in conjunction with borders and immigration controls, to structure the relationship of black people to capital, and to allocate to ethnic minority workers in Britain a distinct position within international divisions of labour.

Interfaces of Racism and Gender in Relations with Capital

Gender and ethnicity combine to give black women sections of the working class a particular relationship to capital, as a super-exploited class fraction. This operates within both their paid and unpaid labour.

The Position of Black Women as Unpaid Labour

Caring and other unpaid types of 'women's work' has been intensified by the frequent acceptance by welfare services in Britain of the myth that black people, particularly of South Asian and Chinese origin, prefer to 'look after their own', leading to the assumption that family networks will provide support and that therefore outside help is neither needed nor wanted (Chahal 2004). This leaves ethnic minority women unsupported where certain types of support are needed even if family care is preferred in other aspects, and in situations where low wages force women to take paid work to maintain family incomes, preventing them from caring for their elders or other family members even where this would be their preference (Craig et al. 2000: 39). The assumption that low take-up of services is rooted in culturally-determined preferences also conveniently distracts from the question of whether black people's experiences of inadequate or inappropriate welfare provision in the past may be a more significant contributory factor.

The Position of Black Women as Paid Labour

In private sector employment, ethnic minority women are disproportionately concentrated in less skilled and lower paid occupations. For example, in 2004 Indian, Pakistani and Black African women were four times more likely than White British women to be working as packers, bottlers, canners and fillers, while Pakistani and Indian women were respectively around six times and four times more likely than White British women to be working as sewing machinists. Over half employed Bangladeshi women are employed in semi-routine or routine work

(ONS 2006b). While there are relatively high proportions of Chinese, Indian and Black women in professional and managerial occupations, the majority of these work in lower managerial and professional roles rather than the higher levels (Heath and Cheung 2006: 16).

Relative to white women, Pakistani and Bangladeshi women have faced fairly consistent employment penalties for the last thirty years, including being less likely than women on average to re-enter work once they become unemployed (Berthoud and Blekesaune 2007: 2). In 2008, out of the thirty countries of origin with the largest populations living in Britain, women from Somalia, Bangladesh and Pakistan had the highest economic inactivity rates[1] and were also among the top four groups for unemployment (Khan 2008: 3–4; Table 2.1):

Table 2.1   Economic inactivity and unemployment rates for working age women by ethnicity in 2008

Country of origin	Economic inactivity	Unemployment
Somalia	84%	39%
Bangladesh	75%	18%
Pakistan	80%	23%

Source: Khan 2008: 3–4.

When controlling for family position, including having young children, Pakistani and Bangladeshi women still face large employment penalties compared to white women (Berthoud and Blekesaune 2007: 28). Together, these figures suggest that the degree of economic inactivity cannot simply be explained by a personal or cultural preference for unpaid work in the home, but that when women from these countries do attempt to find waged work, they are less likely to be successful, discouraging them from trying in the future (Khan 2008: 2–3). What this means is that these sections of ethnic minority women represent a significant potential reserve army of labour, who if work was offered may move from economic inactivity – representing in many cases unpaid domestic work – to also undertaking waged labour.

Some sections of black people have borne a disproportionate brunt of the initial consequences of the economic crisis, with gender marking significant differences. As of October 2009, almost one in five Black men in the UK was unemployed (CIPD 2009b) (see Table 2.2 for increases).

---

1   Those listed as economically inactive include those who aren't looking for work because they have found it so hard to find work in the past, and those who are unable to take work because of long-term illness or disability, which in some cases may be related to poor employment conditions, housing or health.

Table 2.2   Male unemployment rates by ethnicity in 2009

	Unemployment rate	Yearly change
Black men	18.2%	+4.6 percentage points
Asian men	10.8%	+1.4 percentage points
All ethnic minority men	12.8%	+2.3 percentage points
White men	8.3%	+3.1 percentage points

Source: Stewart and Hopkins 2009.

At the same time, inactivity rates for ethnic minorities fell 0.9 percentage points between the first quarter of 2008 to the first quarter of 2009, but still stood at 31.1 per cent compared to 20.7 per cent for the overall population (EHRC 2009: 18). Table 2.3 gives other indicators.

Table 2.3   Change in unemployment indicators for ethnic minorities in the year up to Quarter 1 2009

	Employment rate	Change	ILO unemployment	Change
Ethnic minorities	60.9%	+0.4% point	11.6%	+0.5% point
General population	73.5%	−1.2% point	7.3%	+1.9% point

Source: EHRC 2009: 11.

This is a difference from the recession of the early 1990s, when the employment rate for ethnic minorities dropped by significantly more than for the population as a whole (EHRC 2009: 17). What this may suggest is that a section of the ethnic minority population who were previously registered as 'economically inactive' – for example they may have been doing unpaid work in the home, or been unemployed but not drawing jobseekers allowance, or studying – have now started to seek paid work, and some of these have been successful. For the working age population as a whole, research has demonstrated that the real increase in unemployment since the start of the economic crisis has been under-represented in statistics, because an individual counts as employed whether they are in full-time or part-time work. Large numbers of full-time workers have been losing their jobs, but these have been offset in the statistics by increasing numbers, mainly of women, taking up part-time work (CIPD 2009c: 2). Applying this to black sections of the working class, and taking into account the high levels of economic inactivity among some sections of ethnic minority women (Heath and

Cheung 2006: 11–12; Khan 2008: 3–4), the changing figures for ethnic minority employment and inactivity as a whole, and the high unemployment among ethnic minority men, it seems reasonable to suggest that, as a result of the economic crisis, we may be witnessing a restructuring of black sections of the working class, with increased unemployment among ethnic minority men and an intensification of dual exploitation of ethnic minority women, who were previously engaged in unpaid labour in the home, and are now taking on part time jobs in addition to make ends meet.

Imperialism, Nationalism, Racism and Gender

Physical divisions of labour interact with political and social processes, including ideological discourses of nationalism and racism, which take on particular forms in the context of the imperialist system, and play a role in the management of labour beyond the scope of direct control by the state. Despite the persistence of the idea of races and the evidence of continuing racialised inequalities in outcomes, as Cohen (2006: 4) suggests, 'Even the most naive cursory appreciation of the history of migration (reinforced now by the evidence of the Human Genome Project) demonstrates a more plausible alternative proposition', that of a single human race with common origins in Africa. While much 'commonsense' race-thinking functions in terms of skin colour, the assumption that race-thinking is simply rooted in visible difference is shown to be false by examples such as the recent histories of extreme racialisation of Muslims and Serbs in Bosnia, and Hutus and Tutsis in Rwanda (Miles and Brown 2003: 6), or closer to home the racism directed in different periods of Britain's history against predominantly pale-skinned Jews and Irish Catholics. The consistent role of 'race' has been as a guiding interpretation of the world, suggesting distinct collectives based on sometimes real and sometimes imagined shared biological and cultural characteristics, with an assumed deterministic relationship between the two (Miles and Brown 2003: 89). The vagueness of the concept contributes to its enduring power, by allowing it to mean different things to different people at different times (Barzun 1965: 2).

Challenging the Myth of Racism as a 'Natural' Response to Difference

The argument that racism is a 'natural' response among people not used to migration to 'their' area has a certain common sense resonance in the case of contemporary Newcastle. Some writers have presented a picture of a 'monocultural' white Tyneside, sheltered from contact with immigrants until the 1950s or even later, expressed, for example, in arguments that as of 1980 'Tyneside's parochial conservatism [had] hardly been challenged by contact with other cultures since the area has such a small ethnic minority population' (Robinson 1988: 190). Yet such a picture is far from complete, and glosses over a much longer history of migration, settlement, racism and resistance. In 1874, the North East was the most diverse region of England if measured by country of birth, and only three other cities in England had more Irish-born residents than Newcastle (Renton 2008). In addition to high levels of migration from other regions of England, Scotland, Ireland, Eastern Europe and Scandinavia, there is also a long history of residents of Newcastle with darker skin. According to archival research, 'Black Africans, Americans and West Indians continued to visit, perform, and settle in the North East throughout the nineteenth century' (Archive Mapping and Research Project 2007). In addition to a steady stream of black performing groups visiting Newcastle in the late nineteenth century, there is evidence of a stable black resident population working in a variety of occupations. Black residents of Newcastle were also politically active during this period, including black sailors who played an active role in a notable seamen's strike in 1866. When the British Association for the Advancement of Science held its national convention in Newcastle in 1863, and two speakers made the claim that black people were not fully human, they were rebutted by a local black man, William Craft, who had lived in England for thirteen years after escaping slavery in the US. Craft warned the two supposed 'experts', 'not to try it on in Newcastle where a Negro is treated as a man and a brother'. At the same time, racism was evident from the state, with a publican receiving only a small fine from local magistrates for kidnapping a 'young man of colour', Henry Niles, with the intention of forcing him onto an Italian ship in 1861 (based on research conducted by Nigel Todd, reported in Godfrey 1989). Records of black people in Newcastle continue to surface into the early twentieth century. For example, a 1936 obituary records the death of African-American Charles Johnstone, who had worked the night shift on the gate of the Swan Hunter shipyard in Newcastle for 41 years at the time of his death (The Shipyard 1936: 10). A survey of 88 families in the West end of Newcastle in 1972 found several Indian and Pakistani men who had moved to Newcastle as early as the 1930s, leaving Britain for a period of years and then returning with their families (Atkinson 1972: 135–6).

Such longstanding histories of migration and settlement, repeated in a diverse tapestry across Britain, raise questions about the persistence of racism at personal, local and national levels. The supposed ethnic homogeneity of England, and in particular the North East, has been ideologically constructed on the basis of changes in British capitalism including an increasingly imperialist relation to other countries, which has been justified by racist ideas about those countries' inhabitants. While there is no simple and linear causation between structural factors and particular outcomes of racialised oppression, some structural formations are more conducive to racist outcomes than others (Williams 2005: 40), and play a large role in influencing particular racial or ethnic constructions. The ideological construction of an ethnically homogenous England was part of welding a coherent imperialist 'nation' whose working class would identify with the interests of the national ruling class and would view workers of other countries as sufficiently 'alien' that they would not object to their wholesale plunder and oppression.

The Role of 'Race' in the Management of Labour

Since production and labour relations necessarily entail social relations and labourers as social agents, this requires systems of signification to select and legitimate use of labour, of which race is one historically contingent instance (Miles 1987: 187–8). Race may be regarded as a form of myth, carrying social and political force, despite its non-correspondence with material reality. Studies of the role of myth and magic across different societies suggest that where secular understanding and technique is sufficient to meet human needs, myth plays no role. The propagation of racism is therefore intimately tied to material conditions, and to the absence of a scientific understanding of society and the capacity to act on it (Cassirer 1967: 278–9). As Kahani-Hopkins and Hopkins (2002: 290–91) point out, 'Myths only ever occur as arguments, and as arguments are invariably specific responses to a particular state of affairs or opposing alternatives', and therefore develop at the conjuncture of political struggles. While the particular symbolic content of constructions of racism in Britain have shifted in response to changes in socio-economic conditions, including factors such as demand for labour in Britain, the symbolic role of racism in managing bodies' relationship to capital forms a line of continuity (Goldberg 1994: 53–4; Dominelli 1997: 11–15).

Saxton (1990: 14–18) locates the 'pre-race' basis of race-thinking in the interaction of population and state movements with class relations, relations then requiring justification to fit with Enlightenment morality. Under capitalism, there has been a long history of legislative controls on the movement of poor people, initially internally, with the Poor Law and Vagrancy Laws operating in early British capitalism to control movement from the countryside to the towns, while minimising the costs to the state (Gordon and Newnham 1985: 5). These controls, and the systematic exploitation they played a part in managing, were supported and justified at the time by the idea that class characteristics were transmitted through heredity, and that working class people had inherent and degenerate biological differences (Cashmore and Troyna 1990: 43; Lentin 2004: 51). It was only with the development of the imperialist character of British capitalism from the mid nineteenth century that the majority of the working class in Britain began to be incorporated into the same 'race' as the British ruling class, and the legislative focus shifted to 'external' migration controls (Schuster 2003: 175; Kundnani 2007: 12–13), with Irish Catholics an early focus of anti-immigrant hostility (Hickman 1996: 85–9).

The Connection Between British Nationalism and Racism

Viewed abstractly, there is no necessary conjunction between racism and nationalism, but a particular and close relationship has developed in the context of Britain's position as the first fully-developed capitalist country in the world, and its colonial and imperialist relations with other nations (Cassirer 1967: 232; also Miles and Phizacklea 1987: 133). Since the development of British oppression over other countries began, nationalism has played a dominant role in enabling the ruling class to present their own interests as the 'general interests' of society (Marx and Engels [1845] 1991: 52–3). In this context, racism towards migrants from oppressed countries is generated by the threat they represent to the divide between 'our' wealth and 'their' poverty (Kundnani 2007: 3–4), particularly where much of 'our wealth' was produced by 'them'.

Following previous periods in which labour was moved around the world through direct force under slavery and then indenture, today capital is largely reliant on less direct means of manipulating the movement of labour according to its needs (Kyriakides and Virdee 2003: 285). Racism plays a vital role, informally structuring individuals' relationship to capital in line with international divisions of labour. At the same time, racism diverts attention from the structural causes of population displacement onto racialised and localised explanations, such as 'Holy wars, nationalist wars, ethnic conflicts, genocidal threats, and terrorist activities' (Richmond 2002: 710). For example, in the case of Somalia, which provides one of the largest sections of the refugee population in London: 'It was more convenient to present the Somalis as uncivilised "barbarians", who had a natural propensity to tribal warfare, rather than to acknowledge the West's own hand in Somalia's collapse in the 1980s' (Kundnani 2007: 38).

The early US sociologist of race, Robert Ezra Park, predicted that the increasing integration of the world economic system and interrelationships between modern states would decrease the importance of race in favour of class (Geschwender 1977: 6–7). Hardt and Negri (2001: 236–7) argue that this has indeed happened, and that nation states have become irrelevant, to the point that class struggle acts, 'without limits', directly between an international capitalist class and an international labouring class, without distinction of nation. If this were accurate, then it may be argued that the current stage of capitalism contains no material basis for racism, or that, as Gilroy (2001: 56–7) argues, modernity's racism dependent on nations as bounded and antagonistic entities has been transcended by qualitatively new and post-modern racisms. On the contrary, as the discussion of imperialism in Chapter 1 demonstrates, national antagonisms continue to be a key feature of the present period, and are intensifying as the crisis of the system deepens. In the era of imperialism, struggles for national domination and liberation are an intrinsic part of the class struggle.

Assimilation and the Reconstruction of British Nationalism in the Twenty-first Century

Recent years have witnessed a drive across Western Europe towards aggressive assimilation, based on the view that violence carried out by a tiny minority of Muslims is rooted in their 'cultural difference' (Fekete 2004: 18–19), with the portrayal of 'a slippery slope from segregation to extremism to terrorism' (Kundnani 2007: 124). This has been enforced in Britain through a combination of tightening controls on entry, together with official lists of 'national values' and tests for language proficiency and national loyalty (Back et al. 2002: 446; Kostakopoulou 2010: 830). For immigrants to attain membership of the 'British nation', they are now required to explicitly support the history of British colonialism, with a handbook published by the Home Office to prepare immigrants for citizenship ceremonies describing how 'for many indigenous peoples in Africa, the Indian subcontinent, and elsewhere, the British Empire often brought more regular, acceptable and impartial systems of law and order', and 'disparate tribal areas' were united through access to the English language, healthcare and education. No mention is made in the pamphlet of the massacres and other injustices carried out under British colonialism (Kundnani 2007: 137–8). These developments have formed part of a reconfiguring of British nationalism to also include some black people and existing migrants as members of a 'multicultural nation', alongside continued denial of equal rights to most newcomers (Kyriakides and Virdee 2003: 299). A particularly stark example of the outcome of these changes has been the participation of a small number of black people in the violently anti-Muslim and pro-imperialist 'English Defence League' (Adar 2010; FRFI 2010; Taylor 2010).

The mandatory reconstruction of migrants' values, including their readiness to make 'long term sacrifices', was presented as essential for the 'national interest' under recent Labour governments (Brown 2006: 3). This nationalist agenda was advanced through a citizenship programme involving the re-writing of a historical narrative of Britain as a home of 'liberty, responsibility and fairness':

> And we should not recoil from our national history rather we should make it more central to our education ... not just dates places and names, nor just a set of unconnected facts, but a narrative that encompasses our history. And because citizenship is still taught too much in isolation, I suggest in the current review of the curriculum that we look at how we root the teaching of citizenship more closely in history. (Brown 2006: 14)

The shifting membership of the nationalist project was expressed in the emphasis, in the government White Paper *Secure Borders, Safe Haven* (Home Office 2002), on the need to cultivate a sense of 'active citizenship' in both existing 'working class communities' and those entering these communities as immigrants, reinforced by citizenship tests introduced by the 2002 *Nationality, Immigration and Asylum Act* (Griffiths et al. 2005: 212–13). Alongside the careful cooption of those sections of the working class who could be won over, the same White Paper announced new powers to strip UK citizenship from people with dual nationality if they were considered to be acting in a way 'seriously prejudicial' to the UK's 'national interests', extending the power of deportation and its potential use as a political weapon (Kundnani 2007: 128–9).

As part of this assimilationist shift, multiculturalism came under attack for interfering with national 'governance' (Zetter et al. 2006: 4–6; Però 2008: 74–6). At the time of the publication of the MacPherson Report into the death of Stephen Lawrence, which pointed to institutional racism in areas of the British state, David Blunkett, then Education Secretary, rejected the recommendation for a programme of anti-racist education on the basis that it would undermine national culture (Kundnani 2007: 131). Framed in however 'friendly' and 'welcoming' a way, assimilationist approaches to help black people 'adapt to the British way of life' assume superiority of white culture, render black people's day-to-day experience of racism invisible, ignore their positive contributions and deny their acts of resistance (Dominelli 1997: 3). The consent of migrants to assimilate is frequently considered unnecessary, as with Gordon Brown's 'solution' to migrant unemployment through the imposition of 'mandatory English training' (Brown 2006: 13). Within this context, the overall policy paradigm of recent governments has presented immigration as primarily a security problem (Cheong et al. 2007: 35). This ideological construction of particularly racialised minority immigration, and the response of 'defence of the nation' that it calls for, is enacted through a combination of implicit and veiled 'cultural' racism in the formal political arena, together with overt racism employing older, crude ideological formations on the streets and in the actions of the state's repressive apparatus (Miles 1987: 36–7; also Gilroy 2001: 246–7).

A decisive point in the turn of Labour governments towards assimilationism was the uprisings in Bradford and other Northern cities in the summer of 2001, which represented a response to decades of racism and poverty among large sections of the Asian population (McGhee 2003). Research on the political engagement of Muslims following the uprisings found that large sections of Muslim people felt they had no influence on decisions at a local level, let alone nationally (Jayaweera and Choudhury 2008: 88–90), but contrary to the dominant response of the state that followed, research also found that this related at least as much to material inequality and racism as to a lack of willingness to engage with wider society (Jayaweera and Choudhury 2008: 78). The response of Labour governments focused on promotion of a set of 'British values' as the defining feature for a reconstructed British nationalism, in an approach summed up by then Labour Chancellor Gordon Brown, in a speech to the Fabian Society:

> ... if we are clear that shared values – not colour, nor unchanging and unchangeable institutions – define what it means to be British in the modern world, we can be far more ambitious in defining for our time the responsibilities of citizenship; far more ambitious in forging a new and contemporary settlement of the relationship between state, community and individual ... our success as Great Britain, our ability to meet and master not just the challenges of a global economy, but also the international, demographic, constitutional and social challenges ahead, and even the security challenges, requires us to rediscover ... the shared values that bind us together and give us common purpose. (Brown 2006: 2; also Blair 2006)

This reconstructed British nationalism served to deflect attention away from economic inequalities and onto the values and beliefs of minorities (Cheong et al. 2007: 26), uniting different ethnic groups through opposition to the Muslim and asylum seeker 'other' (Fekete 2004: 18–19), at the same time as second and third generation descendents of immigrants continued to suffer racism (Lentin 2004: 311–12). In this process, long-standing cultural racisms were mobilised in response to particular material conditions and struggles. McGhee (2003: 396–400) suggests that the punitive sentences handed out to young Asian people following the 2001 uprisings related at least in part to a view of them as representatives of a 'dangerous other', ignoring the context of provocations by heavy-handed policing and far-right activity. A key determinant of who is included in such target 'out-groups' is their perceived support for, or simply symbolisation of, forces of resistance to imperialism, and repression of these groups has been brutal and far-ranging, from deportation, to systematic police harassment, to shoot-to-kill (Brickley 2005).

The Displacement of Anti-Racism by 'Anti-Discrimination' Approaches
The shift towards assimilation has been supported by attempts to refocus away from anti-racism and particularly structural elements of oppression, onto a more generalised 'anti-discrimination' approach. More or less radical varieties of 'diversity' initiatives have been promoted in the name of overcoming one-dimensional perspectives, which ignore the interaction of oppression based, for example, on gender and racism, but have been criticised for diverting attention from the specific roots and processes of racism, which are targeted by anti-racist approaches (Butt 2006: 1–2). The conflation of racism with other forms of 'discrimination' follows the post-war 'UNESCO tradition' on race, based on a scientific discrediting of the biological basis of race, and its replacement by an explanation of human difference based on categories of culture and ethnicity, which serves to dehistoricise racism and hide its connection to the state (Lentin 2004: 74–7). This view, strongly influenced by liberal humanism and psychological explanations of racism, makes claims to be 'colour-blind', but in doing so ignores questions of power and the different treatment and social position of black and white people (Frankenberg 1994: 142–9; also Saxton 1990: 10; Hesse et al. 1992: 51). When confronted with the reality of racist outcomes, the assimilationist logic of such a perspective is that greater success by white people is due to individual excellence (Dyer 1999: 9), whereas poorer outcomes for black people is due to some deficiency on their part, such as lack of skills or competencies in order to compete equally, and that they should use 'mind over matter' to overcome their problems, creating the illusion that black people can 'earn equality' if they work hard enough (Williams 2005: 38–44). Simultaneously, racialised depictions of 'ethnic communities' as homogenous blocks deny internal struggles. It is suggested that assimilation is the only road to progress, for example for Muslim women fighting gender inequalities, as though women's oppression was absent from 'White British' communities and values, when an average of two women a day die as a result of domestic violence from their partners in mainstream, 'white' British society (Kundnani 2007: 138–9). Geschwender (1977: 7–8) describes

the assimilationist perspective as concluding in the argument that immigrants themselves, and particularly those showing 'visible difference', are the ones responsible for racism (also Ahmad 1993: 8). The extreme lengths to which the British state has been prepared to carry this argument, when necessitated by their interests, was shown in the late 1930s, when the government refused to accept Jewish refugees from Germany on the grounds that this would increase anti-semitism (Schuster 2002: 54–5).

Links between racism, sexism, homophobia, and other forms of discrimination need to be established through a concrete analysis of each and their interaction, rather than by starting from the assertion that they are all basically the same. At the same time, while maintaining analytical distinctions, we must also keep in sight their coexistent and interconnected nature in material reality. This is not to imply that anti-racist and women's struggles should be subsumed within a simplistic notion of the class struggle, or that they should be pushed back to await redress on its 'conclusion'; rather, it is to argue that the class struggle can only be waged effectively through an explicit and concrete focus on the role of gendered and racialised oppression.

Refugees in Britain and the Management of Migration

A concrete examination of the position of refugees in Britain is impeded by the rigid distinction often drawn between 'proactive' and 'reactive migrants', and between refugees and other forms of migration (Bowes et al. 2009: 24–5). This is reflected in a historical divide between refugee and migration studies (Sorensen and Olwig 2002: 7–10). 'Proactive migrants' are frequently thought of as making a 'free' and independent choice to migrate, while 'reactive migrants' are assumed to be forced to migrate by external conditions beyond their control. In practice, there is rather a continuum between those who have some freedom of choice whether, when and where to move, and those who have very little (Richmond 2002: 708–9). Even for those classified as 'forced migrants', choices are still made, even if within an extremely limited range of options (Crawley 2010: 20–23).

Refugees occupy an ambiguous position in the international division of labour, simultaneously seeking refuge on the basis of human rights regardless of demand for their labour and at the same time forming part of the international reserve army of labour, with the potential to be called on depending on circumstances and the needs of capital (Kay and Miles 1992: 4–7). As Castells ([1975] 2002: 85) suggests, the role of immigration, and by implication immigrants, 'has to be explained, not in terms of the technical demands of production, but by the specific interests of capital in a particular phase of its development'. This includes political, as well as purely economic, considerations. Refugees' situation may be viewed as a particularly acute form of the general contradiction between migrants as units of wage labour and as conscious social and political actors, with interests independent of capital and a spontaneous propensity to form non-market relationships and 'put down roots' (Coole 2009: 380). While Zygmunt Bauman and associated theorists (e.g. Barmaki 2009) suggest that refugees are being criminalised as part of an 'underclass', in a context where a reserve army is no longer necessary for contemporary capitalism, I argue that their criminalisation is instead a reflection of the continuing importance of the reserve army, and the need to discipline those who do not obey its labour market imperatives. This has implications for the wider working class, contributing to divisions that make it easier for the state to impose increased discipline.[2]

Labour Fine-Tunes the Management of Migration, Tightens the Screw on Refugees

While asylum applications did undergo a significant increase, from around 4,000 per year between 1980 and 1988, to 26,205 in 1990 and 80,315 in 2000 (Griffiths et al. 2005: 38), the influence of asylum on public discussions of immigration is out of all proportion to the relative numbers of refugees compared to other forms of population movements (Cohen 2006: 5–6; Crawley 2006: 22–4). Between 1995 and 1999, migration to Britain from other advanced capitalist countries totaled 381,000, compared to 282,000 asylum *applications*, mostly from less economically developed countries, around half of which were rejected. Yet, it is migration from oppressed countries which is problematised in government, media and public discourse (Back et al. 2002: 451–2). Labour's five year strategy, outlined in *Controlling Our Borders: Making migration work for Britain* (Home Office 2005), involved a four-tiered system ranking 'highly-skilled' English speaking migrants above 'low-skilled', non-English speaking workers, and only allowing settlement after five years for the top two tiers (Cheong et al. 2007: 35). Initial results of this strategy unsurprisingly showed the majority of those in the top tiers to be from other imperialist countries, while the middle tiers were predominantly white Eastern Europeans, and the bottom tiers were predominantly black people from longstanding oppressed countries in Africa and Asia (Jameson 2006). Following the onset of the economic crisis, the bottom tier was suspended indefinitely. The majority of non-EU migrant workers are not entitled to state welfare on the basis of need, but only on the basis of direct labour market considerations. As Morris (2007) describes:

> ... economic migration is conducted on a largely contractual basis. Entry into an EU member state for non-EEA [European Economic Area] citizens involves clearly stated terms relating to purpose and conditions of stay. As well as specifying initial duration, these terms usually include any restrictions on the right to take employment, and a condition of no recourse to public funds for a specified period. (Morris 2007: 40)

---

2   For example, through measures such as the Welfare Reform Act 2010, which introduced multiple new grounds for withdrawing benefits from people not prepared to accept whatever work was available, no matter how poor the terms.

The exploitation of refugees is increased through greater pressure to accept undesirable and low-paid jobs, as a result of poverty and the non-availability of pensions compared to the majority of the working class, and through the lower costs to the state and capital due to their disproportionately poorer quality and more overcrowded housing conditions (Phillips 2006). Hewitt (2002) describes the way in which:

> Living outside the main social benefits system, recent asylum policy all but worsened their social exclusion and that means that different agencies find themselves struggling to meet asylum seekers' basic needs. (Hewitt 2002: 8)

This represents a fine-tuning of immigration controls, in order to recruit workers with exactly the skills needed by British capital, on the best possible terms, while attacking the rights of those fleeing persecution and poverty (Jameson 2006).

Ideological Reflections of the Management of Migration

Refugees occupy a distinct position in Britain, both in relation to capital and to other sections of the working class, a position which is mediated by racism. The measures described above are not predetermined by fixed racist ideas. Particular policies are determined by the needs of capital at a given point in time and Britain's economic, legal and political relationships with other countries (Miles and Phizacklea 1980: 14), which are then justified and enforced through racism. This draws on a long legacy of racist ideas arising under previous material conditions, which has led to racism becoming so culturally, economically, and politically ingrained that racist processes and outcomes are produced even if policy makers do not hold explicit racist intentions. Racism is the ideology and practice around which class struggle takes place, rather than simply the ideology of the ruling class, with the potential for different fractions of different classes to have interests served or opposed by racism in different instances (examples are offered by Castells [1975] 2002; Miles and Phizacklea 1987; Sivanandan 1991; Miles and Brown 2003). Different sections of capital may have different interests in the movement of labour and capital, for example manufacturing and communications capital moving to the cheapest labour markets in oppressed countries, while personal service occupations, construction and agriculture seek immigrants to move to the imperialist centres (Richmond 2002: 714). As different stages and conditions in the economic cycle impact, leading for example to changes in demand for labour or the ability of capital and the state to grant concessions, so processes of racialisation must shift and adapt (RCG 1979: 4), and historically have taken a variety of forms.

Recent Labour governments' approach of 'managed migration' made no pretence to accord rights to migrants, but viewed them purely in terms of their economic value, with an inevitable fall-out on treatment of refugees, despite claims to the contrary embodied in the UN Convention on Refugees, of which Britain is a signatory (Kundnani 2007: 7–8). Since the 1990s, there has been a shifting depiction of refugees in Britain, from a group claiming humanitarian protection to 'economic migrants' coming to sponge of the welfare state. Following the removal of access to many state benefits, which did not decrease numbers but created a national crisis, refugees became ideologically reconstructed again, now as 'illegal immigrants', and were responded to with tightened border controls, which in turn created a market for international people trafficking, which was used to further increase the image of criminality. Following September 11 2001, they made a final transformation into potential terrorists, with terrorism seen to be based on cultural difference (Kundnani 2007: 4–5). Patterns of racist attacks support the idea that racial signifiers in Britain have shifted away from a more exclusive focus on skin colour to focus on other visual factors and accent (IRR 2001: 13), with the perception of an individual as an 'asylum seeker' playing a powerful role. The impact of this is strongly gendered, reinforcing the oppression of women refugees as a distinct class fraction. While not exclusive to refugee women as opposed to all women, it is significant that 83 per cent of female refugees who participated in a national survey said they do not go out at night because they are scared of abuse and harassment (NERS 2007: 14).

Labour's Policies for Disciplining Refugees

As the metaphor implies, once refugees have 'put down roots' in Britain, with access to resources and networks of support, they are in a stronger position to resist the demands of capital. Refugees' ability to put down roots and rebuild their lives in Britain was increasingly obstructed from 1999 by key policy interventions, which combined to undermine resistance to being re-incorporated into international divisions of labour on the terms of capital. By the time the Labour Party left office in 2010 it had expanded immigration detention facilities to a capacity of over 3,000, among the largest in Europe, with the most common category of detainees in 2010 people who had sought asylum (Silverman 2011). Gill (2009) found that regular movement of detainees between centres not only disrupted any attempts by detainees to build networks, but also contributed to an attitude toward refugees as fundamentally transient among non-refugees who had contact with them, with little opportunity to form relationships, either with detention centre personnel or local support and activist organisations. This facilitated the dehumanisation of refugees as passive objects to be 'managed', with evidence that those trying to complain or organise with other detainees were particularly liable to be transferred. Outside detention, Temple et al. (2005) report refugees struggling to make wider links, in a context where they faced high levels of individual racism and disruption by the state of what connections they had established. They found that along with dispersal, refugees' attempts to reconstitute communities were restricted by: allocations of resources, which tended to exclude refugees without status from integration initiatives; hostile environments in dispersal areas, which in some cases kept people confined to their homes; and prohibition of paid work (Temple et al. 2005: 23–6). These factors were also identified in my research in Newcastle, framed and given added force by the asylum decision-making process itself.

The Asylum Decision-making Process

The deep-rooted antagonism between the interests of refugees and the British state is reflected in refugees' accounts of the asylum process. In the first quarter of 2010, 76 per cent of asylum applications were refused at their first hearing, and 68 per cent of appeals against previous refusals were also rejected. This is in a context in which 93 per cent of applications for other forms of settlement during the same period were granted, with an increase of 45 per cent in numbers of grants of settlement for employment-related purposes compared to a year earlier (Home Office 2010). BID (2009) suggests that UK asylum policies are implicitly based around a highly unrealistic 'model' refugee, who 'arrives in the UK with their identity documents, declares to the immigration authorities "I would like to make a claim for asylum under the 1951 Refugee Convention", and hands over a dossier of evidence in support of their claim' (BID 2009: 15). The mismatch of reality with this expectation leads to experiences reported by refugees in detention, who talked about 'confusion, misinformation, bad advice, fear and shock that they had ended up incarcerated' (BID 2009: 15). Issues raised by participants in my own research can be grouped into the length of wait for their case to be decided, the mistrust many reported experiencing from the state and the inconsistency, unfairness and lack of transparency of decisions.

The length of wait for a final decision was a frequent concern:

> … the way they are doing this is very slow. I was having hope, but now the hope again is a bit shaky, because it is just taking [so] long … (29 years old, arrived 2006)

> … the immigration [system] is very bad, they keep you waiting … like me eight years now … I [have] family and I left my country, I have [been] traumatised and I have so many experiences … sometimes [it is very] stressful … (arrived 2001)

> … there is this backlog of all these people who have been in this country like I have for seven years, and I haven't heard anything from the Home Office yet, and these people are just stuck in the twilight zone, they can't move on … (20 years old, arrived 2001)

Coupled with restrictions on paid work, studying or even volunteering with many organisations, the length of wait prevented many refugees I interviewed from moving on with their life and created serious uncertainty and anxiety which compounded the trauma many had experienced before coming to Britain. The pressure thus generated from refugees without status for quicker decisions helped the government to gain their support or at least acquiescence for changes to the system in 2007, when the New Asylum Model (NAM) was introduced, which reduced waiting times for decisions, while negatively affecting refugees' interests in other ways, as discussed further below.

Refugees I interviewed reported the mistrust built into the asylum system as a further degrading factor, with a starting assumption on the part of immigration officials that their stated reasons for seeking asylum were a lie. In contrast to the principle of 'innocent until proven guilty' in other areas of British law, in asylum law it is up to the claimant to prove they are telling the truth, and, until they do so to the satisfaction of state officials, they are liable to detention, deportation, and denial of other rights. While refugees are expected to place their trust in the British state, Hynes (2009) surveys the ways in which mistrust of refugees is built into every stage of the UK asylum process and is a barrier that must be overcome by refugees without status in order to be granted permission to stay in Britain. One participant in my research expressed their feelings about the unreasonable nature of the state's demands for written evidence from people who had fled situations of danger, and their frequent refusal to believe that documents were genuine even where they could be produced:

> … they will ask you, do you have any evidence, but that's asking – for example, if there is an earthquake now, suddenly, and you want to save your life, will you take your qualification, will you take your I.D., will you take everything which is important for your life? No, the important thing will be for you to save your life, and then maybe you'll be going back to your house and search for these important things. So that is what happens to asylum seekers. When they came first, maybe they have been persecuted and they don't have enough time to take all of these things, [they just] want to be safe. Even some people who are lucky [because they have documents with them], when they come with these documents, [immigration officials] will just say no, it's fake … (DRC, arrived 2005)

Many other refugees I interviewed reported experiences where they felt an arbitrary decision had been made to disbelieve them:

> I went to the Home Office interview. I had proof that I worked for that man and I was in danger. They said we know that is not your picture, they refused [my case], they even said that this isn't your children … the baby's not yours as well. (DRC, secured status in 2008)

> … they ask you to give them the reason why you left your country … after that they say the reason is failed, how can a reason fail, I don't understand. (Zimbabwe, secured status in 2009)

Both of these individuals were initially disbelieved, but eventually won their case after a legal struggle. This echoes other research, which reports refugees' perceptions that culturally-based misconceptions were a major determinant in judges' decisions, overriding the credibility of accounts by refugees, expert witnesses and other evidence (Chantler 2010: 101).

Related to experiences of willful disbelief by the state, is the perception expressed by many refugees I interviewed that there is a lack of consistency, fairness and transparency in the asylum process. A perception of lack of consistency between decisions for different individuals contributed to a sense of the process as arbitrary rather than based on a thorough examination of each case:

> Sometimes you can see that the process isn't fair, because some people will have left the [same] country … for the same reason as I, and they had their status like straight away, whereas I'm waiting now nine years. (26 years old, arrived 2000)

A lack of access to proper legal representation and translators was reported by this refugee (and several others) as restricting the fairness of decisions:

> … when we went to the airport it was an officer … her French was very broken, and we were trying to explain to her why we came, and she was very impatient and she was very rude, and she just left, and then another man came, and his French was even worse than hers … they asked us to sign [to confirm what they had written down], I wasn't sure but we had to, because we didn't know about anything, we're just in the airport and people were crying. So we just signed anything that they gave us. And then a month later we got refused because we didn't have a good reason to seek asylum. And then we went to a solicitor with an interpreter, and what those officers had written had nothing to do with what we said …

For refugees who do not speak any European language, which is more common for refugees from poorer backgrounds, the lack of proper translation may be even more difficult to overcome. Another refugee explained the frequent lack of legal support:

> … a lot of asylum seekers even for the first time they go to the court by themselves, nobody comes with them, it is more than 50 per cent of cases not successful, and of course it is not right … (Iran, arrived 2002)

Reinforcing the feeling that decisions were arbitrary, was the lack of transparency reported by several participants as to the exact decision-making process and criteria:

> … you don't know who is being given papers and who is not. You'll find that someone has been here maybe for ten years, they're still struggling, someone

> who has been here for two years, is given papers. So they don't have formula really, you never know how they work. (Zimbabwe, arrived 2006)

Of those participants who were aware of changes to the asylum system since their arrival in Britain, the majority felt that in most cases the changes had been to the disadvantage of those 'in the system':

> ... when I started working the new system came in, just Home Office trying to make it as hard as possible for people to get status ... (arrived 2001, started volunteering at VOL in 2007)

> ... [the] first year I came here ... everything [was] ok and every year [the government] make [things] a little bit [more] difficult for asylum seekers ... especially for court, and finding solicitor, interpreter or everything, before is very well, but now every year make it too difficult for people. (Volunteer with CHUR, arrived 2000)

Restrictions on the right to appeal were reported as having a very serious impact on refugees' chances of securing leave to remain in Britain:

> ... when I first arrived here we could have several appeals if our case was rejected, and we could go to High Court, but now it's just one appeal, and after one appeal you are either deported or left in limbo. (Volunteer with CHUR, arrived 2000)

Areas where some refugees I interviewed felt there had been positive change were the reductions in the time taken for decisions to be taken and the greater clarity and consistency of having the same Home Office caseworker throughout each case, which were part of the changes under NAM:

> I think it's actually ok, they're trying to make it better for everybody, not just for themselves. Because at the moment there's a lot of immigrants, so what they've done is introduce new, different models, like now for instance is the New Asylum Model, it's something different. I think they're doing it just to help people to get over as many cases as they can. (Volunteer with VOL, arrived 2005)

Although this individual expressed many other views in sympathy with the actions and perspective of the state towards refugees, on this point their views were shared by a greater range of other refugees I interviewed. Support for NAM among some of those who made applications before 2007 reflects divisions it fostered among refugees, which will be returned to in Chapter 4.

Overall, the refugees I interviewed presented a picture of the asylum process as unreasonable, unclear and unjust. A fog of complexity and bureaucracy covers up for the fact that a process which is 'fair' in formal terms is in practice set up to fail all but a few, regardless of their need. This fulfills two related but contradictory needs of imperialism, which shape the management of refugees' oppression. On the one hand, the absolute priority accorded to capital's demand for labour as the basis for migrants to live in Britain is reinforced by the likelihood of being refused asylum, necessary for the continuation of the imperialist division of labour. On the other hand, the British state's image as an upholder of universal human rights and liberty is maintained by the formal fairness of the system, necessary for the claims to moral authority so often used to justify imperialist interference and domination.

Dispersal

Since 1999 'dispersal' – the forced resettlement of refugees without status to towns and cities across the UK – has been a key element in the British state's attempts to manage refugees. Following the Asylum and Immigration Act 1996, which made local authorities responsible for housing refugees while their cases were being considered, pressure developed from local authorities in the South East of England, where a high proportion of refugees at that time were housed, to relocate them to other parts of the country (Phillimore and Goodson 2006: 1716). The Immigration and Asylum Act 1999 made provision for the compulsory 'dispersal' of refugees to towns and cities across Britain, echoing assimilationist policies involving the dispersal of ethnic minorities in the 1950s and 1960s (Griffiths et al. 2005: 38). Other historical precedents include the dispersal of refugees without status in Germany from 1982, which served to impose new restrictions on movement, reduce access to certain social benefits and worsen overall social conditions, in a process that, it has been suggested, was as much about creating a deterrent to new applicants as the stated aim of sharing costs between regions (Boswell 2003: 319).

The dispersal of refugees without status reflects their status as presently unwanted members of the reserve army of labour, who capital has no place for within Britain. The existence of 'intra-ethnic' social capital has been pointed to in the case of Pakistani communities in London as a set of structures and strategies, such as employment within the ethnic group or with white employers via specialised 'middle men', capable of providing a basic level of subsistence and some degree of 'buffering' from the racism of wider society (Ahmad 2008: 856). The dispersal process has played a significant political role in breaking up such diasporic networks, removing their potential as a basis for resistance, or even a degree of independence from the state. Just as the larger numbers of casually employed workers in Britain prior to the First World War required more directly oppressive policing in order to maintain stable capitalist accumulation (Jefferson 1991: 169–71), in the recent period, the presence of refugees within the imperialist heartlands has posed a threat to the stability of the domestic social contract. Significantly in the context of imperialism, the existence of coherent and self-conscious diasporas with a sense of shared identity between immigrants in imperialist countries and their oppressed countries of origin, rather than with the national ruling class of their new home, poses a threat to national borders on both an ideological and practical level (Gilroy 2001: 124). Behind the prominence of 'social cohesion' in recent discussions of immigration, there lies a concern with real or perceived threats to the state (Griffiths et al. 2005: 212–13). Dispersal has played a role in countering the threat diasporic communities pose to 'social cohesion', by physically separating refugees with status from those without, refugees without status from the rest of society, and refugees without status from one another, often just at the point that they were beginning to form new relationships (Hynes 2009). Refugees' lack of control over where they are dispersed has contributed to particular problems of isolation for some refugees, such as women refugees experiencing domestic violence, with UKBA giving contradictory responses to women's refuges about the resources available to move women experiencing violence at the location they were dispersed (Chantler 2010: 96–7).

Political conditions for dispersal were created by a government and media campaign portraying an 'invasion' of Dover by 'asylum scroungers'. This was based on the presence of less than 1000 Czech and Slovak Roma refugees, who were then targeted with a vicious campaign of racism, enabling the government to begin forcible dispersal under the argument that fewer refugees in any one place would 'provoke' less racism from local people (Kundnani 2007: 81–3). This was a revival of an argument blaming migrants for racism, which had also been employed to justify dispersing Vietnamese refugees in 1979 and 1981 (Boswell 2003: 320–21). Coordination of housing was transferred from local authorities to the National Asylum Support Service (NASS), operating under the direction of the Immigration and Nationality Directorate (IND), and subsistence payments were set at a rate 30 per cent below the minimum unemployment benefits available to British citizens.

Local Conditions in Dispersal Areas
In selecting areas for dispersal, little consideration was given to social and economic infrastructure or existing community networks or resources (Griffiths et al. 2005: 41–2). In the early period of dispersal, research nationally found that 'almost nowhere in the UK is there a coherent, comprehensive local community relations strategy involving a great number of relevant stakeholders in the statutory, voluntary, and community sectors' (Hewitt 2002: 5). This contributed to a situation in which dispersal served to cut off refugees from family, friends, ethnic communities, services and refugee support groups, and to relocate them to areas with inadequate social provision, a lack of qualified lawyers, and high levels of exposure to racism (Boswell 2003: 326; Briskman and Cemlyn 2005: 718; Temple et al. 2005). The main priority driving the dispersal process was the need to find cheaper and more available housing, often resulting in refugees being dispersed to largely white areas with 'high levels of multiple social deprivation, violence and anti-social behaviour'. Reports were common of refugees in NASS accommodation only rarely being moved in the event of problems, and housing contractors getting away with 'blatant abuse' (Hewitt 2002: 7; also Boswell 2003:

324). All seven of the major dispersal areas nationally were in the top twenty most deprived areas in Britain on the Index of Multiple Deprivation (Phillimore and Goodson 2006: 1717). In an indication of how unpopular dispersal was among refugees, in the initial period, up to two thirds of refugees without status took up residence with family or friends in order to avoid being dispersed (Boswell 2003: 322). This may be viewed as a smashing up of existing networks of support and solidarity, and a starting point of extreme weakness and isolation from which refugees tried to rebuild their lives.

In Glasgow, members of community-based organisations reported that the rapid housing of refugees in refurbished housing, in areas where maintenance of council housing had been neglected for many years, made integration with local residents more difficult, causing resentment that took some time to overcome (Bowes et al. 2009: 36). At the time that dispersal began, Newcastle was experiencing serious problems of 'void' or unoccupied council housing, and was the first city to bid to receive dispersed refugees through the North East Consortium, alongside considering the possibility of housing refugees without status in prison ships on the river Tyne (Evening Chronicle 2000). While acknowledging the lower quality of vacant compared to occupied properties, Newcastle City Council justified dispersal to areas with large amounts of vacant properties on the basis of 'good use of resources available to authorities', suggesting that 'there is a basis for providing accommodation which can be more easily upgraded to suitable provision rather than having to provide addition [sic] new accommodation' (Policy and Research Services 2002). Within five months of setting up an Asylum Seekers Unit (ASU) in December 1999, Newcastle had received 100asylum-seeking families. By 2002, the ASU was housing 500 households and working with 2,500 refugees whose claims were being processed (Evening Chronicle 2002). Refugees continued to be dispersed direct to Newcastle until April 2007, when the UK Borders Act made significant changes, including reorganising dispersal to Leeds as Newcastle's local 'hub', from where some would continue to be housed in Newcastle.

In predominantly white and working class areas in the East end of Newcastle, seventy empty properties were opened up to refugees (Interview with a local authority community worker, 2005). A refugee, who arrived in the North East in the early period of dispersal, described the lack of provision that greeted them:

> ... no services were set up to welcome them ... just a person in the council who was dealing with that issue, he said ok, we have some void houses ... and unfortunately most of the asylum seekers have been put in the most deprived areas, even the voided houses [which] no ... British [people would] accept ... So there were that gap ... the cultural barriers [and] a lack of services, even an organisation ... to welcome those people ... (Volunteer with COM, arrived 2002)

As in many other dispersal areas, local professionals report that in the East end of Newcastle support was left largely to a local church-based organisation, which offered a drop-in free shop offering advice, networking and practical support such as warm clothing and cooking utensils, while a local authority-based project focused more specifically on racial harassment (Interviews, 2005).

In the West end of Newcastle, a private company, Angel Group, announced plans to turn a former nursing home into a hostel to house 200 single male refugees without status (Young 1999). 'Angel Heights' became the site of regular protests by its residents. On 10 May 2000, six refugees without status were arrested following a protest in which dozens of men refused to go back into the hostel, claiming they were treated 'worse than prisoners', and were then penned into the courtyard by thirty police. Some were arrested and held for several weeks on remand, before all charges were eventually dropped (Renton 2007: 191–2). The protest had been sparked by Angel Group's reduction of the adult residents' weekly allowance from £7 to £5 per week. A few weeks earlier, on 22 April, a manager at the hostel had made claims to a local newspaper about how happy the refugees living at the hostel were, describing them repeatedly as 'boys', and had dismissed accusations that the hostel was 'like an open prison', saying that residents were free to leave any time they chose (Heywood 2000). Angel Group claimed the 10 May cash cut was to pay for £600 damage done to the centre, while those staying at the hostel said only a table had been broken in previous weeks. Kent Council, at that time still responsible for welfare provision to refugees dispersed to Newcastle, justified the cut, saying that a 'complete care package' was provided and that Angel Group were 'generous' to give residents any cash at all (Hutchinson and Dickinson 2000). On 17 January 2001, fifteen Afghan refugees were arrested at Angel Heights following further protests, according to the police aimed at expressing dissatisfaction with the accommodation, but according to Angel Group owing to frustration at the amount of time their asylum claims were taking, and tensions between different national groups cooped up together (Charlton 2001).

In addition to Angel Heights, Angel Group also housed refugee families in areas of Newcastle previously abandoned for demolition, with a scattered number of properties reopened, and break-ins, fires and serious racial attacks a frequent occurrence. According to the levels of dissatisfaction reported in the council's own survey of ethnic minority tenants in 1999 (Research and Information Services 1999), it is unsurprising that in many cases the promised 'upgrading' of inadequate accommodation does not appear to have been carried out by the time tenants moved in, or for some time after. In fact, dispersal represented a generalisation of much longer-running trends in refugee settlement in Newcastle. For example, in 1972, Ugandan Asian refugees were reported to be housed in the West end of Newcastle in poor quality housing and met with racism from some in the area, with 'Asians Keep Out' painted in letters three foot high along the street, and reports of attempts to set fire to one refugee's door (Evening Chronicle 1972).

Racism played a central role in isolating refugees' experiences from the consciousness of British workers. Refugees dispersed to Newcastle from 1999 encountered an intensely hostile context. An article in the local *Evening Chronicle* is symptomatic, titled 'Police hunt four illegal immigrants: Asylum seekers go on the run', referring to four men who had come from Holland in the back of a lorry and then run away from the driver (Hickman 2002). While there was also a more positive side to local media coverage, refugees in Newcastle, and those alongside them, were also subject to hostility from the national press. When a national lottery grant allowed the National Coalition of Anti-Deportation Campaigns (NCADC) to set up an office in nearby Middlesbrough, Home Secretary David Blunkett responded to a hostile *Daily Mail* campaign by calling for a review of the grant. The Community Fund subsequently made the grant conditional on the organisation 'toning down' what they called 'aggressive campaigning on its website' (Kennedy 2002), and further National Lottery funding was cut in 2005, resulting in the closure of the Middlesbrough office and redundancies. This contributed to a 'taming' of much potential opposition. In 2003, the Chair of a major voluntary sector refugee organisation in the region gave backing to a Home Affairs Select Committee Report, which warned that rising numbers of refugees could 'overwhelm' Britain and lead to a 'backlash' and the election of far right parties, with the Chair quoted in the local press saying 'The last thing we want to see is the British characteristic of welcoming people in to this country disappear' (Marley 2003).

Alongside attacks on refugees, the state and organised racists combined to put pressure on black residents of Newcastle during the early period of dispersal. In 2002, the National Front (NF) leafleted in the West end against a new mosque, while the council threatened to shut down an improvised mosque where people were worshipping while the official one was being built (Marley 2002). Between 2001–2002 and 2002–2003, reported race crimes in the North East nearly doubled from 503 to 934, with anti-racist protests taking place in Peel Street, Sunderland (Redvers 2003), and a march on Sunderland police station by fifty refugees without status, after the fatal stabbing of Iranian refugee Peyman Bahmani (Renton 2007: 206). In 2004, a black family, who had moved from their previous area because of racist abuse, started to receive attacks within a week of moving into their new home in the West end of Newcastle, despite having specifically asked the local housing provider if there were any problems of racism in the area, and had their windows put out three times, suffered abuse in the street, and finally had their home ransacked while they were away (Armstrong 2004). Such individual racism, fostered by the state and media, puts pressure on refugees to either accept whatever terms of support the British state might offer, or otherwise leave Britain.

Capital has no interest in refugees remaining in Britain, because they are driven by imperatives that override demand for their labour, and consequently the state has little interest in providing any but the most basic means of survival. The state has even less interest in helping refugees integrate with other working class people. Such integration could both offer solidarity for refugees' attempts to remain in Britain and advance their rights, and fundamentally threaten the divisions among workers of different countries, which imperialism relies on to undermine resistance to the super-exploitation of oppressed countries. By disrupting connections with other refugees, support networks and other sections of workers, the dispersal system has undermined the potential for collective resistance and increased pressure for refugees to accept the positions assigned them in international divisions of labour. It thus forms a key element in the management of refugees' oppression.

The Prohibition on Paid Work

While some categories of migrant workers have continued to receive encouragement to come to Britain, most refugees without status are prohibited by law from seeking paid work or even accessing work-based training, cutting them off from legal areas of the British labour market (Phillimore and Goodson 2006: 1721). Prior to the legislative prohibition of paid work in 2002, the 'right to work' had already been restricted to refugees with status and to the 'primary claimant' on each asylum application, and even then only once the person had been in Britain for at least six months (Dumper 2002: v). This excluded many women from paid work as 'secondary claimants' on family members' applications, and legally enforced their role of unpaid domestic work in the reproduction of the labour power of family members permitted to do paid work, as a super-exploited section of labour.

In a capitalist society, where survival and self-worth for the majority are tied to the sale of one's labour power, several refugees I interviewed spoke about the negative impact on their self-esteem and mental health as a result of forced inactivity due to being denied the right to undertake paid work:

> If they lose their hope they will kill themselves. I didn't lose my hope yet totally, but sometimes I ... say ok, I finish this university, what [else can I] do when I don't have permission to work? ... Just to sit at home or just look at the television or something like that, it kills everyone. (45 years old, arrived 2002)

Several refugees also described the legal restrictions on funding for refugees without status in higher education, which blocked the majority from progressing with their studies as an alternative to paid work:

> ... in August I'm going to enroll for an economy course, because I think I've done every imaginable course I could do now and economy and business is left ... (20 years old, arrived 2001)

> I went to college when I came here but because of my situation I couldn't go to higher education ... (43 years old, arrived 2000)

In the accounts of refugees I interviewed, the experience of being a refugee, particularly one who has not been granted some form of refugee status or 'leave to remain' by the state, was strongly characterised by insecurity and dependency on the state, enforced by the prohibition on paid work:

... the asylum seeker is limited, he's not allowed to work ... his income is very low, and he doesn't know the outcome of his decision, so any time he can be deported or can be accepted, so he is in limbo ... (arrived 2002)

Relative household poverty rates for people resident in the UK but lacking UK citizenship suggest inequalities may be greater among those most dependent on the state (Table 2.4). This suggests that increased dependency for refugees may contribute to an even greater material division between them and other sections of the working class in Britain.

Table 2.4   Household poverty rates by citizenship and degree of reliance on benefits in 1994

	Primary reliance on wage	Primary reliance on state benefits
UK citizen	4.5%	17.5%
Non-citizen	9.4%	44.8%

Source: Morrissens and Sainsbury 2005: 648.

Several refugees I interviewed vividly expressed the severity of their situation in Britain, compounding traumatic experiences in their country of origin:

... maybe they flee their country because they were persecuted, and when they came here they are experiencing the same thing. Because they will never be at rest, they will never be at peace ... (DRC, arrived 2005)

You come with a really optimistic hope that you will get a peaceful life, and you will get a normal life and you will get rid of all the stressful things in your country, and all the pressure, and all the dangers, but when you come here you face with even more difficulties and more problems. And one of the reasons I had a mental breakdown and I spent fourteen months in a psychiatric ward was because of the problems here, because they rejected my asylum claim and they wanted to deport me ... I saw no hope, I didn't want to go to my country, because that was even worse, and was much more terrible ... I tried to end my life several times ... (Iran, arrived 2000)

Uncertainty over the future was a recurring cause of anxiety reported by refugees I interviewed, and in some cases seemed to be deepened by a sense that they had little knowledge or power to change their situation:

I don't have any knowledge to change it; I don't know what to do ... (Zimbabwe, arrived 2006)

This insecurity, and the legal restrictions on many kinds of action which might have improved their situation, contributed to an intense sense of dependency:

> I've always been independent ... but now it's as if I'm in prison ... there's nothing that proves that I'm an adult, I am just at home, just wait[ing] for somebody to give [things to me] ... (Cameroon, arrived 2008)

By coming to Britain under imperatives other than the labour market, refugees have broken discipline with the reserve army of labour. Asylum policies thus combine to disempower refugees and enforce their dependency on the British state and with it their responsiveness to be re-disciplined into the reserve army. This both keeps them in an oppressed position, and manages this situation by enforcing compliance with the terms of their oppression.

The Long-term Impact of Asylum Policies on Refugees with Status

Government policy since 1999 has consistently acted to separate refugees with and without status, despite the lived reality that 'what happens to people before their claims are settled and what faces them in settlement are intimately connected' (Temple et al. 2005: 7–8). Entitlement to housing has been increasingly restricted and tied to immigration status, and changes in 2005 which limited initial periods of leave to remain, to five years, removed the option of taking out a mortgage (Dwyer and Brown 2008: 205–7). Policies targeting refugees while their cases are being considered continue to impact on their experience of the labour market if and when they are granted status. In some cases, refugees have been subjected to repeated re-dispersal in the years since 1999, with one study identifying individuals who had been forced to relocate to three different cities in four months. This leaves a 'legacy of dispersal', where applications for credit and employment are jeopardised by so many changes of address (Hynes 2009). The forced gap in employment while a person's claim is being considered, which has now reduced on average, but for some has lasted more than ten years with no response, leads to a loss of skills and, in some occupations such as medicine, makes it particularly difficult to resume a former career. In research focusing on refugees and healthcare professionals in London, 63 per cent of interviewees had professional qualifications but only 15 per cent were working, with significant levels of long-term unemployment, despite 80 per cent having the right to work (Cowen 2003: 4,12). Additionally, increased threats to employers of fines and prosecution for taking on employees legally prohibited from paid work have contributed to a reluctance among some employers to take on any refugees in order to avoid having to check documents, or for fear of accidentally breaking the law (Bloch 2007: 22).

This contributes to a situation for those who have been granted some form of refugee status where, although they can legally seek paid work, the work that is available is generally significantly deskilled and limited compared to the work performed in their countries of origin, concentrated in catering, interpreting and translation, shop work and administration and clerical jobs (WLRI 2005: 32), and higher proportions are unemployed than in their countries of origin (Bloch 1999: 190–91). A survey of 1600 refugees dispersed to the West Midlands found high levels of motivation to seek work and a range of qualifications, but also found individuals frequently left with little choice but to accept low-skilled and low-paid work, even where their qualifications and past experience were above this. Of those working, 79 per cent were employed as process, plant and machine operatives or in elementary occupations. Compared to a regional average wage of £19,296, more than half earned less than £9,600 and none earned more than £13,000 (Phillimore and Goodson 2006: 1725–7). Another study found an average hourly rate of £7.29 among refugees, compared with an average of £11.74 for the general population, and 11 per cent of refugees paid less than the minimum wage. 25 per cent of refugees in work were found to be in temporary jobs, compared with 6 per cent of the working age population, and 35 per cent compared to 23 per cent were working part-time, mostly because they could not find full-time employment (WLRI 2005: 31–2). It is estimated that, on average, refugees in paid employment earn only 79 per cent the level of ethnic minorities overall (Bloch 2007: 24). More than one refugee I interviewed who had secured leave to remain described lack of language skills, deskilling and lack of access to resources as continuing their material insecurity, particularly in comparison to their previous class position:

> I've lost my skills at the moment ... I need to improve my English, and then back to finding some choice ... dishwasher, cleaner, I can't work in [that kind of work for a] long time. For ... higher education my English [is] not [good] enough, for open[ing] my personal acupuncture clinic I haven't got finance support ... (former professional, 39 years old, with status)

While English language skills have repeatedly been identified as a key factor in employment outcomes, in the West Midlands survey cited above:

> ... one of the issues repeatedly raised by interviewees was the difficulty they had accessing English classes. They often experienced long waiting lists, overcrowded classes, lessons aimed at low levels, limited progression opportunities and a lack of emphasis on vocational language. (Phillimore and Goodson 2006: 1726)

In the absence of rewarding paid work, many refugees have little option but to undertake work for no pay, with a Department of Work and Pensions study finding 29 per cent of refugees engaged in formalised voluntary work (WLRI 2005: 34).

Dispersal has been found to further limit access to employment and social networks even after securing leave to remain, and to decrease opportunities to move to where there are greater opportunities (Bloch 2007: 24). In 2005, unemployment rates for refugees with status were estimated to be around 36 per cent nationally, with far higher levels in particular areas, and estimates of 60 to 90 per cent unemployment among refugees in London (Phillimore and Goodson 2006: 1720–21). In one survey, 43 per cent of refugees had been unemployed for more than six months (WLRI 2005: 31–2). As one refugee said:

> … once you have your status, you're like in a golden cage. So you have a better cage, but it's still a cage … you can see all the doors that can be opened … but then you can't open them … you can work, well look for a job, there's no jobs. Well you can travel, but if you don't have your passport you can't travel. You can send your child in the crèche, but then you have to have health visitor … if you move from another city there is no health visitor, so you have to look for one …
> (woman refugee, 26 years old, with status)

Women refugees face particular barriers to finding paid work. Among a survey of 400 refugees in five localities around Britain in 2002, women refugees were more likely to be out of work, and of those out of work they were less likely to be seeking work, and more frequently because of childcare or other responsibilities. For those in work, women were more likely to be in different jobs to their country of origin, and on average lower paid and more likely to be in part-time and casualised work. Employment levels were also far lower for those without a UK qualification, and 26 per cent of women compared to 1 per cent of men mentioned lack of available childcare as a barrier to undertaking training or education (Bloch 2007: 27–9). This demonstrates once again the ways in which class, racism and gender oppression have the potential to act not simply as multiple discrete lines of oppression, but to interact and compound one another in complex ways.

Adult refugees to Britain thus experience significant downward class mobility compared to their position in their countries of origin. A combination of factors result in refugees beginning their economic existence in Britain as long-term unemployed, with few prospects of becoming self-supporting, and therefore unlikely to be able to move out of the deprived areas to which they were dispersed (Phillimore and Goodson 2006: 1730). Younger refugees also encounter significant barriers on entering the British labour market, frequently leading them to accept casualised and insecure work in the hope that this will lead to something better, although often these hopes are not fulfilled (Centrepoint 2004: 27). The inclusion of English for Speakers of Other Languages (ESOL) classes in the Job Seeker Allowance restriction of 16 hours of learning a week further limits the kind of jobs many refugees are able to train themselves for (Centrepoint 2004: 11). Meanwhile, the introduction of the 'five-year' rule in 2005, only granting five-year leave to remain followed by review rather than indefinite refugee status, further reduces refugees' sense of security and may act as a disincentive to invest time and energy in training (Bloch 2007: 22–3). This results in a situation where, even for refugees granted status, for many their acceptance into the British labour force is only as 'second class workers', and they will always bear the mark of the reserve army, under pressure to accept whatever work is offered.

Conclusions

The racism required to justify and 'manage' international divisions of labour within the imperialist system extends beyond immediate migrants, impacting variously on anybody associated with or identifying with the populations of oppressed countries, including many black people within Britain, as part of a dialectic of racism and national oppression. Recent Labour governments promoted a reconfigured British nationalism based on a value-based assimilationism. At a policy level, this has been implemented through a fine-tuning of immigration controls, including declarations of loyalty and demonstrated contributions to 'the nation' as prerequisites for admittance. Thus, oppression is managed through a conditional approach to rights which stratifies the working class along multiple levels.

Refugees occupy an intermediate class status, particularly acute while their cases are under consideration. They are part of the international reserve army of labour, but a 'part out of place', with a potential to disrupt the normal functioning of the division of labour on a political as well as an economic level. Their trajectory is in most cases from countries oppressed on a national basis, within which they may have occupied a relatively privileged class position, and with which they may maintain connections in identity, communication and transfer of resources. Their present position is among the poorest sections of the working class in Britain, in conditions which hold the potential to forge alliances across racialised divisions. From 1999, government policy specifically mitigated against this, by breaking up existing networks based on refugees' countries of origin, through dispersal, and impeding the formation of new ones based on common elements of class position within Britain, through a prohibition on paid work. With the exception of individuals who 'escape' the collective position of the majority, for example through paid employment in the refugee sector, the trajectory of most refugees after arrival in Britain is either inclusion into a more regularised but super-exploited section of the working class in Britain, or for many deportation back to the situations they have fled.

Chapter 3
Refugees and the British State

This chapter investigates the relationship between refugees and the British state, both in the objective sense of their relative locations within the imperialist system and in the subjective sense of refugees' perceptions of the British state in the light of their experiences.

Introduction

The chapter begins by presenting the Marxist theory of the state in the context of international class struggle, and develops this understanding through a brief overview of the history of the British state's relation to asylum policy. The chapter goes on to look at some of the differences between the British state and the states of countries many refugees have fled, drawing on refugees' own stories. This is followed by discussion of repressive and welfare aspects of the British state and their relation to immigration and asylum, alternating between the literature and refugees' accounts of their experiences and understandings in order to draw out complexities and contradictions. The chapter concludes by reflecting on changes in the British state currently underway and the implications for refugees.

The term 'state' does not merely describe a set of interlinked institutions, but is defined by its exclusive claim to legitimacy as the sole representative of the 'national interest' (Jones and Keating 1985: 1). In a class society this 'national interest' is not the interest of the whole of the population, but that of its dominant sections, who use their dominance to present their own interests as the interests of everybody in the country. Discussions of immigration and citizenship take place within this highly politicised context. As the ultimate governor of citizenship, it is therefore misleading to view the state as a neutral arbiter in relation to immigration (Ahmad and Atkin 1996: 44). Rather, the state polices entry and settlement, and in many cases other aspects of life, in line with the interests of the ruling class. Yet as with the US, the long historical continuity and ideological dominance of parliamentary democracy, or more specifically bourgeois parliamentary democracy, in Britain has contributed to the lack of an intellectual tradition of conceptualising the state, and even to arguments that the state does not exist (Jones and Keating 1985: 1–2). In particular, there has been a persistent failure within post-war anti-racist movements in Britain to historicise the relationship of racism to the state (Lentin 2004: 308–10). As A. Sivanandan put it during the last Labour government: 'the academics, caught up in yesterday's mantras, are unable or loath to speak truth to power; the think-tanks speak to the New Labour agenda and the activist Left is still idealistically looking for a borderless world' (Preface to Kundnani 2007: vii). This chapter aims to move beyond these approaches, to situate the relationship between the British state under Labour and refugees within longer-term trajectories of British imperialism. In contrast to liberal political discourse, which frames questions of power within the subjectivist focus of who has power over society, and economic theories that ask how much power different actors have to carry out their objectives, Marxism offers one approach which focuses primarily on the nature of power and how it is exercised (Therborn 1980: 129–32), and that is the approach that will be taken here.

The Class Basis of the Imperialist State: A Particular Kind of Capitalist State

First I will consider general features of capitalist states, and then the particular features of the British state as a capitalist state occupying an imperialist position within the capitalist system. Engels theorised the modern state as not arising from outside society or from an abstract idea, but from within society, and proceeding to alienate itself in order to fulfill its purpose, not of reconciling opposing classes, but rather holding in check the conflict arising from their irreconcilable interests (Lenin [1917] 1972: 8). As Roberts (2004) puts it:

> [T]he separation of the state from civil society is in fact based upon the fragmentation of society inherent within the capital–labour relation. Unlike other social relations such as feudalism, capitalism is not structured in the first instance by extra-economic coercion in order to procure surplus-labour. Rather capitalism is structured through the formal freedom of labour to sell its labour power to whoever will purchase it. The state arises as a means to regulate the contradictions and struggles around this relationship. Thus the capitalist form of the state first and foremost emerges internally from the contradictory relationship between capital and labour. At a high level of abstraction we can say that the capitalist state is required to ensure that the dominance of capitalist property remains intact. (Roberts 2004: 480)

Under capitalism, the capitalist and working classes are interdependent and both alienated, but the capitalist class 'feels happy and confirmed in this self-alienation, it recognises alienation *as its own power*, and has in it the *semblance* of human existence', while the working class 'feels annihilated in its self-alienation; it sees in it its own powerlessness and the reality of an inhuman existence' (Lenin [1895–1916] 1972: 26–7, emphasis in the original). From this arises a conservative impetus on the part of the capitalist class, towards preserving this relationship, and a destructive impetus on the part of the working class, towards annihilating the same relationship.

These class antagonisms are fundamental to capitalism. Unchecked, however, they threaten to produce a level of constant conflict which would prevent the profitable accumulation of capital. In other words, if left unchecked, the class antagonisms fundamental to capitalism would themselves make capitalism unworkable. The interests of the ruling class and the working class cannot be reconciled, but the state fulfills the role for the ruling class of holding these antagonisms in check. The state is thus formed in the midst of class struggles, resulting in the formation of the state as the state of the most powerful, economically dominant class, who, through the exercise of a state apparatus specifically tailored to its needs, maintains itself as the politically dominant class (Lenin [1917] 1972: 13–14). State courts produce officially sanctioned national narratives (Hirsh 2003: 139), backed up when necessary with the officially sanctioned physical force of the police, military and prisons of various kinds. Alongside this, welfare services both morally sanction class rule through the services they provide and achieve a form of physical coercion through the threat of withholding these services. Diverse aspects of the state thus contribute to the management of the oppression of the working class.

This can be observed in practice throughout the history of capitalism, although the discussion here will focus on the relationship of the capitalist state to international migration. The Peace of Westphalia in 1648 established principles of territorial integrity and the right of a sovereign to control entry to their country, including the ability to grant asylum as a gift (Schuster 2002: 45–6). The principle of the right of ruling classes to regulate the territory and inhabitants within 'their' country's borders continues to be a central element of modern states. This takes a particularly acute form in the states of imperialist countries, as they attempt to police the divide between the extremes of poverty, war and repression which characterise many oppressed countries where capital owned by imperialist ruling classes is invested, as discussed in Chapter 1, and the wealth and freedom which characterise the imperialist countries where the profits return. As Kemp (1967) states, 'Historically the development of capitalism has been inseparable from the formation of national states as the political expression of the various ruling classes' (Kemp 1967: 74). This has led to a particular character for the state of Britain as the oldest imperialist country, including deeply entrenched racism in many of its institutions, and mechanisms for foreign intervention which span military, financial, intelligence, diplomatic and welfare institutions.

The development of imperialism has been synonymous with the fusion of banking and manufacturing capital and the state apparatus of imperialist countries, taking the form of 'state monopoly capitalism'. This contributes to a particular division of labour within the national ruling classes of imperialist nations (Kemp 1967: 22–3). In comparison to capitalist owners exercising direct control in capitalism's earlier periods, under imperialism both a large part of the social product and control of capital 'seems more usually to lie with men whose special powers derive from specifically financial control and manipulation – particularly control of money capital placed at their disposal by rentier-shareholders' (Lenin

[1916] 1975: 24–6). The custodian of these interests is the imperialist state, performing vital and complex roles both within Britain and internationally in order to defend the interests of the City of London and maintain conditions for continued accumulation. A vivid reminder of the extent of this fusion between the interests of the imperialist state and finance capital was the massive bail-outs of banks and financial institutions by state institutions in Britain, the United States and many other countries since 2007.

The History of British State Policy Towards Refugees

The 1951 UN Convention on Refugees created, at least in principle, a safety net to catch those who fell through the cracks in the supposed care exercised by each state for its citizens, and to reassign them to a nation. It was precipitated by the Nuremberg trials of Nazis, with an associated assumption that the Convention's purpose was to safeguard white Europeans in the event that a state not only failed to care for a section of its citizens, but threatened their very existence. The Convention represented an exception, created under exceptional circumstances, to the principle of national sovereignty wherein each nation state is free to govern its borders without any external interference (Kundnani 2007: 24–5). At the same time, it served in principle as a corrective mechanism, assigning displaced people to the responsibility of a state, and by doing so avoiding demands for care and welfare on a universal basis of human need, which might undermine the ideological dominance of the capitalist state's provision as conditional on welfare recipients playing the role of 'loyal citizens'. The Convention has been criticised as inappropriate to contemporary situations, having been drawn up to respond to specific circumstances during and after the Second World War, and to vary widely in interpretation between states, with a blurring between persecution and systematic discrimination (Richmond 2002: 718). It has also been criticised for failing to account for the impact of gender on experiences of persecution, simply assuming equal protection for men and women, and open to interpretation as excluding violence against women as a 'private' concern (Chantler 2010: 108–11). Furthermore, the Convention was drawn up by imperialist states, with no consultation with then socialist countries, and reflects the priority imperialist ruling classes assigned to 'higher order' political and civil rights, above rights they took for granted, such as rights to housing, healthcare, food and education (Schuster 2003: 98–101). In practice, British policy has not acted consistently in line with even the limited principles of the Convention, for example frequently breaching the key principle of *non-refoulement* by deporting people to countries where they face persecution and/or violence (Chantler 2010: 112), and has followed a conflictual course, often based on more short-term priorities.

In a speech to the Confederation of British Industry in April 2004, then Labour Prime Minister Tony Blair referred to two cases intended to illustrate Britain's benevolent history towards refugees, but which actually demonstrate a history of racism and hypocrisy. The first example was the case of Nicholas Winton, who, after visiting Prague in 1938, arranged for special visas to be granted to Jewish children and their placement with foster parents – while their parents were refused entry and many presumably died in the gas chambers. The second example was the case of 'East African Asian' refugees, who were British subjects and sought refuge in the 1960s and 1970s – many of whom were blocked from entering Britain by emergency legislation rushed through by a Labour government in 1968 (Kundnani 2007: 67–8). A survey below of other such key points in the history of British asylum policy demonstrates the priority consistently given to the interests of the British ruling class and the needs of British capital above the interests of refugees.

As Schuster (2002) documents, from the first introduction of the concept of the 'political refugee' in Britain, initially for members of the French ruling class fleeing the revolution of 1789, the British state has constantly shifted its approach depending on political considerations. This has included both the granting of asylum to citizens of other countries, and acceptance of the legitimacy of asylum granted by other countries to citizens of Britain and to countries it has oppressed. For much of the middle part of the nineteenth century, under conditions of growing demand for industrial labour and high levels of emigration to the colonies and America, asylum was championed for the sake of refugees' labour, carrying the additional benefit of legitimising class rule by presenting the ruling class as liberal and humane. By contrast, the Jewish refugees who fled to Britain from Russia and Eastern Europe in the late nineteenth century came at a time of economic crisis and high unemployment. They were met with the Aliens Act (1905), whose provisions only applied to 'steerage passengers' on ships carrying more than twenty 'aliens'. This enabled the Act to specifically target Jewish refugees from Russia and Poland, especially poorer refugees, without naming them (Schuster 2002: 46–50). Cohen (2006: 146) gives examples of Jewish refugees refused entry in the decades following 1905, whose memory has been erased in the claims of the ruling class to a history of welcoming refugees.

The attitude of the British state towards refugees before and during the second world war is telling of a recurring pattern in which the British state has pursued strategies aimed at minimising costs while maximising benefits to British capital. In preparation for the possible receipt of refugees from Belgium and Holland in the event of a German invasion, the British government expressed an overriding concern to avoid any expenditure by the British state, and to maximise 'voluntary' contributions and support (Ministry of Health 1940: 11–12). In line with this, when a Polish ship carrying 170 refugees, 58 of them carrying no money whatsoever, was requisitioned by the British admiralty at Newcastle on 2 October 1939, the Corporation of Newcastle used the fact that the majority of passengers were Catholic or Jewish to transfer responsibility for support to Catholic institutions and the Jewish community. Despite an initial understanding on the part of the religious bodies that the Corporation of Newcastle would pay the costs of all refugees' board, to be reimbursed by the Home Office, the Corporation later denied that this had been the agreement, and stated that it would only support the Catholic families. In the end a compromise was reached, with the Catholic Church, Jewish community collections and the Home Office all contributing something. By the end of October several refugees had left for London, America, and one to Palestine, and support for the remainder without their own means of support was transferred to the Unemployment Assistance Board (Tyne and Wear Archives 1939). A particular strategy employed by the British state from 1937 and through the war years to use the desperation of European refugees to the advantage of British capitalism was its unofficial policy of admitting refugee industrialists, merchants and specialists on the understanding that they would invest in designated 'special areas', which included the North East, where British capitalists were reluctant to invest and there was high unemployment. The Ministry of Labour admitted in a letter to the Aliens Branch of the Home Office on 11 March 1936 that:

> It is recognised that there might be objections to pressing the statutory powers of the Aliens Orders to the length of refusing permission to a foreigner to establish himself in the UK solely on account of the proposed situation of his factory, but there seems no good reason why advantage should not be taken of these powers to persuade employers in the desired direction.

> Our suggestion is that in response to any enquiry on the part of a foreigner as to permission to come here and set up a factory, the earliest opportunity should be taken of raising doubt whether permission will be given, if the foreigner proposes to establish his factory in London or the Home Counties. (Tyne and Wear Archives)

The following day the House of Commons passed a resolution that the government should 'discourage the undue concentration of modern industries in the Southern Counties and to encourage new industries, where practicable, to establish themselves in the older centres' (Loebl 1978: 121–5).

War-time labour was recruited by rather different means. During the First World War a 'village' of Belgians was established at Birtley in County Durham just South of Newcastle to produce munitions, with its own Belgian administration and hospital, school, sewer system, courts and jail. 6,000 people lived at the village at its peak, and were rarely allowed to leave, purportedly to prevent 'clashes with the locals' (Godfrey 1982: 7). Immediately after the Second World War, around 75,000 displaced persons were rebranded as 'European Volunteer Workers' and brought to Britain to work for a limited period, rather than being granted any kind of leave to remain as refugees (Schuster and Solomos 1999). More than a quarter of the European Volunteer Workers were women, recruited to work in the textile industry and in hospital domestic work, which were areas of high demand for low-paid, unskilled labour (Kay and Miles 1992: 9).

The powers confirmed under the 1971 Immigration Act, for the Home Secretary to issue Immigration Rules without the sanction of Parliament, and for Immigration Officers to refer cases to the Home Office, beyond the reach of the courts, have ensured that decisions on immigration have remained 'unapologetically subject to domestic and foreign considerations' (Schuster and Solomos 1999: 58). This reinforces the Leninist analysis that, while the policies of the state may at times conflict with particular ruling class interests, at the long-term level of the whole class system, the state is anchored in the class relations of the society over which it stands, which are in turn shaped by relations of production (Kemp 1967: 13).

From the Second World War up until the 1990s, most refugees arriving in Britain did so under a specific programme, responding to events such as the 'Bosnian crisis' or the expulsion of Asians from Uganda. Under pressure from tightening controls on other routes to move to Britain, this changed during the 1990s, with increasing numbers of 'spontaneous' or uninvited refugees arriving and applying for asylum (Phillimore and Goodson 2006: 1715). These 'uninvited' refugees arrived at a time of crisis in state welfare provision and high unemployment. Together with the removal of the 'Cold War' imperative to demonstrate the superior humanity and benevolence of liberal democracy, this contributed to a reduction in the usefulness of refugees to the state, prompting increasing restriction. While Kosovan refugees settled under a specific programme in 1999 were portrayed as victims of atrocities by Serbia, with whom Britain was in a state of war, and were automatically given exceptional leave to remain (Sales 2002: 468), refugees outside an organised programme were increasingly excluded and refused leave to remain. This was publicly justified by the ideological construction of refugees as 'disguised economic migrants', who it was argued harmed the interests not only of British citizens, by stealing their jobs and resources and placing demands on tolerance, but also 'genuine asylum seekers', by clogging up the system and creating mistrust (Schuster 2003: 145–7, 173–5).

Since the late 1990s, the increasing replacement of a multiculturalism, based on a view of homogenous 'ethnic communities', with an aggressive assimilationism, has contributed to the previous predominance of fragmented service provision by communities themselves being displaced by increased centralisation and state intervention (Griffiths et al. 2005: 24–6). As has often been the case with assimilationist approaches, this has also required forceful means of exclusion, of which deportation is one of the most extreme. From September 2004, the government publicly geared its immigration policy to deporting more 'failed' refugees each quarter than the number of new applicants (Prior 2006: 19). As discussed in Chapter 2, other policies have systematically excluded refugees who remain within Britain's borders, and have offered even those who secure status narrowly circumscribed conditions for inclusion. These antagonistic structural relations between refugees and the British state do not translate directly into social and political relations, but are mediated by subjective factors, including understandings and priorities arising from refugees' movement between the states of oppressed and imperialist countries.

The Position of States in the Imperialist System

The relationship of refugees to the British state is an active process, influenced by refugees' experience and relationship to the state in their countries of origin (Miles and Phizacklea 1980: 193–5). The nature of states occupying oppressed and dominant positions within imperialism needs to be considered in the context of a complex of interacting systems, with states developing as systems situated at different points within imperialism, and social classes and ethnic groupings developing and taking on meaning within and across these (Geschwender 1977: 2–3). Back et al. (2002) suggest that there was a contradiction between New Labour's programme for economic growth, based on neo-liberalism and globalisation rhetoric, and a desire to maintain the social integrity of the nation state (Back et al. 2002: 450). Yet, this underplays the centrality of population displacement in state formation and that the history of modern states demonstrates that 'the ability to control a citizenry through selective uprooting, removal, resettlement and containment is pivotal in maintaining state power' (McDowell 2005: 1). The power of multinational corporations and the movement of people and capital around the world associated with globalisation and neo-liberalism, which some incorrectly see as 'transnationalisation' leading to the erosion of nation states, are entirely consistent with the history of states, and should not suggest their imminent demise, but rather:

> Just as capital becomes more mobile and 'fluid' in the current era of globalisation, so is it the case that states must become more 'statist' in their orientation towards policy provision. The increasing dominance of global capital in the world requires local administrative powers to regulate the flow of capital. (Roberts 2004: 481)

Within this general picture of tightening state control there are of course exceptions, notably in the deregulation of the financial sector, and the failure to impose significantly tighter controls even after the global financial crisis.[1] This is entirely consistent with the class interests which I argue are represented by the British state. The role of the British state is not to regulate the activities of finance capital, but to regulate everything else in accordance with its needs. As the modern capitalist state organises and divides its subjects according to territory and creates 'special armed bodies of men' apart from society in order to enforce the authority

---

1   The new banking rules agreed in September 2010, known as 'Basel III', increased the minimum required size of capital reserves against total holdings from 2 to 7 per cent. However, this represents no real limitation on the big UK banks, who already exceed the new requirements, with Barclays holding reserves equivalent to 13.7%, RBS 11.2%, HSBC 10.2% and Lloyds Banking Group 9.2% (CEBS. 2010. *2010 EU wide stress test exercise*: Committee of European Banking Supervisors; Yaffe, D. 2010. Paying for the Crisis. *Fight Racism! Fight Imperialism!* (217 October / November 2010).).

of this separation (Lenin [1917] 1972: 10–13), the states of both exploiting and exploited nations facilitate the penetration of foreign capital in search of profit, yet in very different ways.

In imperialist countries in Western Europe and North America, the size of the state grew from around 10 per cent of GDP at the beginning of the twentieth century to nearly 50 per cent by the 1980s (figures from Fukuyama 2004: 3–4). The Second World War facilitated a massive expansion of the British state, with increasingly centralised control over production and massive increases in taxation, which were justified by the war but maintained afterwards, and an influential report 'Social Insurance and Allied Services', known popularly as the Beveridge Report, published in 1942, calling for increased state provision. This laid the groundwork for the massive expansion of state welfare and wide-ranging nationalisations in industry following the war. The expansion of state welfare was a concession forced on the ruling class by unrest and the threat of rebellion among a working class who had endured sustained economic crisis and two world wars, many of whom were looking to the Soviet Union as an example of a real alternative. The expansion of welfare was funded to a great extent through the exploitation of Britain's colonies, both in the form of migrant labour who performed low-paid work in the new National Health Service, and within the colonies themselves, such as Malaya which provided a crucial source of exchange currency while the wages of workers on rubber plantations were reduced by 80 per cent over ten years (Clough 1992: 88–90). Nationalisations in industry were primarily driven by the needs of capital, concentrated in inefficient areas or those requiring massive capital investment to survive, and in many cases were managed by the same business executives who had run them as private companies (Harling 2001: 156–64). Many of the nationalisations were in areas of industry producing vital inputs for manufacturing, such as coal, and therefore acted as a subsidy to capital.

In oppressed countries, the state frequently acts as the main guarantor of access for foreign capital, where necessary enforcing acceptance of poor terms for the population's sale of their labour. Hoogvelt (2007) argues that globalisation is exerting contradictory pressures on the state, requiring a reorganisation 'to suit global rather than domestic capital accumulation priorities', which in turn creates a tendency for a break-down in the integrity of some (oppressed) nation-states, increasing unplanned population movements. She goes on to argue that this in turn creates the contradictory pressure to maintain the integrity of other (imperialist) nation-states and strengthen their military capabilities to defend their interests directly in regions where local states are breaking down (Hoogvelt 2007: 18). Recent examples contradict this model of sole reliance on direct intervention by imperialist states, including action by imperialists to also strengthen local states where they are compliant rather than intervene directly, but to intervene to the point of military invasion where states may be strong but non-compliant:

- In the Democratic Republic of Congo (DRC), which has had a high level of both mineral exploitation by multinational companies and 'unplanned population movements' in recent years, imperialist countries have not intervened militarily from outside, but have attempted to reinforce and legitimate the local state. EU monitors verified elections in October 2006 as genuine, for which only incumbent President Kabila had been able to use UN vehicles, planes and helicopters for campaigning. In addition, he received $450 million in funds via the Comité International d'Accompagnement de la Transition (CIAT), which is made up of the US, UK, German, French and Belgian Embassies (Kayembe 2007).
- In Haiti, military action instigated by the US and France in 2004 was prompted, not by a breakdown in the local state, but by a government with a reformist agenda and popular participation, which was seen to threaten imperialist interests (FRFI 2004; Pina 2007).
- In Iraq, where the largest military intervention of recent years has taken place, this was also not prompted by a break-down of the local state, but by a government no longer compliant with its former US backers (Rayne 2003). Since then, the failure of the US and British-led occupation to re-establish a viable local state has created major problems for their extraction of profits from the region, despite their military presence (Craven and Rayne 2008; Cordesman and Burke 2010).

In other cases, strong local capitalist states have operated to some extent as a barrier to imperialist exploitation:

- In China a strong centralised state remains as a legacy of a socialist revolution despite the reversion of the country to capitalism, and prevents outright plunder by imperialist multinationals while also advancing an independent agenda internationally (Hart-Landsberg and Burkett 2005: 617; Cerni 2006).
- In Venezuela, a principled anti-imperialist President has formed an alliance with movements rooted in some of the country's poorest communities, and together they have made inroads against the influence of imperialists and the local capitalist class, including nationalisations of banks and oil production and the use of oil revenues for welfare programmes, and together with Cuba have launched wide-ranging initiatives for regional cooperation with other oppressed countries (Wilpert 2007; Muhr 2010; Yaffe 2011).

This range of examples demonstrates that local states in oppressed countries continue to be important sites of struggle and are crucial to the effective operation of imperialism in the current period. The underlying force driving these struggles is economic, but they play out through complex interactions between economic interests and forces of politics, culture and identity. This shapes the forms of exploitation and resistance which distinguish imperialism from earlier forms of capitalism. Class exploitation takes on a national character, backed by the national state and racist ideologies, contributing to forms of resistance which have frequently included positive affirmations of denigrated cultures or religions, and anti-imperialist movements which have included elements of the local capitalist classes.

The relative position of countries within the imperialist system impacts on not only the practice of states, but also their image. Many participants reported the abrupt shock of their treatment in Britain, which stood in stark contrast to their expectations based on dominant conceptions of Britain in their country of origin, with further distress caused at times by the contrast between the politeness of British state officials and the inhuman outcomes of the policies they implement, as indicated by a refugee without status I interviewed in Newcastle:

> … everybody I think all over the world knows Britain because of probably the empire it had … it was very powerful, I mean still is powerful, economically, politically, and its reach, and the language [that is] international. So I think it's a dream for everybody to live in Britain … when you come here you realise that it's completely different, it's the opposite, especially when your claim with the Home Office and everything is rejected … (Iran, 38 years old)

Crawley (2010) found a similar pattern, with many refugees having little or no knowledge of the British asylum system before arriving in the country, and in most cases assuming that if they explained their situation to the authorities, they would be allowed to stay, or in some cases relying on religious faith or the 'moral responsibility' of the British government for the causes of their problems (Crawley 2010: 39–40). This limited the preparedness of some refugees I interviewed to defend themselves against attacks from the state:

> … the problem I was running from, I was expecting to get friendly people, understanding people, things like that, but I found completely the opposite … After you've suffered persecution in your country … you wouldn't expect to come and be persecuted with sleepless nights, no future, no hope, no nothing … (Kenya, 28 years old)

While for some of the refugees I interviewed, comparison with the more openly repressive state in their country of origin encouraged acceptance of their treatment by the British state, for others the contradiction of expectations by reality appeared to contribute to a sense of not only inequality but injustice, which formed part of the motivation for more political and confrontational forms of action.

Repressive Aspects of the British State and Refugees

There is a long-running dispute between reformists and revolutionaries as to whether the state is a means of class reconciliation or repression (for example, as surveyed at the time of the Russian revolution by Lenin [1917] 1972: 9). This argument takes on particular resonance in relation to the more obviously repressive elements of the state. When considering the disproportionate wealth obtained by members of the ruling classes illegally compared to members of the working class - through means such as tax evasion, corporate fraud (Spalek 2007), and the corruption of UK politicians' expenses exposed by journalists in 2009 (The Telegraph 2009), for which only a small minority have received prison sentences - the harsher treatment and demonisation of perpetrators of 'blue collar crime' demonstrate a clear class character of the British police and courts in favour of the ruling class, even in periods of relative social stability, when the working class does not pose an immediate threat to the state (Jameson and Allison 1995; Bauman 1999: 123–6). In periods of heightened class conflict, such as during the Chartist Movement in the early nineteenth century, or during the miners' strike of 1984–1985, the police and courts have taken on an even clearer role in the service of the ruling class, meting out repression collectively to sections of the working class associated with resistance (Coulter et al. 1984). This demonstrates the fallacy of Thomas Hobbes' argument that the monopoly of legitimate power held by the state allows individuals to escape 'the war of every man against every man' (cited in Fukuyama 2004: 1). Rather, it is a powerful weapon in the hands of the ruling class against the working class in general (Lenin [1917] 1972).

The super-exploited position of black workers and the interests of the ruling class in racism, both outlined in Chapter 2, are reflected and defended by the racism of the police, exhibited by their frequent indifference and insensitivity when dealing with reports of racial harassment, at times treating victims as perpetrators, racially abusing them and detaining them in cells (Hesse et al. 1992: 66–7; IRR 2001: 14). Historically, black people have been over-represented as recipients of 'social control' aspects of state intervention, such as prisons and compulsory psychiatric detention, and under-represented in 'welfare' aspects of state intervention, such as counselling, group work, support for carers, and services for the elderly (Ahmad 1993: 31–2). Ethnic minorities continue to be over-represented at every stage of the UK criminal justice system, from stop and search, to arrests, to prosecutions, to sentencing, with 25 per cent of the prison population from ethnic minorities, more than double their proportion of the general population. This is in spite of offending rates which are equal to or lower than those for white people (Goodman and Ruggiero 2008: 56–8).

A number of well-publicised insights into the internal organisation of the police at a local level also suggest ongoing racism. In Newcastle in 1998, Rishi Johri left Northumbria Police claiming his career had been ruined by racist abuse from other officers (McKegney 1998). Following this, high profile claims of racism within Northumbria police were made by another officer, dating from the mid-1990s

(Neil 2004). This is part of a national pattern, with a BBC documentary in October 2003 uncovering continuing racism among police trainees in North Wales, and an inspection in the same year by Her Majesty's Inspectorate of Constabulary into policing in south Manchester finding a sexist and racist culture among officers (Townsend et al. 2003). In 2008, the most senior Asian police officer in Britain lodged a case of racial discrimination, sparking hundreds more complaints (Sawer 2008).

The modern British state employs a complex division of labour, both between and within different agencies. The police are divided internally, with some sections focusing on 'community relations' and the negotiation of social order at a local level, while other sections are held largely in reserve, to restore order with brute force where necessary, regardless of the law, and the damaging consequences of resort to the latter section being mitigated by employment of the former (Jefferson 1991: 171). Following the urban uprisings of 1980 and 1981, which had significant involvement by young working class black people, the state cultivated the appearance of making concessions by both setting up public bodies for monitoring and taking action on racist harassment and drawing in a section of black leaders into relatively well-paid 'race relations' and community posts (Sivanandan 1991: 118–21), as discussed in more detail in Chapter 5. Alongside these 'carrots', the 'stick' was deployed in targeted interventions backed by the media to link race to crime, and by doing so to criminalise whole communities that had been the basis of resistance (Solomos and Rackett 1991: 43–5). Parallels can be drawn with the state's recent approach to the opposition of many British Muslims to British imperialism's military actions in the Middle East, combining punitive sentencing of peaceful protestors with demands that 'community leaders' 'root out extremism' (McGhee 2003; Davidson 2006; Irving 2010).

The British State and the Criminalisation of Asylum

Since at least the early 1990s, there has been a steady trend of increasing criminalisation of refugees. The 1993 Asylum and Immigration Appeals Act was the first primary legislation to deal with asylum in the UK. Its measures included reinforcing carrier sanctions and introducing fingerprinting of refugees and their children (Griffiths et al. 2005: 38–9). The Immigration and Asylum Act 1999 extended the powers of search, arrest and detention of refugees without status (Sales 2002: 463). The routine detention of refugees without status, who have been accused of no crime, but at most the infringement or expected infringement of an administrative rule, increased significantly between 1997 and 2010 (Crawley 2010: 14). One episode in this expansion was linked to the attacks on the World Trade Centre and the Pentagon in September 2001, with levels of detention increasing alongside proposals to exclude suspected foreign 'terrorists' from the asylum process, running together the categories of 'asylum seeker' and 'terrorist' in public discourse (Sales 2002: 473). In recent years, more than 30,000 people have been imprisoned in UK immigration detention centres each year, 70 per cent of whom had claimed asylum at some point, many of whom report complying with everything authorities had asked them to do, yet still had their doors broken in and were forcibly taken into custody (BID 2009: 7–8, 15). As of 31 March 2010, there were more than 2,800 people being detained solely under Immigration Act powers, more than half of whom had sought asylum, with 220 people having been detained in this way for more than a year (Home Office 2010: 19). Widespread use of administrative detention compounds the trauma, uncertainty and fear that characterise the backgrounds of many refugees before reaching Britain (Briskman and Cemlyn 2005: 717). Added to this is the increasing 'double punishment' of foreign nationals who have been convicted of a criminal offence, by deporting them at end of their sentence, which in many cases has included people whose only crimes are related to survival needs, such as using false documents to enter or leave the UK, or undertaking paid work without permission (BID 2009: 21– 6). BID (2009) collected accounts of the trauma and terror caused by indefinite detention, with no automatic right to judicial oversight or application for bail, and found problems in contacting legal representation, severely restricted access to healthcare, and trauma and health-related problems continuing in many cases even after release.

The effective criminalisation of the act of seeking asylum itself was established in the UK through legislation in 2004, making it an offence to be unable to produce a valid passport when approached on or after arrival in Britain. At the same time, asylum tribunals took the view that a valid passport constituted proof that the holder was not a genuine dissident and refugee, as they would not then have been granted a passport by the country they were fleeing (Kundnani 2007: 69–70). Because of entry restrictions to European countries, it is impossible for many refugees to enter Britain to claim asylum without using illegal routes, thus criminalising refugees at the point of entry and fuelling a 'migration industry' of agents providing services to smuggle refugees across borders (Stewart 2008: 224–5; Crawley 2010: 18–19). For many refugees I interviewed, requirements to sign at a local Immigration Reporting Centre (IRC), for some as often as once a week, provided a powerful material and symbolic experience which deepened the sense of criminalisation:

> ... when you go to sign you have to put your fingerprint ... they don't trust anybody ... (DRC, arrived 2002)
>
> ... this thing of always going to sign, we [are] treated like ... criminals ... (Zimbabwe, arrived 2006)

As a convenient and frequently-used opportunity for refugees without status to be taken into detention, IRCs were perceived by many refugees to have a very direct link to immigration detention. For areas of the country where there is no local IRC, refugees without status may be required to sign at a police station (UKBA 2005), further emphasising the link between seeking asylum and criminality. While some

IRCs include their own short-term detention facilities, Newcastle's local IRC in North Shields has been reported to lack its own facilities and instead place those detained in the cells of the adjoining police station (Loraine 2008, and confirmed by the personal account of a refugee I spoke to who had been detained there). There was evidence that experiences of criminalisation influenced refugees' subsequent actions, with some refugees who had been involved in campaigning against deportations expressing a fear of police on demonstrations:

> Sometimes when we are demonstrating ... I find it difficult ... at the end there will be police, you know, you will be scared that they might arrest you or something. (Zimbabwe, arrived 2006)

The sense of criminalisation, the constant threat of detention and deportation at a moment's notice, and uncertainty over the duration and basis of the decision-making process combined to create a sense of fear, anxiety and persecution among many refugees I interviewed:

> Being an asylum seeker is torture, they torture you psychologically and physically and all that. And I found it terrorising because of the dawn raids, you can't sleep at night, it's very, very traumatising ... (Kenya, arrived 2004)

> I'm always depressed, every day, because I'm always thinking we don't even know what is going to happen tomorrow, and sometimes you get some people being snatched by immigration officers ... you're always in fear, at night, even if you hear any sound you are scared, maybe it is them coming for you ... (Zimbabwe, arrived 2006)

There was a wide range of understandings among the refugees I interviewed as to the nature and basis of these repressive measures, from acceptance and justification to political opposition. These differences were broadly in line with differences in forms of action. An individual volunteering with several state-related projects and with intentions to pursue a career in criminal forensics expressed one of the most accepting attitudes towards state repression of refugees without status:

> ... sometimes they can be a little bit harsh against some people, but I suppose they have to follow the procedures and the law ...

On the other hand, a refugee who was an active participant and organiser of demonstrations for refugee rights, and who expressed an intention to move into an advocacy role after securing leave to remain, related an anecdote which celebrated an act of 'everyday' resistance by refugees against degrading treatment by immigration officials, and suggested that refugees needed to stand up and demand their rights:

> ... if you call the Home Office, for example, and you say something like I know
> my rights, they speak to you differently ... There was one woman [working at a
> local IRC] ... she was being a racist ... she would speak to people as if they were
> animals, and then a man told her you are not going to speak to me like this, I am
> not an animal ... she didn't say anything, but she just did whatever she had to do,
> but it's just the fact that he did it in front of people and how she reacted, I think
> people were just smiling in the room ... (26 years, arrived 2000)

The refugee reported that since this incident, reporting procedures have been
changed to require those signing to attend at more specific designated times,
forcing them to disperse their attendance and avoiding the potential for acts of
collective solidarity and resistance such as the one described above. This provides
another example of the approach to managing oppression by breaking up potential
bases for collective resistance, rather than by simply increasing the severity of
repression.

British State Repression in the Context of Forced Flight

Despite the racist character of the state's repressive elements outlined above,
and the specific measures targeted at refugees without status, the relief of finding
safety in Britain cannot be underestimated for its impact on refugees' perceptions
of the British state. This was emphasised in my research in Newcastle, for example
as expressed by a refugee who took part in a focus group:

> ... we want really to contribute to this great nation ... first of all to be thankful
> for being accepted ... and given that haven, of safety and security, that was a
> luxury, from where we come from ... (DRC, arrived 2002)

This participant showed a high level of awareness elsewhere of the role of
imperialist countries in contributing to the situations which cause many refugees
to flee, but was nevertheless grateful for being granted refuge. Despite individual
and collective experiences of denial of rights, detention and threatened or actual
deportation, several other refugees in Newcastle spoke positively about the relative
democratic rights allowed by the British state:

> ... it's very safe to be [in Britain], it's free to stay, and free to speak and to work
> as well, that's why it's very good to be here ... (Chad, arrived 2001)

In part, some accounts may have been influenced by what has been referred to
as the 'immigrant story', where situations of insecurity result in pressures such
that: 'relative newcomers do not feel they have the right to project anything other
than a positive interpretation of their experiences in Britain' (Roberts et al. 2008:
36). This reflects a relationship of dependency, rooted in the material relation
of Britain to refugees' countries of origin, which plays on the vulnerability of

refugees as a result of their oppression and is reinforced through specific practices and processes.

The accounts above also reflect fundamental differences in the character of states occupying oppressed and imperialist positions within the capitalist system, which lead some refugees to regard the British state positively in comparison to the state they have fled. Compared to the states of oppressed countries the repressive elements of imperialist states contain contradictions, less frequently having to resort to naked force. The relationship of the police to the British working class developed in the period following the First World War, from naked confrontation to increasing negotiation. This took place hand in hand with the consolidation of a 'labour aristocracy' (Clough 1992), and a decline in the numbers of informally employed sections of the working class, who had more distinct norms of their own for behaviour and law, which were largely independent of the bourgeoisie (Jefferson 1991: 169–71). The absence of these conditions in non-imperialist countries, and the lack of super-profits to buy off a section of the working class, has frequently resulted in their states operating through more directly repressive measures. Among refugees I interviewed in Newcastle, such experiences of repression contributed to a tendency for refugees fleeing these states to regard the behaviour of the British police as positive by comparison:

> ... the police interviewed us ... he asked my date of birth and then I said Christmas day 1969, he smiled and tapped on my back, 'lucky person'. He was a very good policeman and I ... felt how different ... the policemen [in Britain are compared to] our country. In my country they hit, they swear, they use very, very offensive words, provoking words, but here the police [are] very polite ... (Iran, 38 years old)

Another refugee described the presence of police at anti-deportation protests in a positive light, viewing their role as protecting protesters from individual racists. This was despite their experiences of having been forced by the British state to live underground and destitute with their small children for an extended period, and later being detained. For some refugees interviewed, such views had been added to by observing particular instances of repressive agencies of the state playing what they saw to be a positive role:

> ... these wardens in the streets, from the local authority ... it made a big difference, a big impact in the relationship with the newcomers and the people who were making trouble ... (COM management committee member 1)

This reflects the state's need to manage racism, to create structures for 'mediation' between oppressed groups and thus remove any impetus towards independent organisation. At the point of immediate experience, however, this is seen by many refugees as the state playing a positive role. These views of the repressive elements of the British state in general contrasted sharply with views of repressive measures specifically targeted at refugees without status, as discussed above. This reinforces the findings of other research (Hynes 2009) which found common perceptions among refugees that the British state operates 'double standards', with a level of democracy and human rights for British people which is not available to those denied citizenship.

Racism and Politics in British State Welfare

There is a contradictory relationship between the working class and 'welfare' aspects of the British state, including institutions delivering education, health and social services. Welfare services provided by the state represent both a deduction of a portion of wealth away from capitalist profits towards the maintenance of the working class, and a means of social control. Disagreements with the Leninist conception of the state typically concern the argument that the British state either enjoys 'relative autonomy' from capitalist pressures, and is neutral with regard to different sections of society, to be fought over by competing interest groups (Jones and Keating 1985: 2–6), or that it is not coherent, with different interests served by different sections of the state. In Britain the latter argument has been associated historically with the Fabians in the Labour Party, who differentiate between a 'good' side of the capitalist state, including social services, health, education and nationalised industries, and a 'bad' side, including defence, law and order, and aid to private industry. Yet, in many cases those giving and receiving supposedly 'welfare' aspects of the state experience the way things are given as a further means of oppression, regulation and social classification, and a distraction from the question of why people need 'benefits' in the first place (LEWRG 1980: 52–3), with a long-standing ambiguity in social work between a duty of care and a mission of social control (OU 1978b: 41).

A Political Role for Welfare Provision

The social control element of welfare is particularly acute where interventions are made into people's lives by welfare professionals and agencies in a way that objectifies people into a clutch of 'problems', rather than engaging with them in an attempt to increase their agency. British welfare practices have often included the imposition of middle class values and understandings of the world, delegitimising understandings arising from working class experience and interests. Since the reorganisation of policing in the 1980s, the divide between welfare and repressive aspects of the state has become further blurred, with efforts to 'incorporate social and welfare agencies into the policing process' (Kundnani 2009: 32), in line with the emphasis placed on low-level intelligence gathering by leading police figures based on experience of counter-insurgency in colonial settings. These strategies were increasingly applied within Britain following the urban uprisings of the early 1980s, with Frank Kitson, the author of the classic handbook on counter-insurgency (Kitson 1973), appointed Commander-in-Chief of UK Land Forces in 1982.

The impact of the British state has at its best been very far from the 'welfare state' ideal, of an organised effort to modify the outcome of market forces, not only guaranteeing a minimum level of income and support at times of crisis, but also access as a right to the best quality services available (Harling 2001: 154). Instead, from 1948 state welfare in Britain involved a combination of means testing and universal provision which resulted in the maintenance and at times extension of existing inequalities. This was influenced by factors such as the greater confidence with which middle class people could navigate the NHS and make use of the full range of services, and the flat rate national insurance which effectively forced the working class to pay for their own services, while universal benefits were set so low that large numbers of people had to supplement them with degrading means-tested benefits (Harling 2001: 171–4). Low levels of benefits have further served to keep wages low, by presenting even poverty-level wages as a preferable alternative. In the recent period Prime Minister David Cameron has justified further reductions of benefits on the basis that if they are too high then they may act as a disincentive to seek paid work (Cameron 2011). The other solution to this question, to raise wages above benefits, is not even considered by the ruling class.

Gösta Esping-Andersen uses 'decommodification' as a measure of the degree to which welfare provision guarantees access to the necessities of life as a right, independent of the sale of labour power (cited in Morrissens and Sainsbury 2005: 639–40). It is a measure of the extent to which state welfare meets the 'welfare state' ideal cited above. This measure also allows us to pose the question of the role of welfare structures in affecting social stratification, including the way that welfare is delivered impacts on political relationships between and within classes. Welfare regimes across different capitalist countries have the common feature of intervening to structure relations of gender and race, such as the 'male breadwinner', although this structuring differs according to context, and takes place in interaction with political mobilisations (Williams 1995: 138–9). In Britain, the use of welfare in conjunction with immigration controls to divide the working class along racialised lines has a long history (Gordon and Newnham 1985; Ahmad and Bradby 2007). Similarly, restrictions in access to welfare services at particular points in history have played a role in managing gendered oppression, by forcing women either into paid employment or back into economic dependency on men (Dominelli 1999: 16–17). Gorodzeisky and Semyonov (2009) distinguish between public support for excluding 'foreigners' from the country and excluding them from certain 'rights and privileges', and place the latter as temporally following the first, and coming into play when the former fails (Gorodzeisky and Semyonov 2009). At a state level, Freeman (1986) suggests that welfare provision may be seen as a form of national protectionism, underscoring their role in national competition and the sheltering of privileged levels of wealth within the imperialist nation (Freeman 1986: 53–4).

Welfare and Citizenship: Twin Strategies of Cooption and Division

Historically, a line of continuity can be drawn from the granting of suffrage to working class men in the nineteenth century to the establishment of the National Health Service and other institutions in 1948, in a process of incorporating working class people within Britain into a nationalist alliance with the British ruling class, through the twin exclusive strategies of citizenship and welfare. As early as 1596, at a time of economic depression in what may be considered the pre-history of British welfare, Queen Elizabeth I ordered the deportation of all 'negroes and blackamoors', so that resources would only be consumed by white citizens (Craig 2007a: 608). The first forms of collectivism from 1900 included old age pensions, school meals and public housing, partly in order to appease an increasingly militant working class, to ensure a healthy working class for the army and factories, to control migration, and to create an elevated status of 'motherhood', keeping women tied to unpaid domestic work and in a form closely tied to the ideology of the development of 'race and nation' (Williams 1995: 151–5). The term 'welfare state' first appeared in common usage during the Second World War, in order to contrast the British state's care for its citizens with its fascist rivals (Harling 2001: 154). From the first, it was thus linked to ideas of national superiority. After the war state welfare provision supported post-war rebuilding by maintaining mass consumption, drew women back into unpaid domestic work under the concept of the 'family wage', and afforded limited concessions demanded by the balance of class forces in order to pacify the working class, while assigning a second-rate status to low paid migrant workers (Williams 1995: 151–5).

The concept of 'humanitarianism' as a 'benevolent duty' consistently resurfaces within the ideology of British welfare capitalism, concealing the fact that inclusion within the state's benevolence also implies excluded groups, serving to maintain the state's legitimacy by relatively privileging large sections of the British population, and to some extent all British citizens (Kyriakides and Virdee 2003: 301). The first 'concern' with the health of ethnic minorities arose within tropical medicine. This was driven not by concern for members of ethnic minorities themselves, but by the aim of preventing 'foreigners' from infecting British citizens, both in the context of migrants coming to Britain and in the context of British citizens settling in Britain's colonies. The roots of this concern were therefore bound up with British colonialism and racist fears of immigration. This began a tradition in which normal diagnostic approaches in health were sidelined, in favour of explanations based on cultural deficiencies, such as the special designation of 'Asian rickets' in the 1970s, which neglected the lessons of measures that had largely eradicated rickets in the 1940s, and more recently attempts to explain away health inequalities through unproven culturalist suggestions about marriage between cousins (Ahmad and Bradby 2007: 801–2). At its creation, NHS services were formally available to anyone present in Britain regardless of their nationality, and exceptional in this among other countries, but this quickly changed (Kundnani 2007: 18). William Beveridge, the 'founding father' of the NHS, made clear the racism underpinning his conception of welfare by speaking in unequivocally positive terms about the British 'pride of race', and the need for a welfare system 'to plan society now so that there may be no lack of men or women of the quality of those early days [of Marlborough, Cromwell and Drake], of the best of our breed, two hundred and three hundred years hence' (cited in Kyriakides and Virdee 2003: 287). This demonstrates the direct and racialised interest taken by the ruling class in managing the reproduction of labour power, and the contradictory impacts this has had on the history of state welfare in Britain (OU 1978a: 17–19; Williams 1995).

Racial Narratives in Welfare

The exclusionary role of state welfare in Britain has been masked by the racialised conception that 'certain identifiable categories of individuals are less able to "cope" than others, and that particular groups are more prone towards deviant or anti-social behaviour' (Bryan et al. 1988: 111). For example, in mental health there has been a history of damaging stereotypes associating black men with physicality, aggression, and dangerousness, which has seriously affected their provision (Newbigging et al. 2007: 113). Pathologising black families and labelling them as 'deviant', in comparison to a supposed white, two-parent, middle class, heterosexual norm, through a process of being 'social worked', has been a key aspect of racialised control by the state. Desires of black people to improve their social position are portrayed as 'overambitious', or as pressuring their children. Images are cultivated of black families constantly on the verge of collapse, while the context in which immigration controls, poor employment prospects and bad housing severely hamper the self-definition of many black families is ignored (Dominelli 1997: 94–8). Where black social workers have attempted to challenge this, they have frequently come under attack, accused of 'over identification with the client' or of 'oppressing the individual with family and community expectations' (Ahmad 1993: 14–15). One aspect of increasing conditionality in welfare in recent years has been the tying of benefits and pensions to earnings, which has reduced access for migrants as they tend to spend a shorter amount of time directly employed in the British labour force, particularly those claiming asylum (Sales 2002: 460). Figures for the 1990s show only 62.6 per cent of elderly migrant households in the UK in receipt of pensions, compared to 88.2 per cent of elderly non-migrant households, and only 21.2 per cent of unemployed migrant households in receipt of unemployment benefits, compared to 46.9 per cent of unemployed non-migrant households. Like other imperialist states surveyed by Morrissens and Sainsbury (2005), in the UK a far greater proportion of income for migrants is dependent on stigmatised means-tested benefits than universal benefits, and for countries where data is available, this is even more pronounced for ethnic minority migrants (Morrissens and Sainsbury 2005: 650–53).

Research has identified a serious lack of information of entitlements and services among ethnic minority people in Britain across a range of services, even where there are no language barriers, including a particular lack of awareness about direct payments for disabled people, with the consequence in many cases that people give up on trying to access formal provision (Chahal 2004: 5–6). In social care, assumptions that ethnic minorities, and particularly South Asian people, prefer to 'look after their own' have served to justify a situation in which 'nearly one in five Pakistani women aged 30–pension age, and one in ten British Pakistani or Bangladeshi men aged 16–29, are also carers', among some of the most deprived sections of the British population. This seems likely to increase as the trend nationally is one of rising thresholds for entitlement to statutory support, yet 'BME carers have been given little attention within legislative and policy documents, with no explicit mention of these groups in any of the Carers' Acts and only fleeting references within National Service Frameworks' (NBCWN 2008: 10). Research addressing the lived experience of South Asian carers found that in the majority of cases, rather than a cultural preference for home care, it was rather an absence of support and low expectations based on past experience that contributed to an inclination not to fight for more effective support, and to resign themselves to the fact that it was up to them to care for themselves (Mir and Tovey 2003: 471).

Disempowerment and Discrimination in Refugees' Experiences of Welfare

The dominant narrative among refugees I interviewed in Newcastle about their receipt of state welfare spoke of disempowerment, with a minimal level of support combining with prohibition of paid work to create a sense of dependency and powerlessness:

> They give us support, house, all this stuff, it's fine, but the time is going, it's not good. Because we also want to work for ourselves, and know our future, how our future is going to be. But we're not allowed to work, we are being asked to go and sign, all those things and they are taking long with the case. (29 years old, arrived 2006)

> … not find a job or not find a hobby, is always sadness and is sometimes like a prison here … (38 years old, arrived 2000)

Hynes (2009) characterises the experience of dispersal by 'waiting, not wanting to "bite the hand that feeds" and an unwilling patron/disadvantaged client relationship'. The majority of refugees interviewed in my own research volunteered examples from their personal experience of the substandard support provided under the separate welfare system for refugees without status, which was established as part of dispersal in 1999:

> … they put us in a flat, everything was broken in that flat, and we just came from [a country] where it was 30 degrees, and it was in May … that year was very cold,

and there was no heater or anything, it was just horrible. And then they moved us to somewhere better, but still things were broken, I think that's actually why [the private housing provider] lost their contract, because everything was broken in that house, I mean the doors would just fall off … (26 years old, arrived 2000)

Dependency on the state, enforced through government policy, combines with stigmatisation through separate support systems and media portrayals of 'asylum scroungers' to fuel racism on a personal level, further isolating refugees without status, who in some cases have as their first priority avoiding meeting people who may attack them (Temple et al. 2005: 32–4).

Discrimination and lack of resources were also reported in aspects of 'mainstream' state welfare provision:

… when I was pregnant the first week they said to me – I mean she said it very nicely, she said oh I hope that you speak English, because we don't have time to have an interpreter, unless you wait for three more weeks … it wasn't her fault, but it's just how things are happening, and I know some people that have to wait a long time … and in the meantime they don't know anything about their pregnancy … (26 years old, arrived 2000)

Another refugee reported a case where the practices and expectations of different elements of the state had combined together to produce a powerful web of institutional racism, whereby a woman was forced into poverty, then criminalised for lacking the means to provide for her children, and then targeted for deportation on the basis of this supposed 'criminality':

… when the social services will be coming to your house to check, and when they will say no, this child is not well dressed, he doesn't have enough toys, [this] happened to one [refugee I knew] … after that your child will be registered in child protection, and that means you will be in danger, they will say … this person is a bad person … when they are doing the legacy cases [if the state has it on record] that you will neglect your child, that you abuse your child, that means you are under this category of person who can pose a risk [to] British society, so they want … to remove you … They are … themselves creating this kind of situation. (Refugee and founder of local African women's group)

This reflects a situation in which the kind of state welfare provision experienced by refugees and other migrants is frequently different on a qualitative level from that encountered by many people born in Britain, and this furthers the super-exploitation of migrants and the material divide in the working class, with its consequences for undermining international class consciousness and contributing to the management of oppression.

Refugees and Conditional State Welfare

Recent refugee experiences of welfare provision have been formed within a wider context which has seen rapid change. Since the 1990s, the British state has undergone a decisive moment in a longer-term transition to a concept of welfare based on surveillance and coercion, away from the concept claimed in 1948, of welfare as a right rather than a privilege. State welfare has been reorganised from a professional/bureaucratic order to a system of conditional state welfare (Dwyer 2004), with a managerialist regime that views service users as individualised consumers and integrates the market into provision of key services (Williams 1995: 151–5; also Sales 2002: 459). This new arrangement leaves those who have no money to pay for services with little choice but to provide for themselves as best they can, with the largest part of this burden falling on working class women (Dominelli 2007).

Privatisation of some areas of state welfare, in order to open them up for the production of surplus value (Byrne 2001: 245), has combined with the delegation of other areas to parts of the voluntary sector which are willing to work directly for the state, and regulated on a contractual basis, with 'voluntary sector compacts' established at a country level in 1998 (Morison 2000). In this process, the scope of activity for the voluntary sector has been shaped largely towards areas 'outside the reach of state bureaucracy and beyond the interests of the private sector' (Morison 2000: 105), including areas from which the state wishes to disengage, but which are unattractive for profitable private investment. This restructuring has also impacted on the nature and priorities of the voluntary sector, as organisations have come under pressure to adopt a more professionalised and managerialist approach in order to compete with private companies for contracts (Roberts and Devine 2003: 312–13). This has brought with it a devaluing of professional decision-making and principles (Banks 2004: 149) and displacement of questions of power (Bunyan 2010: 114–15).

Mayer (2003) traces a process, beginning in the 1980s in many advanced capitalist countries, of non-state organisations, which began with missions of empowerment and transformation, coming under increasing pressure to provide basic services and substitute for the state, with little time or resources left to do anything else, and a practical focus on individuals' 'inclusion' in the labour market – often in low-paid and highly exploitative positions – replacing the goal of poverty alleviation (Mayer 2003: 120–21). The shifting treatment of refugees and the conception of asylum as a privilege or act of charity instead of a right have gone in line with this trend and provided one of its most extreme expressions (Kundnani 2007: 74–5). Refugees pose an implicit challenge to the conditional and market-tendered approach to welfare, by claiming an absolute right to sanctuary based on membership of humanity (Morris 2007: 50–51).

Welfare Restrictions and the Policing of Asylum

In the recent period, restrictions on access to welfare have been viewed as a key element of the strategy of reducing asylum applications, under the justification that many refugees without status are attracted to Britain by its welfare provision (Bloch and Schuster 2005: 116; Gibney and Hansen 2005: 75–9). This is not without precedent, for example following the revolution in Iran in 1979, many visiting Iranians stayed in Newcastle, unable to return for fear of persecution, but found themselves refused work permits and access to unemployment benefits (Evening Chronicle 1984a: 16). Successive immigration acts have removed access to mainstream benefits and welfare support from those in the asylum process, claiming that their needs would still be met by the National Asylum Support Service (NASS), despite its own assertions that it was primarily a housing provider, not a welfare service (Grady 2004: 135–8). In 1996 and 2002, Conservative and Labour governments went as far as attempting to remove welfare support from refugees without status who had failed to claim for asylum immediately upon arrival, although in both cases the implementation of these measures were prevented in the courts on human rights grounds (Morris 2007: 52–3). For those refused asylum, however, British courts have permitted the withdrawal of all support except on severely limited, exceptional grounds. Among the refugees I interviewed there was a widespread view that, while aspects of the decision-making process may have improved, the living conditions and access to services for those awaiting a decision or who had been refused had worsened in significant ways in recent years:

> … since I've been there I think things tend to be worse, for example they will ask you to stay six months before [you can] access ESOL, which was not the case, they will say to you once you've been destitute you can't access … health [care] … (DRC, arrived 2005)

> When I first arrived here there wasn't eviction or benefit cut when your asylum claim was rejected, and now if your asylum claim is rejected they stop your benefit and they evict you from your house, they remove you from your flat. And people are really in difficult situations, I've seen people who are sleeping in metro stations, parks, things like that, or asking friends to stay over for a couple of nights, it's very difficult. (Iran, arrived 2000)

Among refugees without status, there are extreme levels of destitution, which have been found to exacerbate existing needs relating to the conditions of refugees' forced flight, and to also create new ones, such as mothers unable to breastfeed because of lack of food, or mental health problems linked to high unemployment (Patel and Kelley 2006: 5–6). In December 2005, there were an estimated 300 destitute refugees without status resident in Newcastle, with twenty to thirty sleeping outdoors on a given night, and several thousand more who had had their cases refused and support withdrawn, but who were supporting themselves by working illegally, in situations extremely vulnerable to exploitation (Prior 2006: 7). In a situation where reductions to legal aid have reached the point where proper preparation of a case is often impossible, the status of 'failed asylum seeker' is the eventual fate of many refugees (Prior 2006: 15). As of 2009, it was estimated that numbers in Britain in this situation exceeded 500,000 (British Red Cross 2010).

The changes in welfare provision for refugees described above have paralleled a similar intensification of a militaristic and aggressive dimension to British foreign policy under the banner of the 'War on Terror', including the full scale invasions of Afghanistan and Iraq and widespread allegations of collusion with torture and participation in the United States' 'extraordinary rendition' programme (Kundnani 2007; Tran 2008; Vertigans 2010). Both of these developments have taken place in the context of the increasing crisis of capitalism. This crisis has driven the ruling classes of the major imperialist powers towards more direct means of confrontation, as they compete to increase their share of global profits, while also increasing pressure towards tightening their control over working class people who produce those profits, including their movement across borders and their access to services.

With the exception of those with young children, for refugees who have been refused status, even the limited subsistence and housing support available while cases are being processed is withdrawn, usually with twenty one days warning at most, or in some cases as little as seven days due to late notification (British Red Cross 2010). Hardship housing and food vouchers are available to most only if they sign up for a 'voluntary return' programme. For many, a return to the situations they fled is an even worse prospect than destitution, and consequently there is a low take-up rate (Prior 2006: 19; Home Office 2010: 17). At the most extreme, poverty and lack of access to services is such that for some refugees in Britain their health and living conditions are worse than in their 'third world' countries of origin (Cheong et al. 2007: 34). Even for those with a technical right to support, the fear of detention and deportation forces many underground and therefore out of touch with supporting services:

> ... first time they try to catch me, they didn't get me, they cancelled all my support, [I] stay one year here with my boy, no support, I was all the time running to people to get eat, get sleep ... in my country I didn't think I was going to be here one day asking people to give me something to eat, but I try my best after that again, they refuse then they get me and my children, two of them there [and put us in detention] ... (arrived 2004, secured status 2009)

This emphasises the extreme human cost of enforced destitution as part of the state's management of refugees' oppression. By keeping refugees without status under constant threat of detention and deportation, these measures deter refugees from participating in public political activity and further isolate them from resources and potential allies in other sections of the working class, reducing their capacity to resist the dictates of their oppressors.

Far from being an issue limited to an earlier period, when relatively larger numbers of refugees were applying for asylum each year, there are indications that levels of destitution have increased since the fall in numbers of applicants and the introduction of NAM. Since 2007, Leeds has been Newcastle's designated local 'hub' for dispersal. A four-week survey of four agencies supporting destitute refugees in Leeds in early 2009 found 232 destitute individuals, including 21 families, with a total of 30 child dependents, and cases of long-term destitution, in some cases more than two years. This is more than double the level of destitution found in a similar survey in 2006, before the introduction of NAM, and is likely to be an under-recording of actual need or demand, as the survey only recorded those actually receiving services, and these are massively overstretched (Lewis 2009: 8). In early 2009, two hardship funds in Leeds closed as a result of reductions in funds and resources since the start of the recession and simultaneously rising demand (Lewis 2009: 21). The projects surveyed reported that, although the Home Office claim support is available to those who need it under 'Section 4', many who are destitute would not qualify under its five conditions, and of those who do, many do not access it because they are either not aware of what is available or are avoiding state agencies for fear of deportation (Lewis 2009: 11–12). The Red Cross reports a similar picture of increasing needs for support nationally, with their centres directly assisting 7,920 destitute refugees in 2004 and 11,600 in 2009, even as numbers of refugees entering Britain declined, and numbers being deported increased (British Red Cross 2010).

During this period, the state continued to reduce its support. Total numbers of refugees without status who received some form of state support in the first quarter of 2010 was 27,455, 17 per cent lower than a year previously, with a steady fall since 2007, and numbers receiving Section 4 support were 8,660, down 20 per cent on a year earlier (Home Office 2010: 14–15). In order to qualify for social services support, refugees who have been refused leave to remain must not only be destitute but 'destitute plus' under a community care, community mental health or Section 17 Children's Act assessment (Islington Local Authority 2007). In contradiction to the government's stated purpose for these restrictions, to discourage people coming to Britain to seek asylum, a number of studies suggest that most refugees without status have very limited information on entry and welfare policies in the European countries where they later seek asylum, in many cases having little choice anyway over which country they flee to (Bloch and Schuster 2005: 117; Crawley 2010: 26–8). Even where migrants have left conflict regions for economic reasons, many have sought alternative routes rather than claim asylum (Stewart 2008: 229).

Political Purpose in the Denial of Welfare to Refugees without Status

Among those refugees I interviewed who perceived a denial of support to be intentional rather than a result of accident, incompetence or lack of resources, the view was expressed that this was part of a government strategy to restrict settlement of refugees in Britain by making life so hard that people would decide to leave:

> … maybe just to force them to leave the country, make them tired … (Angola, arrived 2002)

> … the main reason I think is to discourage people who are not in Britain, and who intend to come to Britain … The other reason is to change people who are already here to get back to their country … I've seen people who prefer to live in their own countries, within war zones or difficult situations, [rather than] stay here and be destitute or lose their reputation … I've seen people from Iran, from Baghdad, who is still under heavy control of the military, they prefer to go back, even though it's not – the life is not so easy. (Iran, arrived 2000)

The evidence above suggests that the primary purpose of welfare restrictions may be less as a deterrent and rather as both a pressure for those already in Britain to leave the country, and a measure for keeping them divided from British working class people, by placing them with separate housing providers, separate benefit systems and separate offices for signing on. Refugees who participated in a focus group I organised in Newcastle in 2010 reported experiences of exclusion from mainstream welfare provision continuing to an extent even after they achieved status, through a lack of access to information:

> … sometimes when I've got a problem I just suddenly realise that I have … limitations … people have to get more information, because integration is about also culture, it is about social, it is about economic, it is about politic … [For example] when I knew about Sure Start it was just when I gave birth, and it was just by random [chance] that I met people [who told me about it] (DRC, arrived 2005)

Research into experiences of women refugees from Pakistan found similar patterns of exclusion from access to support in Britain following domestic violence, with a lack of resources for these services compounded by frequent lack of sympathy, cultural awareness and culturally appropriate provision:

> … the prevailing perception was that the system of asylum and immigration control determines and 'regulates' provision to women asylum seekers and women with insecure immigration status, heightening women's vulnerability to harm. (Chantler 2010: 95)

British Welfare in the Context of Refugees' Journeys

In general, welfare functions performed by the state in imperialist countries are left to Non-Governmental Organisations (NGOs) in oppressed countries, the largest of which are based in imperialist countries. In general, these NGOs operate within a narrative of benevolent charity, in contrast to the concept of welfare as a right which has been dominant in the state welfare of many imperialist countries in recent decades (Hessle 2007: 356). NGOs have also played a key role in microfinance and microcredit initiatives, which shift responsibility for poverty alleviation from the state onto individuals engaged through the market. These have had a tendency to divert the focus from structural causes of poverty and collective responses to an 'active individualism', in which it is suggested that the cause of people's poverty is their previous inability or unwillingness to engage in established structures (Burkett 2007: 151–2). While such projects divert challenge from capitalism's fundamentally exploitative basis by co-opting leaders into projects designed to allow a successful few to escape its worst consequences, these projects also contribute to a tendency for members of oppressed nations to view imperialist countries from which the biggest NGOs originate as a source of benevolence, which perpetuates colonial attitudes. As a worker with refugees in Newcastle said in an interview I conducted in 2005:

> ... many of our clients come here thinking we are the mother country, because of our past interference, and our past empire ... they genuinely believe that we are well-mannered, friendly, welcoming ...

Far from 'helping', 'community development' across borders has frequently used scarce resources to employ professionals from imperialist countries on even higher wages than they would receive in their home country, and who may lack approaches appropriate to local conditions and/or a serious commitment to engage local people. At times, such work has been taken over by multinational companies or other organisations whose top priority is to maximise profits rather than meet peoples' needs (Dominelli 2005: 703–4).

The perspectives of some refugees I interviewed contained contradictions relating to welfare provision, which may be seen as arising primarily from such differences between their countries of origin and Britain. One refugee reported that even the limited welfare support they had experienced in Britain was beyond anything they had expected:

> ... when I first came in this country ... my priority was my safety, I wanted just to protect myself, to save my life, I didn't know that once I come there they will give me accommodation, or that I will be entitled to receive some support ... (DRC, arrived 2005)

The oppressed position of refugees' countries of origin was such, that even substandard conditions in Britain were, for some, an improvement. To borrow a metaphor used by Sivaram Dharmeratnam to describe state strategies used to subdue Tamil resistance in Sri Lanka (cited in Whitaker 2007: 152–3), some refugees in Britain are like a prisoner who is beaten repeatedly until he shows gratitude to his jailor that the beatings have stopped, even if he is still denied adequate food and water, in that their experiences have reduced their expectations to a bare minimum. Experiences of inadequate provision in their countries of origin, oppressed under imperialism, in turn influenced refugees' expectations and views of their entitlement in Britain:

> I am sure that in all countries … refugees … haven't the same conditions and help which we have here. For example in Iran it is … more than three million [refugees], one million have papers, and two million are asylum seekers … nobody gave to them … buildings or money. And they work, they work very hard, but they were very happy because of that. (Iran, 45 years old)

> … in my country we don't use benefit, benefit is not part of our daily life, you have to work hard … (DRC, female)

In line with this, some refugees I interviewed viewed the British state as essentially well-meaning towards refugees without status, by comparison to the states in their countries of origin, with instances of lack of support or unfairness of decisions seen as arising primarily from laziness or inefficiency rather than political intention:

> The British government … they give me somewhere to sleep … really they are nice to refugees … (DRC, arrived 2002)

> [At the charity there] is too much care, and Home Office is saying 'Oh, I'm really busy' or 'That's a policy', or something, and here it's too much care, [that's] the difference … Both of them just looking after the law, but [the] Home Office is just [a] little bit lazy, here [there] is too much care. (Iran, arrived 2000)

These views appeared a powerful factor influencing less confrontational strategies in securing rights against the state, making it easier for the state to manage their oppression.

This illustrates some of the ways in which the relations of oppression and dependency between refugees and the British state mirror those between refugees' countries of origin and Britain. The impact of this dependency is reflected in the accounts above, where some participants expressed gratitude for support provided by the state, when they are in need of this support primarily because of the same state's prohibition on paid work, or where participants were prepared to accept more readily what they considered to be negative aspects of NAM because it also included a shortening of waiting times for decisions, again bringing gratitude to the state for solving a problem it was responsible for creating in the first place.

It may be argued that these latest developments in welfare represent a resolution of the tension already identified in the 1970s, between professional values developed in an earlier, more autonomous phase of competitive capitalism, and the need for more direct state manipulation of labour under advanced monopoly capitalism (OU 1978a: 18–19). These earlier values have not merely been rejected, but appropriated and reconstructed, exemplified by the use of 'empowerment' and 'participation' to represent the performance of functions delegated by the state (Shaw and Martin 2000: 408). That such a resolution of this tension in capital's favour should be possible at this point in time, may owe in part to the negative balance of class forces for the working class following the successful offensive carried out under the Thatcher government during the 1980s and continued under Labour from 1997, together with the collapse of the majority of the socialist countries at the beginning of the 1990s. This has serious implications for social workers, particularly in light of their assigned role in enforcing immigration controls internally by policing black people's access to welfare (Dominelli 1997: 27). If social workers are to develop effective and genuine anti-racist practice, an understanding is therefore needed of the context of social work within the state, and of the state's relationship to racism (Dominelli 1997: 19).

The British State in a Period of Bank Bail-Outs and Public Sector Cuts: Implications for Refugees

The bail-out of banks and financial institutions in response to the global financial crisis beginning in 2007 represented a massive transfer of wealth from the public to private sector and from the working class to the ruling, capitalist class. During 2009 over 25,000 public sector workers were made redundant, and all the main political parties entered the 2010 General Election committed to massive public sector cuts. Labour's plans set out in its pre-election March 2010 budget opened the way for a massive programme of privatisation and reduction in services under the incoming Conservative–Liberal Democrat Coalition government. The £81 billion welfare and spending cuts announced in the June 2010 budget (HM Treasury 2010a) was followed in October by the announcement of 26 per cent cuts to local authority funding over four years (HM Treasury 2010b). The government has justified public sector cuts on the basis that the public sector deficit is 'unsustainable'. In fact, at 57.2 per cent of national income as of September 2010, Britain's accumulated net debt is lower than it has been for much of the last 200 years, having averaged 112 per cent of national income between 1688 and 2010 (Rayne 2010). Following the direction of Labour governments in transferring responsibility for non-profitable areas of provision to the voluntary and community sector, the Coalition has branded this the 'Big Society', divesting responsibility from the state at the same time as voluntary sector funding is also reduced (BVSC 2011; http://voluntarysectorcuts.org.uk).

Refugees and other migrants are facing targeted cuts which threaten to exclude them and divide the working class even further. These have included the cancellation of councils' provision of housing to refugees without status in many cities including Newcastle, Glasgow and Birmingham, with NASS contracts transferred in many cases to private providers like Jomast and Y–People (Burnett 2011). At Homerton hospital in Hackney, London, language services are being removed, including the Kurdish language service, in a borough with a sizeable Kurdish population, many of them refugees (Londra Gazette 2011). These examples are just the tip of the iceberg. Funding for ESOL (English for Speakers of Other Languages) is being reduced, with English lessons no longer free for those who need them, but reserved for 'priority groups', primarily those registered unemployed and those on income support. The majority of people on low wages will have to pay at least 50 per cent of the cost of lessons, a charge which many will be unable to afford alongside basic living expenses. Refugees without status will be expected to pay at least 50 per cent of the cost of their lessons, even where they are prohibited from paid employment (http://actionforesol.org). Overall, cuts to funding for specialist services have included a 62% reduction for asylum support services in 2011 and the cancellation of all support for integration of refugees with status (RRF 2011: 34–45).

This reduction in services has combined with a further tightening of restrictions on immigration. The points based system introduced by the Labour government has been retained, but has been added to by the Coalition with a 'cap' on the maximum number of migrants entering under each tier per year. The repressive apparatus of immigration detention and removal has been maintained, with the Liberal Democrat's commitment to end child detention fulfilled in name only. While an end to the placement of children in existing detention centres was announced in December 2010, they are to be replaced with a purpose built 'pre-departure accommodation centre' to be run by the charity Barnardo's (Lepper 2011), a detention centre in all but name.

Conclusions

A contradiction which was central to the approach of recent Labour governments is the claim to oppose social exclusion as a key factor in inequality, simultaneous with the systematic exclusion of refugees and other migrants in the name of maintaining the privileges of those benefiting from state welfare (Richmond 2002: 724). This is expressed through a racialised narrative which presents public services as constantly under threat of being 'swamped' by migrants seeking to take advantage of 'our' services. As discussed above, this is a general contradiction which has always existed in British welfare, but has been exacerbated and brought into prominence in response to the intensifying crisis of imperialism. Changes in welfare have reflected shifts in the wider policy agenda, from 'race relations', through community relations, multiculturalism, and most recently assimilation of selected black people into a reconfigured 'British nation' (Craig 2007a: 615–16). Already, before 2002, the existing restriction on refugees without status taking paid work for their first six months in Britain had been identified as a serious contributing factor to divisions between refugees without status and others living in the same area, by preventing contact and reinforcing an impression of refugees as 'idle' and 'scroungers' (Hewitt 2002: 11). The wholesale withdrawal of the right to work for the majority of refugees without status in 2002, together with the removal of access to statutory housing and forced dispersal around the country since 1999, was a key point in their deepening exclusion and subjection to control by the state, creating strong pressure to conform to official and formalised channels merely in order to survive (Griffiths et al. 2005: 202). This forced engagement with the state has been of little benefit to refugees and other migrants. This is part of a wider pattern, with analysis of data for the UK from the Luxembourg Income Study finding that social policies targeting poverty had far greater impact on the situation of non-migrants than that of migrants, lifting 70.9 per cent of non-migrants out of poverty compared to 49.8 per cent of migrants (Morrissens and Sainsbury 2005: 646).

It is important to also acknowledge the shifting and unreliable nature of formal citizenship in Britain, exemplified by instances such as the recruitment to Britain of black Commonwealth citizens in the 1960s, who were later denied access to the social rights of citizens (Williams 1995: 143). For refugees without status, occupying an intermediate position between possible deportation back to the international reserve army of labour and inclusion in a super-exploited section of the British working class, the shifting and unreliable nature of their relationship to the British state may be particularly acute. The accounts of the refugees I interviewed in Newcastle show that refugees' responses to their experiences of the state are diverse and complex, with evaluations of the British state both influenced by their experiences of the state in their countries of origin and reflecting the relations of dependency and false 'benevolence' characteristic of the relation between Britain and oppressed countries. That the divides between what may appear clear class fractions are not absolute or static suggests possibilities both for points of cooption and diversion, and for points of alliance and resistance. As the recurring urban uprisings of the early 1980s, early 1990s, 2001 (FRFI 2001; Amin 2003), and 2011 (Roberts 2011), demonstrate, the symbolic reassurances, depoliticisation, cooption and promises of future reform employed by the state can only be successful for so long, and resistance will continue (Solomos 1993: 239). The state cannot be oblivious to this, and has made careful interventions to structure their relations with refugees, drawing on longer-standing approaches to the management of black populations' oppression through the creation of a race relations industry, which forms the focus of Chapter 4.

Chapter 4

Introducing the Refugee Relations Industry

This chapter sets out to expose Britain's 'refugee relations industry': what it is, the role it plays in the oppression of refugees, and its origins in the race relations structures which were established in response to earlier resistance movements.

Introduction

Since the 1990s, an increasing array of state agencies and voluntary and community sector projects have emerged specifically targeting refugees, extending in national coverage with dispersal from 1999 (Figure 4.1 outlines the main components of the refugee relations industry).

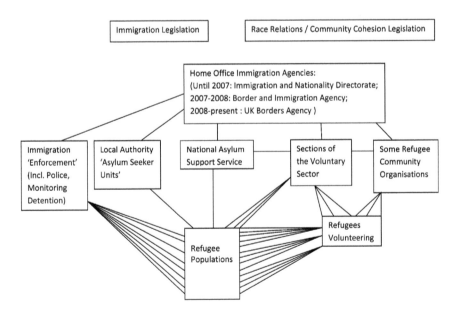

Figure 4.1

This framework of control did not develop in a vacuum, but built on existing projects and a tradition of 'ethnic minority' and 'race relations' initiatives through which the British state has intervened to influence the responses of black people to racism over decades, in order to manage their oppression.

The chapter begins by sketching some key elements of the history of 'race relations' in Britain since the 1960s. Several case studies are then drawn from the history of race relations in Newcastle, based on archival research and qualitative interviews with key informants, which I undertook as part of a series of research projects between 2005 and 2010. These local case studies are intended to illustrate the local tensions and contradictions inherent in the operation of these processes at a local level. They also provide a backdrop to the more recent developments in the management of refugees in Newcastle which are explored later in the chapter. The chapter goes on to respond to some of the main arguments suggesting that the position and rights of black people in Britain have improved since the 1960s. I show that apparent advances for some black people also represent the development of new mechanisms of control, with the establishment of a small black middle class inseparable from the continued oppression of the majority of black people.

The general line of development of the refugee sector under recent Labour governments is discussed, and local case studies are presented for two different models of organisation, which the state has engaged with in different ways in its attempts to 'manage' refugees. Devine and Roberts (2003) point to the importance of first-hand accounts of the experience of participation in networks, in order to fully understand their impact on norms, including trust (Devine and Roberts 2003: 97). Refugees' experiences of engaging with the state as volunteers are used here to begin a discussion of the wider impact of their role as agents mediating the antagonistic relationship between the state and refugees, and to begin to draw out dilemmas and contradictions in this process.

The chapter concludes with a discussion of the wider relevance of this understanding of the potential role of voluntary and community organisations in mediating the state's relationship to oppressed groups, in the context of public sector cuts and the 'Big Society'.

The Historical Role of Britain's Race Relations Industry

Race relations policy and practice began as an integral part of the management of colonial exploitation, combining racism, repression and accommodation (Geschwender 1977: 217). Within Britain, the state has engaged actively since at least the 1960s in defining 'ethnic communities' and structuring who should speak as their legitimate representatives (Ahmad and Atkin 1996: 37–41). The 'race relations' approach, exemplified by the original Institute of Race Relations prior to its takeover by black staff in 1972, places academic endeavour firmly in the service of capitalism, serving not to challenge racism but to manage it in pursuit of profits (Sivanandan 1974: 4–7). Implicit in the race relations paradigm is a myth of assimilation and uniformity in British society prior to 1945, subsuming gender, cultural, regional and class differences in a white 'Englishness' (Hickman 1996: 2–4). Implicit in this presentation is a posited threat from internally homogenous immigrant 'communities' (Lentin 2004: 133–5). This implies a common sense 'naturalness' to race and the resistance of white people to 'racial mixing', suggesting that the 'race relations problem' is rooted in immigrants' presence in Britain, and should be resolved by the dual solutions of repatriation and assimilation, the latter sometimes dressed up as 'integration' (Solomos 1993: 193–4; also Miles and Phizacklea 1987: 4–5).

The modern history of 'race relations' interventions by the British state began with the increasingly restrictive immigration acts passed in 1962, 1965, 1968 and 1971, alongside high profile, but ineffective, race relations legislation in 1965, 1968 and 1976. Urban aid programmes targeted at inner city areas where many immigrants had settled were initiated in 1966 and 1968, but had little lasting impact (Bulpitt 1986: 30–33). NHS 'special initiatives' were typical of this period, operating on the basis of a crude multiculturalist view of 'cultures' as static, homogenous blocs, encouraging the establishment of separate provision as a cheaper and higher profile alternative to ensuring that mainstream services met the needs of all (Ahmad and Bradby 2007: 804). What the early race relations legislation did achieve was the establishment of structures for the co-option of 'black militancy', and mediation between sections of the ruling class, between the ruling class and black people, and between black and white workers. This contributed to the acceptance of racist power structures by a large part of a generation of black people in Britain (Sivanandan 1991: 118–21). As in the US, in Britain it has frequently been 'members of oppressed, objectified groups who are expected to stretch out and bridge the gap between the actualities of [their] lives and the consciousness of [their] oppressor', while the 'oppressors maintain their position and evade responsibility for their own actions' (Lorde 1996: 162–3). Beginning in the 1960s and accelerating following the inner-city uprisings of the early 1980s, the British state has influenced racialised identities and classifications through targeted interventions, delegitimising oppositional identities and isolating anti-racist movements' most radical sections.

A pattern observed in earlier generations of black migrants to Britain is that of adaptation and acceptance of racism by first generations, followed by resistance by later generations (Williams 2007: 400). In order to forestall future resistance, the ruling class must attempt to ensure that 'The injunction to be moderate is ultimately the precondition for inclusion within the space offered to minority communities' (Back et al. 2002: 450), where to be moderate means to accept the racist status quo. This is reinforced by regularly resurfacing attitudes, such as that explicitly articulated by police in Waltham Forest in London in the 1980s, that racial harassment only happens to those who have not 'integrated well' (Hesse et al. 1992: 10–11). Threats to the racialised structure of British capitalism, posed by developments such as the takeover of the Institute of Race Relations in the early 1970s by A. Sivanandan and other staff, who began linking race to class and gender

(Lentin 2004: 104–6), and the urban uprisings in the early 1980s, were responded to with the cooption of a section of black leadership into relatively well-paid jobs in the funded projects and local authority posts of the emerging 'race relations industry'. Shared experiences of racism, which held importance for many people as a basis for reversing subordination and turning racialisation into a point of pride, expression and solidarity (Gilroy 2000: 12–13), were used by some to build support for the subjectivism of identity politics and black perspectivism, which presented personal experience as the only legitimate source of understanding of racism (Shukra 1995: 10). In practice, identity politics have often operated on the basis of an 'inward-looking, reductive and conservative notion of identity', which has at times been taken to imply a need to guard against 'contamination' between fixed and organic distinct cultures (Kundnani 2007: 49).

These developments contributed to the increasing dominance, within self-consciously anti-racist approaches from the mid-1980s, of an approach which limited itself largely to a local and personal level, operating mainly through professions and mainstream politics (Shukra 1995: 15–16), focusing on superficial 'political correctness' (Skellington 1996: 132–3), and involving 'the provision of culturally appropriate services taking the place of campaigning against racism' (IRR 2001: 18). As Kundnani (2007) puts it:

> Multiculturalism in this sense [as an element of government policy since the 1980s] referred to a set of policies directed towards taking African–Caribbean and Asian cultures off the streets – where they had been politicised and turned into rebellions against the state – and putting them in the council chamber, in the classroom and on television, where they could be institutionalised, managed and commodified. Black culture was turned from a living movement into an object of passive contemplation, something to be 'celebrated' rather than acted on. (Kundnani 2007: 44–5)

Approaches advanced under the guise of 'black perspectivism', such as 'celebratory multiculturalism', were often theorised from the perspective of the 'white consumer' (Parker 2000: 74), in a form of domestic tourism that reified racial difference. During the 1980s and 1990s, many groups initially set up by black people in order to resist racism were professionalised and brought under state control, either directly or indirectly through dependence on funding (IRR 2001: 18). For example, an initial wave of community-based racial harassment monitoring and support projects, which had included a substantial focus on harassment by the state, were supplanted in many cases by local authority projects advocating a 'multi-agency approach' from 1989, which demobilised grassroots activists and shifted the focus onto individual acts of harassment (Chahal 2003: 4).

The significance of the mediatory role played by such race relations bodies arises from the contradictory pressures on the ruling class and their state, both to accommodate opposition to racism by British-born black people and anti-racist campaigners, and at the same time to maintain a cheap supply of labour at home and abroad (Kyriakides and Virdee 2003: 299). Just as colonial management depends on the balancing of 'useful' consequences of racism with its limiting effects (Allen 1995: 52–66), so racism within Britain may prove a destabilising force to the smooth running of British capitalism. The motivations of the state for engaging with racism can be seen in the comments of William Whitelaw, Home Secretary at the time of the Brixton uprisings in 1981, speaking on the benefits of introducing a 'multicultural' series of television programmes:

> If you are Home Secretary in any government, you are going to take the view that there are a lot of minority interests in this country, [for example] different races. If they don't get some outlet for their activities you are going to run yourself into much more trouble. (Cited in Kundnani 2007: 45)

This is echoed by the 1985 Force Goal of the London Metropolitan police, where one of the main factors given to support the need for state action against racial harassment was that inaction may lead to organisation and mobilisation within Asian communities (Hesse et al. 1992: 52). During the period since then, Però and Solomos (2010) survey a range of examples from across Western Europe, in which processes of 'rolling back the state' and establishing alterative regimes of governance have included the contracting out of governmental functions to NGOs, offering opportunities for migrants and minorities to enter mainstream political processes, but with ambivalent results, and a dominant trend in which 'migrants and minorities were encouraged to organise around ethnicity, forming associations and NGOs in exchange for resources and recognition from the state (national and local) that saw them as governmental tools for social cohesion and status quo maintenance' (Però and Solomos 2010: 5). Some have conceptualised this contradiction as ambivalence around the 'melancholic desire for an imperial past', in competition with the need to maintain a social democratic model for economic growth in a globalised economy (Back et al. 2002: 447). I argue that this can be more fully understood as arising from the efforts to maintain an imperialist present.

Case Studies from the History of Race Relations in Newcastle

The history of the early race relations industry in Newcastle points to some of the complexities and contradictions within the developments discussed above. Following a meeting at Leicester in September 1965, organised by the National Committee for Commonwealth Immigrants, Newcastle City Council set up a joint committee with representation from Education, Health and Housing 'to prepare and prescribe policies for, and also encourage the welfare activities among, the Commonwealth immigrant' (Telang 1967: 1). The 'Special Committee as to Commonwealth Immigrants', later renamed the 'Commonwealth Immigrants Working Group', immediately sought representation from immigrant communities (Special Committee as to Commonwealth Immigrants 1966), and undertook activities such as production of a 'Handbook for Immigrants' to inform new arrivals about local services. In April 1968, the working group was criticised as ineffectual by non-council members, in response to which councillors argued that they saw no 'racial problems' in Newcastle, and that the existence of the working group was proof of the council's commitment to deal with such problems should they arise (Commonwealth Immigrants Working Group 1968a). Some black residents clearly felt differently, organising a protest march against racial discrimination on 11 May. The working group made the decision to actively disassociate itself from the march because, although they admitted there was no indication there would be violence, the group felt that the possibility 'could not be ruled out' (Commonwealth Immigrants Working Group 1968b). This indicates the refusal of the local state in this period to grapple with the lived experiences of racism among black Newcastle residents, and in particular a fear of organisation by black people outside official structures. After this march the council working group never met again, and was superseded by Newcastle-upon-Tyne Community Relations Council (Renton 2007: 117).

Newcastle Community Relations Council, 1968
On 26 November 1968, the day the Race Relations Act of that year became law, Newcastle Community Relations Council (CRC) was formally established at a meeting at Newcastle Civic Centre attended by 117 people including representatives of the council, police, Labour, Liberal, Conservative and Communist parties, voluntary sector organisations, religious bodies and black community organisations (Community Relations Council Newcastle upon Tyne 1968). This was one of many such bodies set up during this period across Britain (Renton 2007: 111–12).[1] The role of Newcastle CRC increased in 1969, when the short-lived local office of the Race Relations Board was closed down (Community Relations Council Newcastle upon Tyne 1969). A conference at Newcastle Polytechnic on 2 May 1970 gives some indication of the close relationship between the early CRC and sections of the local ruling establishment in spite of its formal independence from the state, with sessions on employment led by a Personnel Manager from Rowntrees, on housing led by the Principal Officer from Newcastle City Council's Housing Department, on youth led by the chair of Tyneside Young Liberals Association, and on education led by the Headmaster of St Paul's Church of England Primary School (Community Relations Council Newcastle upon Tyne 1970).

However, for the first few years of its existence Newcastle CRC was no simple puppet of the state. The full time Community Relations Officer was, Chris Mullard,

---

1 The government stipulated that community relations councils could only be initiated by local residents, at least on paper, but were eligible for funding from the national Community Relations Commission, which had been established by the 1968 Act. In 1976 the Community Relations Commission was merged with the Race Relations Board to form the Commission for Racial Equality, but many local councils continued beyond this change in national structures, including Newcastle CRC.

a black man who had experience of anti-racist organising in the Campaign Against Racial Discrimination. His appointment was actively opposed by members of the national CRC, including several Tory MPs and police officers, and funds for his wages were withheld (Renton 2007: 118–23). In 1971, there was a significant split in the Newcastle CRC, with members of the organisation's executive council passing a vote of no confidence in the chairman, including the accusation that he had failed to make contact with 'the black communities' (implying that the 'community representatives' on the CRC were not in fact representative). The representatives of Sikh, Pakistani and West-Indian community organisations opposed this, and at an Extraordinary General Meeting overturned the executive's motion and passed a motion of confidence in the chairman (Community Relations Council Newcastle upon Tyne 1971). This suggests potential for the CRC to be contested by different forces. While necessary from the perspective of the state in order to maintain the image of an 'independent' organisation distanced from the racism of the state, this presents limitations in the reliability with which such a body could be expected to act in line with state priorities. Mullard suggests that for a period the CRC was able to employ 'a politicised model of community development', exposing that 'The issue was race, not friendship', and repeatedly confronting the police over its inaction on racist harassment (Renton 2007: 121). In 1972 Mullard described a change in local community relations policy since the CRC's inception from an 'international event, social work approach, to a political campaigning approach' (Community Relations Council Newcastle upon Tyne 1972). Examples of this included support for a campaign by the Supreme Council of Sikhs for exemption from crash helmets, and plans to organise a demonstration, against the Commonwealth Immigration Act 1971's retroactive elements and calling for an amnesty for all 'illegal' immigrants who had arrived prior to 1 January 1973 (Community Relations Council Tyne and Wear 1973a). In 1973 Mullard, was quoted in a local newspaper saying that in the previous decade racists had dictated race policy, and that now a black approach was needed (The Journal 1973: 5).

The CRC's turn towards political campaigning was short-lived. Mullard (1973) describes the direction the Community Relations Commission (the national umbrella body for local CRCs) was heading at this time:

> Less qualified, less controversial, mostly white officers have been appointed, with the effect of lowering both the Commission's standard of work and its status. The Commission has concentrated on the middle ground of race, pushing forward inoffensive non-policies ... black communities have lost all confidence in the Commission and its work. (Mullard 1973: 110)

In 1973, the local CRC faced major financial crisis and had to be bailed out by several local authorities after the wages of the Community Relations Officer, the CRC's only full time employee, were stopped, with the Chairman reporting that, since its inception, the CRC had 'always been labouring under a burden of a considerable financial deficit' (Community Relations Council Tyne and Wear 1973b). Mullard's (1973) account of the eighteen month battle to get his first paycheque from the Commission national office suggests that even this may be understating the problems (Mullard 1973: 106–9). This insecurity undermined the efforts of members such as Mullard who saw the need for a more militant anti-racist approach. The CRC was re-established in 1974 on a very different basis, described by the new Community Relations Officer, who replaced Mullard, and who I interviewed in Newcastle in 2008 (subsequent quotations are taken from the same interview):

> It was agreed first of all that we would actually work on the principle of cooperation rather than confrontation. And I gave examples; I said people get fed up when we start confronting one another. But through cooperation we can actually create understanding, and through understanding we can actually take action about the issues that we're facing in this area.

In 1975, the CRC opened a youth club in the West end of Newcastle, specifically targeted at 'bringing shy immigrants out' and letting them mix with British young people (Lockley 1975: 13). Other initiatives included the introduction of 'anti-racist education' into schools, work with employers and interview panellists, and joint programmes with religious leaders. On 6 April 1976, the CRC established the Tyneside Committee for Racial Harmony, with the stated aim of involving 'prominent personalities in industry, the trade unions, political parties and religious and community organisations' (Northern Echo 1976: 3).

The work of Newcastle CRC spanned decades. In 1983, a week-long multicultural festival organised by the CRC marked the 25th anniversary of the first 'People-to-People Week' in Newcastle in 1968, including 'musical entertainment, lectures and talks and special open-house sessions at the places of worship of different religions', and an exhibition where people from different cultures were asked to set up stalls 'showing items they use in the home' (Evening Chronicle 1983: 17), in an intense reification of culture. In September 1984, a scheme the CRC had set up a year earlier, involving volunteers teaching people English in their own homes, reported they had matched 100 volunteers with students. The CRC described the scheme as particularly beneficial due to the fact that many Asian women were so afraid to leave their homes for fear of attacks or break-ins that they could not attend the usual classes (Evening Chronicle 1984b). Thus services were brought to black women excluded as a result of racial harassment, without the basis of their exclusion being challenged. The overriding role played by Newcastle CRC, in common with much of the rest of the race relations industry across Britain, was to channel responses to racism into official and 'respectable' channels, which would not disrupt the status quo, promoting accommodation instead of resistance. As the CRC's Officer since 1974 put it:

Because of all the steps we have taken since those days, since '74, we haven't had one demonstration in Tyne and Wear ... demonstration, flags, walking up the street and all that, and attacking people, saying you're racist and all that. We told community leaders and representatives if you have a problem let us know ... we went to the authorities and say look we've got issues, they said tell us, so we developed that kind of rapport, relationship, with the key institutions. And whenever we telephone them they say please come, we'll sit down and talk ... We set up a group in 1974, brought leaders from all the main communities together, and the chief [police] officers, and we met for the first time and we said look, lots of things have happened in the past, you have criticised us and we have criticised you, but we really want to work together in partnership ... So whenever something happened in London we did not respond to events ... As soon as something happens [a senior police officer] would ring me and '[Name], we've got to meet, there was a problem in London, we've got to make sure that doesn't happen here'. So we would just straight away get together and say what is it, he would say it's the East end, there is a riot going on, or there is a scuffle going on there. (Interview, 2008)

This describes a process of managing the responses of black people to racism, in partnership with the police, to within channels acceptable to the ruling class. In particular, this Community Relations Officer saw a role for the CRC in preventing any political response in Newcastle to events in migrants' countries of origin, thus explicitly undermining any potential for migrants to contribute an internationalist influence to local politics:

Taking steps before something happens, that was our policy. So if something happens in Nigeria and all that we would bring the Nigerian community in, if something happened in Oman, you know, or Yemen, I would have brought all Yemeni Arabs together.

The Officer went on to explain the role of the CRC in encouraging local black people to trust the police and cooperate, and the structures they used to disseminate the views of the police among ethnic minority communities:

So that kind of relationship between the police and ourselves is even stronger now [in 2008] ... When people know that the police take notice of what we are saying, then they will cooperate with them, provide information, provide support, and again when police want members of the community to know everything, what we say, we've got ten shops in Newcastle, and you leave that information, and when the customers come to buy their foodstuff and all that, they tell them, so it's faster than television.

Thus the local CRC served to form a strong network with high levels of trust, involving both the police and trusted members of black communities, in order to mediate the relation of these communities with the state and manage their oppression. This represented an approach which would become further perfected and generalised under Labour following 1997, and is echoed in the Conservative–Liberal Democrat Coalition's conception of the 'Big Society', as discussed later in this chapter.

During the period of the CRC's existence racism persisted, in Newcastle and elsewhere, taking a myriad of forms. The CRC did not challenge this, but instead managed the responses of black people. Examples of racism in Newcastle's West end which were reported in the local press – which represent just the tip of an iceberg in experiences of grinding day-to-day racism experienced by many black residents – include April 1982, when an arson attack gutted an Asian-owned chip shop (Evening Chronicle 1982b). In the same year, a black tenant was quoted in a local newspaper, reporting persistent harassment of local black people, with gangs using two-way radios to track targets and attack with stones and half-bricks, leading to many black people moving out of the area (The Journal 1982). In June, another black family had their flat in the West end of Newcastle broken into and set on fire, with NF slogans daubed on doors and windows (Evening Chronicle 1982a). A community centre which had pioneered service provision for black young people in Newcastle, was described in the 1980s as 'fortress-like, with windows boarded and bricked up after regular break-ins and racist attacks' (Young 1989), and young people coming under attack on their way to the centre, as a youth worker from that period recalls: 'they used to set dogs after them, throw stuff at them, they'd just get abuse' (Interview, 2008). Council minutes in 1987 refer to recent fires at two mosques in the North and the West of Newcastle, and a funding request for armour glaze glass for the windows of one of the mosque's community hall following vandalism (Local Government and Racial Equality Subcommittee 1987). Of 223 ethnic minority residents of Newcastle interviewed in a council survey in 1990, 58 per cent reported experiencing one or more incidents of racial harassment in the previous year, 12 per cent on a daily basis, and one in ten reported physical attacks at least a few times a year (Newcastle City Council 1990: 3). In 1991, following a spate of racist attacks on visitors to a mosque in the West end of Newcastle (Andrews 1998), Khoaz Aziz Miah was beaten to death on his way home from prayers. The CRC Officer quoted above told me he worked closely with the murdered man's family in an attempt to prevent them saying anything to the press that might provoke a community response. During the same period there were doubtless also countless acts of day-to-day resistance and solidarity, and neither these experiences of racism or acts of resistance should be taken to define the lives of those who experienced them. What these examples are intended to demonstrate is the hollowness of the CRC's claims to have prevented more collective or public acts of resistance to racism, when they offered no effective alternative against these levels of experienced racism.

Neither do the CRC's claims to have prevented demonstrations against racism and increased cooperation with the police reflect a lack of experiences of racism from the state for local black people. Instead the CRC, a community organisation which claimed to be opposed to racism and involved prominent ethnic minority 'community leaders', covered up for the racism of the state and blocked effective resistance. Instances recorded by the local press – again, just the tip of an iceberg – include a 'security operation', launched in 1971 at Newcastle airport to target Indians entering the country via Amsterdam (The Journal 1971), and coordinated dawn raids on restaurants and workers' accommodation in 1977, during which around thirty Bangladeshi men were detained until they could prove their right to be in the country. Five were deemed to be in the country illegally (The Journal 1977). In 1990, 11 per cent of 223 black Newcastle residents surveyed reported that either they or their families had been investigated by an immigration officer, 65 per cent of whom had been living in the UK for ten years or more, and some of whom had been living in the UK for as long as 27 years. Half of those investigated felt that the investigation had been totally unnecessary, and several reported feeling that questions asked during the investigation were inappropriate and unnecessary, amounting in some cases to harassment and in one case including questions such as: 'Why did you marry a person from Bangladesh and not someone from here?' Four reported being held in a detention centre or prison under Immigration Act powers, two for 25 days or more, one of whom was also subsequently deported (Newcastle City Council 1990).

The Campaign for Black Direction, 1986
Significantly to the left of the CRC, the Campaign for Black Direction (CBD) developed in Newcastle and Sunderland for several years in the mid-1980s. The campaign was sparked by the sacking of a black worker from a voluntary sector organisation, as someone working in the sector at the time recalled in an interview I conducted in 2005:

> Single Homeless on Tyneside ... SHOT employed a black worker ... as a homelessness officer, and subsequently finished him. He shouted racism, SHOT said 'ooh, not us' ... there was a massive, massive rift in Newcastle from activists and workers, professionals ... there was a massive campaign across the West end ... demonstrations outside of offices and agencies.

The campaign included newsletters, letter writing, demonstrations, posters, graffiti campaigns and meetings, leading to a boycott of SHOT and some of those associated with them by several other voluntary sector organisations. SHOT responded that it was attempting to set up an independent inquiry and had contacted the Federation of Black Housing Organisations in London to ask them to mediate (The Journal 1986), but the worker was never reinstated. Following a high profile campaign, which lasted more than a year and forced anti-racism onto the local agenda, particularly in relation to employment practices, the CBD came under attack from a number of directions and went into decline, as one activist and councillor from the period recalls:

> It sort of disappeared. The mechanics of it was the vilification of it really, the vilification of it by a lot of people that I thought should be supporting it, really much on the lines of we don't use these methods in this country ... I think the whole of the Labour group [on the council] had begun to see the anti-racist struggle as an enemy, actually, that these people were their enemies. And so their response to it was to set up the Race Equality Sub-Group, which in essence gave out grants to little community groups to have lunches for pensioners and things. (Interview, 2008)

This account was corroborated by another councillor from the period I spoke to, who described a widely held perception by the dominant members of the Labour group of councillors that the CBD was the creation of a 'Black Power Commissar' sent from London. The CBD is highly significant, both in its own time and in historical perspective, as a rare example of an initiative which punctured the smooth management of racism in Tyneside, yet has been largely written out of history. To deal adequately with this history would be no small task, as the details are highly contested, and would have to include the accounts of all those who played a leading role, some of whom are reluctant to speak about this period. For these reasons it is beyond the scope of this book to deal with the CBD more fully, but the brief consideration above of how the campaign was received – and the fact that so many seem keen to bury memory of its existence – demonstrates the threat it posed to the racist status quo.

The Black Youth Movement, 1985
One group that secured funding from the council's Race Equality Sub-Group following these developments was the Black Youth Movement (BYM), which had begun as an informal grouping of black and white young people, meeting at a primary school in the West end from 1985, initially once and then twice a week. In 1986, a confrontation took place involving a spokesman of the BYM at a meeting of Newcastle City Council's Youth and Community Recreation Sub-Committee. The BYM spokesman reported that black young people were being excluded from current council youth centres in the area, and put forward the demand for separate recreational facilities and support in converting a derelict building in the West end. He said the council had been doing nothing to help the situation of black people in Newcastle, and that people had lost all faith in the CRC after it issued a statement that there was no serious harassment in the area. The BYM spokesman was quoted in the local press as saying: 'Kids are being abused and harassed, doors are being kicked in and people are being beaten up – if that is not large scale harassment I don't know what is' (Young 1986).

By July 1987, attendance at the BYM youth project was regularly eighty to ninety per session, with ages between 6 and 19 (Director of Education 1987: 1). Alongside service provision, the aims of the BYM included: 'To promote and organise activities which challenge racism and develop members' understanding of racism' and 'To provide advice and support to members suffering racism and develop activities which promote anti-racist policies and action' (Black Youth Movement 1987). By the time applications were made to the local authority for Section 11 funding in 1987, the BYM had already been receiving local authority funding for more than seven months for a full-time 'organiser', and were granted funding for a further full-time youth and community worker and some sessional work, this money being dependent on the submission of a full constitution for the group (Local Government and Racial Equality Subcommittee 1987: 1–3). The securing of local authority funding contributed to what an activist and councillor from the period (also cited above on the CBD) saw as a diversion away from an approach of political struggle and resistance:

> It was turned into a youth club ... it came round keeping them off the streets, and table tennis, and all that crap, and it stopped being a movement. And in a sense it was ridiculous, because it started in an attempt to get [access to a youth centre where black young people were being excluded], and it got distracted by that, by being given a completely crappy building and a broken table tennis table somewhere else. (Interview, 2008)

Trends of Resistance and Incorporation

The cases above are important examples of a trend during the 1970s and 1980s, in which many initially radical initiatives, in Newcastle and elsewhere, were effectively incorporated in state funding regimes and their associated constraints, and eventually completely 'professionalised', with their community and activist base demobilised and their most radical elements attacked and isolated. Yet the same issues continued to resurface, with complaints over lack of provision for Bangladeshi young people leading to the establishment of a Bangladeshi Youth Forum in August 1998 by five restaurant workers in one of their homes (Dickinson 1999). A similar process was reported in the case of local organisation against racial harassment in Newcastle, which began on the basis of grassroots networks of phone trees and community mobilisations to defend people under attack, but was taken over by the council from 1991. One of its former members reflected:

> Maybe that's in a sense how you get defeated, in the sense that those sorts of movements are taken over and bureaucratised. So now you have things like [a local authority racial incident reporting service], it is very professional, everybody involved in it is paid, and it's very much seen as them doing something to a community, whereas the West end Racism Monitoring Group was about communities doing things together. (Interview, 2008)

In the 1980s, local authority policy in Newcastle largely followed the national trend of increasing legal sanctions against racism. In 1985, Newcastle City Council set a precedent by requiring every chief officer to attend a two-day course on the authority's duties under the Race Relations Act (CRE 1985: 2), and in 1987 introduced a specific clause into council tenancy agreements prohibiting racial harassment (Local Government and Racial Equality Subcommittee 1987: 5). In the same year, there was a demonstration by Newcastle Community Law Centre, Newcastle University Students Union and the Commission for Racial Equality (CRE) outside the Civic Centre, calling on the council to provide funding for immigrant residents who could not afford to pay a new citizenship registration fee before the deadline (The Journal 1987). This demand was granted. There also appears to have been discussion and involvement by Newcastle City Council in the Anti-Apartheid Movement, with a representative co-opted onto the Local Government and Racial Equality Subcommittee by March 1987, and the right to take a political stand justified by reference to Hugh Greene, former Director General of the BBC, who had argued that: 'a man who speaks in favour of racial intolerance cannot have the same rights as the man who condemns it' (Head of Policy Services 1987). In 1989, Newcastle Council's Racial Equality Subcommittee sent a letter of protest to the Home Office following the forced removal of refugee Viraj Mendis from the church in Manchester where he had claimed sanctuary for two years (Evening Chronicle 1989).

Together, the role of the CRC, the effective co-option of radical elements into a relatively vocal local state, the vilification and isolation of those who refused to be co-opted, and the strong influence of the local Labour Party, all contributed to the relative absence of radical black or anti-racist movements on Tyneside, in contrast to many other urban areas across Britain during this period,[2] and despite high levels of deprivation and racism (Robinson 1988: 203–4).

Race Relations Today

Arguments for political advances in combating racism in Britain since the 1960s seem to rest on the questionable impact of race relations legislation and state-sponsored bodies such as the CRC and CRE (Bulpitt 1986: 38–9). Race relations legislation in Britain has in general represented both a concession to pressure from black and anti-racist movements and an attempt to manage opposition to racism in such a way that fundamental racist structures are left intact. The embarrassment to the government of the Stephen Lawrence Enquiry and the uprisings in northern cities in the summer of 2001 (Kundnani 2007: 52–4) coincided with the Race Relations (Amendment) Act 2000 and the Race Relations Act 1976 (Amendment) Regulations 2003, which had been shaped by long-running processes of resistance

---

2   For example, the Asian Youth Movements in places including Bradford and Southall (Ramamurthy, A. 2006. The politics of Britain's Asian Youth Movements. *Race and Class*, 48(2), 38–60.), monitoring projects which targeted police racism in places including Newham (http://www.nmp.org.uk/about.html), and the uprisings in Bristol, London, Liverpool, Birmingham and many other British cities, but not Newcastle, in the early 1980s (Fryer, P. 1984. *Staying Power – The History of Black People in Britain*. London: Pluto Press Limited.).

and negotiation inside and outside the state. Among other new provisions, these Acts placed specific duties on public authorities to promote anti-racism, and established legal protection from a wide range of racial harassment. Yet while carrying a high profile and therefore enhancing the appearance that the British state is serious about tackling racism, legislation alone has severe limitations in its ability to tackle racism, even in the case of overt racist incidents (Chahal and Julienne 1999: 10–11). In many cases anti-racist legislation, at both a national and local level, has represented part of an opportunist approach which prioritises being seen to do something rather than making concrete achievements, as described by an experienced black professional employed by Newcastle City Council who I interviewed in 2005:

> ... some authorities ... talk about equality, they don't genuinely believe in equality, but they do so because the Act says so, the law says so ... If the councillor happens to represent ... [a ward] which has about 25 per cent electorate from the BME communities, they'll have equal opportunities. Somebody ... they might have twenty BME [constituents], they don't talk about it.

Other arguments for advances in the situation of black people in Britain focus on recent Labour governments' engagement with organisations such as the Muslim Council of Britain (Back et al. 2002: 449). However, often such 'consultation' has been done entirely on the terms of the state, with no obligation to act on what those consulted say, and has largely involved select ethnic minority organisations whose views are palatable to the government and who are then assumed to represent the experiences and needs of all members of that ethnic category (Ben-Tovim et al. 1993: 202–6). Rai-Atkins et al. (2002) make an observation in the case of mental health provision, which is indicative of a wider trend, that involvement of selected black service users in forums and consultations have often operated in a context where a lack of support makes it very difficult to present any perspective other than that of the dominant institution, and particular users are assumed to be representative of the views of all other users of the same ethnic group (Rai-Atkins et al. 2002: 9). This kind of engagement may simply reinforce power inequalities, ruling as illegitimate the views of black people who did not take part in the consultation and marginalising issues of racism by compartmentalising them as a 'community issue', while mainstream practices continue their perpetuation (Ben-Tovim et al. 1993: 202–6). Engagement in consultation exercises and funding regimes by black groups since the 1980s has often included the requirement that, in order to gain recognition and a share of resources, black people must define themselves as easily identifiable groups in terms of dominant discourses (Shukra 1995: 12–14), in a process of intense self-racialisation. Paul Gilroy has described this as the 'boiling down of groups into their ethnic essences', with each ethnicised group competing with others to be the most 'genuinely representative' (cited in Lentin 2004: 192).

The above account of dominant forms of engagement by the state with black people reflects a contradiction within multiculturalism, in which decentralised *cultural* diversity and expression have combined with centralised and forceful assimilation to the *politics* of dominant capitalist interests. This has been expressed through attempts to reconfigure mainstream British nationalism to include diverse religions, cultures and skin colours, bound together by the pursuit of a 'national interest' which continues to include aggressive imperialist expansion and increasingly punitive treatment of new migrants from oppressed countries. Although there has been a sharp turn away from multiculturalism towards an assimilationist approach since 2001, elements of multiculturalism remain, as in the advocacy by the Labour government for faith schools (Flint 2007).

The overriding need for government continues to be the balancing of racism in order to avoid provoking destabilising acts of resistance, as indicated in comments by Gordon Brown in 2006 locating the need for action against racism firmly in the context of national security (Brown 2006: 13). This has been obscured in many discussions of the relationship between the state and civil society which are framed in terms of 'social capital'. This framework, which is explored in more detail in Chapter 5, became increasingly popular under recent Labour governments and continues to surface in the Coalition's concept of the 'Big Society'. Dominant versions of social capital theory rest on the assumption that institutions exist prior to and independently of civil society, and may therefore act impartially towards its different sections and interests (Roberts 2004: 479–80). This diverts attentions from the way state institutions are shaped by the interests of particular groups and their need to manage the responses of those they oppress. Factors that are often ignored in social capital theory include the context in which engagement takes place, the balance of forces, and its consequences for the overwhelming dominance of particular discourses.

Where public authorities have achieved the appearance of making concessions to the anti-racist critique, this has frequently represented in practice the co-option of black leaders previously struggling against structural causes of racism into 'manageable, bureaucratic procedures' (Williams 1992: 102–3). For example, Anderson (2010) relates the Labour government's engagement in 1997 with the self-organised migrant domestic workers group Waling Waling and their supporters' organisation Kalayaan, in a process of case-by-case regularisation based on a stringent set of requirements. Engagement in this process combined with new pressures and opportunities for individuals in Waling Waling as a result of regularisation, such as having family members join them, to lead to an individualisation of responses. Forms of activity changed from weekly meetings of more than 200 people in 1997, to Kalayaan becoming a registered charity providing advice and other services, while the members of Waling Waling took on the more passive role of clients (Anderson 2010: 67–9). Thus, what some present as the development of 'linking social capital', connecting marginalised groups to established power structures, may serve to neutralise collective struggles. Others have avoided such cooption, including in the recent period the Latin American

Workers' Association (LAWA) in London. Però (2008) reports LAWA's founders to have been determined to avoid public funding and the political restrictions associated with charitable status and economic reliance on the state, based on a view of the British state as not promoting the interests of workers and, in particular, of migrant workers (Però 2008: 83).

The Management of Racism and the Black Middle Class

Formal race relations structures operate in interaction with shifting class configurations among ethnic minorities, acting together to shape relations with the state. Funded ethnic community organisations in Britain have frequently played a role in covering up for the deficiencies of the local state rather than directly challenging racist institutions, and have protected themselves from challenge through relatively closed memberships (Ben-Tovim et al. 1986: 69–71). Whereas earlier black movements in Britain had engaged in strengthening group identity in order to engage with wider society from a position of strength, and had begun to challenge oppressive practices within black communities, state-sponsored 'community leaders' from at least the mid-1980s sheltered black communities within a static view of their 'culture' as a means of maintaining their own power, and in general were neither accountable nor interested in challenging oppressive structures on which their status depended (Kundnani 2007: 47). The incorporation of a section of black and immigrant communities into the ruling establishment has thus facilitated the labelling of understandings of racism concerning factors other than culture, and methods of action other than bureaucratic process, as 'extreme' (Ben-Tovim et al. 1993: 204–5). The theory of the internal colonial or submerged nation model of racism, developed in the US by the Communist Party from 1928–1957 and later taken up by organisations such as the Black Panther Party, offers important insights here on the importance to the ruling classes of structures for indirect rule, employing a black middle class in a similar role to that the a 'comprador bourgeoisie' in oppressed nations (Geschwender 1977: 14–15). Even with Britain's relatively small ethnic minority population when compared to the US, this has relevance to processes of cooption in Britain, particularly given the role of black sections of the working class at key moments in Britain's history, out of all proportion to their numbers.

From 1997, Labour went beyond previous governments in its cultivation of ethnic minority middle and even upper classes, to cooperate in 'managing race relations'. This included the establishment of a Race Relations Forum in the Home Office, bringing together ethnic minority professionals and politicians as unpaid part-time advisers at the heart of government. Of the 26 black and ethnic minority individuals with peerages in the House of Lords as of 2002, 19 were awarded by the Labour government since 1997. Historically, it may be argued that the main influence of 'ethnic community representatives' with government has been based on 'their capacity to restore social order at times of unrest or their ability to deliver a block vote' (Back et al. 2002: 449–50). This makes them of particular use to local authorities in their role of managing 'conflictual pressures and interests' (Solomos 1993: 96), and has doubtless influenced the preference of local authorities employing 'municipal anti-racism' to work with 'individual "race relations" officers, or "ethnic entrepreneurs" of religious or "ethnic minority" communities', leading to the marginalisation of black anti-racist groups and collective modes of struggle (Lentin 2004: 134).

Splits between the majority of working class black people and a small but privileged and 'well-connected' minority have been added to by the points-based immigration system introduced in stages in the final terms of the 1997–2010 Labour governments. 42 per cent of the increase in foreign-born workers from 2001 to 2008 represented workers in higher-paid occupations (ONS 2008: 6), and the lowest-skilled tier was indefinitely suspended following the onset of the economic crisis (Home Affairs Committee 2009). Of employers who stated they were planning to recruit migrant workers in the third quarter of 2009, 43 per cent said they were looking for highly skilled workers, 28 per cent for skilled workers, and 25 per cent for low-skilled/unskilled workers (CIPD 2009a: 8).

While on the one hand, there has been recruitment to Britain of highly-skilled workers in professional positions, for many other migrants and for black people born in Britain, there are barriers to advancement far greater than for white people. Even for those in management positions, there is evidence of racial targeting by higher management. A study employing a range of case studies in small and medium sized businesses (Roberts et al. 2008), found a common management tactic to involve the diversion of attention from racism in the organisation onto conflicts between members of ethnic minority groups, for example, between Afro-Caribbean and Somali workers, and to present diversity itself as the problem. Where the study found racism to have been acknowledged in some form by senior management, there was a common tendency for responsibility to be dumped onto black junior managers or team leaders to 'sort it out' (Roberts et al. 2008: 37–8). Multiple studies have demonstrated an 'ethnic disadvantage', not only in direct recruitment to management positions, but also in internal promotion processes, which rely on practical skills and experience more than qualifications, and at times include 'hidden criteria' favouring white culture alongside ethnic stereotyping by managers (Roberts et al. 2008).

Britain's black middle class is based to a large degree on employment in the public, voluntary and community sectors. This ensures that their relative privileges are very directly dependent on the British state, either directly as their employer or indirectly through state influence over funding. Overall, ethnic minorities working in managerial roles in the public sector are significantly more likely than to be in such positions than ethnic minorities in the private sector, particularly in lower managerial and professional roles (Heath and Cheung 2006: 41). However, there are considerable differences between specific ethnic minority groups, and these more privileged sections of public sector workers exist alongside large numbers of black workers employed in the public sector in low paid and precarious roles. Within the public sector as a whole, 30 per cent of workers who were born outside

Britain are on temporary contracts, which is double the proportion in the private sector. Within the NHS, the proportion on temporary contracts is 84 per cent (CIPD 2009a: 8). This seems likely to have very serious consequences for concentrations of unemployment as the government implements its programme of public sector cuts.

The above picture, of decades of resistance and struggle by black people responded to with attempts to co-opt and divide, is an important part of the context for the more recent development of the 'refugee relations industry'. This has included a sharp stratification between a 'refugee elite', with secure immigration status and well paid posts, an intermediary layer with greater opportunities but in many cases working for free, and finally an increasingly excluded and insecure mass of refugees, many of whom are destitute or detained indefinitely in immigration prisons.

The Role of Organisations Managing Refugees' Relationship to the State

Since the early 1990s, refugee community organisations have been increasingly incorporated into the race relations framework of devolved responsibility from the state, with its discipline of funding regimes (Griffiths et al. 2005: 22–3), and numerous voluntary sector projects specifically targeting refugees have been established across the country (WLRI 2005). The Home Office has stated that it views strong refugee organisations and 'involvement in the host society' as positive signs of integration, and has actively encouraged voluntary work by refugees who have been granted status (Wilson and Lewis 2006: 16). In many ways, funded refugee sector organisations have become part of the delivery of the state's punitive immigration system. While some voluntary sector organisations publicly criticised the process of forced dispersal across Britain, there was no sustained campaign, and organisations from the voluntary sector, and in some cases Refugee Community Organisations (RCOs), ultimately took the front line in implementing dispersal, sacrificing much of their independence from the state and inhabiting 'the most visible and contested space within the NASS system' and its intended role as a deterrent to residence in Britain (Hynes 2009). Briskman and Cemlyn (2005) conducted interviews with a range of asylum teams and voluntary agencies and concluded:

> There is a mixed picture among those [NGOs in Britain] with government funding between maintaining independence and advocacy on behalf of asylum-seekers' rights, and becoming enmeshed in managing an unsatisfactory situation. Individual workers, statutory and voluntary, seek to make a difference, but provision is under-resourced and uncoordinated, leaving basic needs unmet. (Briskman and Cemlyn 2005: 719)

Refugees who participated in a focus group I organised in Newcastle in 2010 emphasised the importance of collective organisation by refugees, but also the vulnerability created by reliance on funding, with funding empowering but creating a dependence which lead to disempowerment when it was withdrawn:

> [We aim] to create a platform for individual groups, RCOs, the refugee-led organisations which are just composed of refugees and asylum seekers, to come and to have one voice, to influence, to bring forward the different evidence with the problem, issues they are facing in their communities ... those small organisations, they were quite empowered through the different funding, so the sector now have lost a big chunk of money. (Former volunteer, now a paid worker with an independent RCO forum)

Beyond this vulnerability, two focus group participants, who each had extensive experience across the refugee sector, confirmed the power of funders to influence forms of action:

> ... when you get funding through some government agency, you are not free, there are so many limitations, it's the same with ... some refugee community organisations, we've got some groups, sometimes we get funding, but there are restrictions, they say to you, you do these things, you can't do this. (Female refugee with status, arrived 2005)

> ... now the great money which is available is from the government. As a collective voice, how can you really advertise the work and the kind of action we are doing? The government [says]: 'I give you my money, but with a string of conditions attached, alright you work for me, because this is the money ... I know that ok, you want to defend people who I oppress, but if I give you money you have to be limited in the action. I can give you a room of action, but no hundred per cent'. (Male refugee with status, arrived 2002)

Thus, the state uses its monopoly position in granting funding to shape even the activities that aim to oppose its policies.

1980s–2008: A Context of Increasing Resistance

The context for increased attention to refugee organisations by the state was increased resistance by refugees and their supporters against state interventions, particularly in opposition to deportations and also, at times, targeting the use of vouchers for subsistence payments and the practice of immigration detention (Sales 2002: 470). From the mid-1980s, the Viraj Mendis Defence Campaign and other high profile campaigns against the deportations of particular individuals drew wide support, engaged in active street campaigning, formed alliances with people engaged in other anti-racist and working class struggles, and received backing from trade union branches, religious leaders and some Members of Parliament (VMDC 1986;   1988). In Newcastle, such campaigns included opposition to the deportation of Surjit Singh Lally away from his family to India in 1988, in a campaign involving Benwell Law Centre and supported by local MP David Clelland, which collected more than 6000 signatures and won one year leave to remain in Britain, after which he could apply for permanent leave to remain (Welford 1988: 9). In 1994, the Tahir family in nearby Blyth were deported to Pakistan despite a campaign supported by thousands of people, including 170 MPs, but later managed to return to Britain and were granted the right to stay permanently (Gledhill 2004). In 1998, protests against the deportation of Greg Otigbah to Nigeria, which involved 'Youth Against Racism in Europe', forced the transfer of the flight from Newcastle to Teeside airport (Ford 1998). On 30 September 2000, the North East Campaign for Asylum Rights (NECFAR) organised a march through Newcastle from the quayside to a rally in the Bigg Market, involving local, national and international campaign groups and trade unions (Kennedy 2000). In 2004, the Croatian Bamburac family, who had come to live in Newcastle in 1998 and had been refused their asylum application in 2003, secured the right to stay following a campaign and petition submitted by MP Nick Brown signed by 1,400 'friends and neighbours' (Evening Chronicle 2004). These examples demonstrate the recurring difficulties experienced by the state in trying to implement its immigration controls in the face of organised community-based opposition.

As the numbers dispersed to different areas increased and networks developed and matured, so did forms of resistance (for example, Eskovitchl 2006 reports collective resistance in working class communities in Glasgow). Many of the refugees arriving in Britain in the late 1990s and early 2000s came from a greater diversity of countries than earlier periods of migration from predominantly former colonies in South Asia and the Caribbean, and in some cases were dispersed to different parts of Britain. As a result, they were often outside the scope of the established structures for the management of 'race relations' discussed above. This was a contradictory consequence of refugees' marginalisation, as they were excluded from vital rights, services and official political channels, but also less liable to have their struggles immediately neutralised and their leaders co-opted by well-developed structures. With a peak between 2005 and 2008, refugees across Britain began to mobilise in a new wave of collective opposition to deportations, often around a shared country of origin, including in Newcastle significant mobilisations at different points by groups of refugees from the DRC, Eritrea, Ethiopia, Zimbabwe, Côte d'Ivoire, Cameroon, Iran, Turkey and Iraq, sometimes organising together with non-refugees, for example as part of Tyneside Community Action for Refugees, and sometimes in separate organisations, some of which were directly connected to organisations in refugees' countries of origin. These responses took place at a time of transition from limited recognition to assimilation as the dominant approach of the state to ethnic minorities, contributing to levels of exclusion that provoked political and conflictual forms of mobilisation. In particular, unusually for the recent period, mobilisations by members of 'new' migration flows have at times linked ethnicity to class and gender, such as in collective resistance to people's treatment in immigration detention centres and in organisation within low-paid and insecure workplaces (Però and Solomos 2010: 5–6). Because of this, they have posed a distinct threat to the state because of their potential to form alliances with other sections of the working class, and as a consequence have received special attention in order to neutralise their struggles.

1999–2007: Labour's New Strategies of Control

Removal of the right to work from the majority of refugees without status gave a major boost to the prominence of formalised volunteering. Young refugees have also been reported as being encouraged to volunteer in order to keep them 'off the street' (WLRI 2005: 59), providing both an indirect means of social control and a source of free labour for the asylum system. Attempts by the state under Labour to influence forms of activity and 'manage' responses to racism and oppression extended even to the point of legislating to prohibit unpaid employment for which 'some non-monetary benefit' is received, and to restrict voluntary activity to a state-approved 'charity, voluntary organisation or body that raises funds for either, or in the public sector' (Wilson and Lewis 2006: 18).

Many refugees volunteered with refugee sector service providers as the projects they were most familiar with. Meanwhile, the increasing destitution of refugee communities brought about by state interventions increased the pressure on voluntary organisations and RCOs to provide basic services, limiting potential to engage in other activities such as campaigning, managing coherent volunteering programmes, or even applying for funding (WLRI 2005: 29). Insufficient resources and funding have been reported to keep RCOs frequently on a 'defensive' footing, restricted to filling gaps in basic service provision rather than engaging in community development or long-term integrationist work, and potentially maintaining the marginality of refugees, by engaging in mutual adaptation with statutory services (Griffiths et al. 2005: 201–2). The politicised nature of asylum further exacerbates the pressure on refugee sector organisations by increasing the vulnerability of funding. Fears of the consequences of mounting a political response grew further following the racist campaign by the *Daily Mail* against funding for NCADC (WLRI 2005: 29), discussed in Chapter 3.

Following the introduction of the New Asylum Model (NAM) in 2007, large sections of refugees with children, who had been at the centre of many anti-deportation campaigns, were granted leave to remain as part of a 'legacy exercise', aimed at clearing the backlog of applications, while the process under which many new arrivals were refused and deported was made faster and more centrally controlled, with asylum applicants divided into seven categories, predetermining the outcome of claims and speeding up the deportation process (Hynes 2009). In some ways, NAM represented a victory, with the securing of leave to remain for many people who had been engaged in a long struggle, and for many other refugees around them. Yet, it also carried a negative aspect, in the diffusion of resistance at a time when large numbers of refugees continued to face deportation, including those arriving in Britain later. Two refugees who were volunteering with an organisation which provided information on the immigration system described their initial experiences of NAM in a focus group in Newcastle shortly after its establishment in 2007:

> When the NAM [system] came in and we had the training about NAM, it specifically said on the sheet that came from [the] Home Office that NAM ... is there to ensure that there are more refusals, and that there are not such big chances of appeal, and that was what we were told, that NAM is there to make sure that more people are refused and deported, don't stay in this country, and that people don't get a chance of appeal. (VOL volunteer 2)

> They won't leave the asylum seekers to become illegal, they are straight deporting them, and they know straight [away] where they are, and their case worker know everything about them ... the people who arrive in 2001 and 2002 and 2003, they are still living there, but [people] who arrive after 2005, they are not [still] there, they are straight away [getting] kick[ed] out of the country if they didn't have the right to live in this country. And they gave more positive decisions very soon and very quick. (VOL volunteer 4)

While some who had been waiting a long time have secured their status through the legacy exercise, for many new applicants it has meant entry into a 'fast track' system of claims. Intended in theory to be used for straightforward cases, the fast track involves initial cases being heard in three days, and all appeals completed by 21 days. BID (2009) reports that people who have been through this system describe feeling like confused bystanders in the process. In the first quarter of 2009, 29 per cent of all applications for asylum were granted, but for those assigned to the fast track the success rate was between 2 and 3 per cent. Factors which seem likely to influence this higher failure rate include less time and options to find legal advice as a result of imprisonment, less time to prepare a case and assemble evidence, which may include the need for documents to be sent from another country, and the unspoken assumption that if a case has been placed in the fast track system it is probably not valid. The Labour government's stated aim prior to losing the 2010 General Election was to have 30 per cent of all asylum claims considered under the fast track, despite widespread criticism of the process by mainstream bodies including the Independent Asylum Commission, the UN High Commissioner for Refugees and the National Audit Office (BID 2009: 18–20).

The developments around NAM and the legacy exercise contributed to a decrease in political mobilisations by refugees resident in working class communities, while inside immigration detention centres hunger strikes, break-outs and other forms of protest have continued at a high level of intensity, although largely ignored by the media and isolated from outside support (Jameson 2010). It is therefore reasonable to suggest that the contemporary situation of refugees fits the wider pattern, in which 'All the signs are that a migrant aristocracy which does not threaten to puncture the moral limits of the nation will be allowed continued entry, while a migrant "underclass" will only be let in on the pretext of "benevolent duty"' (Kyriakides and Virdee 2003: 302). Genuine anti-racist practice, precisely because it challenges dominant institutional and societal norms, will continue to be labelled as 'extreme' and pushed as far as possible to the margins (Ben-Tovim et al. 1986: 105).

Two case studies of organisations surveyed in Newcastle between 2007 and 2010 illustrate some of the various ways in which voluntary and community sector organisations play a role as part of the refugee relations industry, which has been cultivated to help manage the state's relationship to refugees.

Direct Contracting by the State: The Case of VOL

VOL is a large, regional voluntary sector organisation, delivering substantial front-line contracts for the Home Office since 1999, as part of a wider portfolio of service delivery and integration work. It offers an important case study here, of an organisation delivering contracts directly on behalf of the Home Office, but relying to a large degree on the unpaid labour of refugees without status. At the time I conducted my research with the organisation, between 2006 and 2008, it had premises in several cities and a large number of paid workers, alongside an even larger number of volunteers, mostly in front-line roles but with some in administrative roles including a management committee.

In 1999, the Home Office contracted local voluntary sector projects to set up 'one stop services' in the areas where refugees without status were being dispersed, as a means of delegated front line contact between refugees and the state. VOL was one organisation which took this role, contributing to a dramatic increase in the scale of the organisation:

> It's grown so big from a small organisation with a few volunteers and perhaps one or two people to overnight a big organisation with … fifty-five employees and about 300 volunteers. (VOL manager)

While formally in the voluntary sector, the work of the one stop service at VOL involves a high level of engagement with the state, both in the involvement of refugees as volunteers delivering work contracted by the Home Office, and in facilitating contact between the Home Office and large numbers of other refugees as users. One volunteer reported the organisation acting simultaneously as a social and networking hub and as a trusted intermediary with the state:

> I think for refugees and asylum seekers, for them [VOL] is just like, for some of them it is just like a social gathering, it's a meeting point, and it's a point they feel very comfortable to come, and they have the confidence in whatever they

get, that they can come any time, and they come, they complain, you know, they
come and they demand, they want the service … In fact sometimes we have to
explain to them just hang on, I'm also just volunteering … it's a place they feel
they can go for help, whatever time, anywhere, anytime, or they can just ring.
(VOL volunteer 5)

VOL's role includes provision of vital services for individual refugees, such as
translation and help with applying for subsistence support, but also mediation of
the conflict and hostility arising from the contradictory interests represented by
refugees without status and the state:

… when I am on reception, and people sometimes swear at you, and you can
see that they're angry, and they shout at you like it's your job, you have to help
them … you can understand why they're so frustrated … I'm an asylum seeker
myself … I did all these things for myself and now I'm doing it for other people,
it makes it easier. (Refugee without status, 20 years old)

… sometimes [a] client is angry, others they wait [a] long time, and some has
children … I am an asylum seeker … I'm very, very understanding [of] people
… I know what happened, what they're worried [about]. (Refugee with status,
39 years old)

Thus, trust and understanding among refugees, based on shared points of
experience, is used to facilitate engagement with the state, sometimes to the point
of substituting for the state. This relieves pressure on the local and national state
from those affected by their policies:

If there was not [a VOL] office in Newcastle, all asylum seekers and refugees
[would be] running to the council, if there were not that office … the destitute
people and everybody [would be] at the door of [the council] and … the system
[would be] totally un-working … If [the council] know they are foreign [and]
they are not citizens of the EU, they automatically give them our address and our
map and send them to our office. (VOL volunteer 4)

A manager indicated the contradiction that even as VOL uses refugees' labour to
carry out the work delegated by the Home Office, volunteers could disappear at
any time as a result of detention or deportation by the Home Office:

65 per cent of our volunteers are our clients … And if they're from the asylum-
seeking community, then they've not got control of whatever happens to them,
they're here today, they're gone tomorrow … even if you motivate them, and
the Home Office wants them gone, it's like there's nothing you can do about it.
(VOL manager)

Refugees as users may benefit individually from this engagement, by being able to access a point of contact equipped to understand them, both in terms of language and experience, and who may be highly motivated by a sense of solidarity to try and secure for them the 'best deal' available within the limits of the legal system. At the same time, the state benefits from more effective incorporation of refugees into its systems and structures, including those whom it continues to deny official refugee status, with implications for the maintenance of their subordination to the state's dictates and priorities.

Delegated Management of Refugees: The Case of COM

COM is a community advice and signposting organisation, established by refugees mostly from the same country of origin but providing services to refugees from a wider range of countries within the North East and to non-refugees in the local geographical neighbourhood. It is discussed here as an important case study of an organisation operating at a greater distance from the state than cases like VOL, run by refugees yet occupying an ambiguous position in relation to the interests of the state and the interests of refugees. At the time of my research with the organisation, between 2008 and 2010, it had funding for one full time worker and a building, supported by an active management committee and a small number of formal volunteers, and was attempting to secure funding for a second paid worker.

COM was established by dispersed refugees in 2001, in response to a general lack of preparation and services in dispersal areas and to a specific gap in information and contact between many refugees and established agencies:

> ... it was a new area for us, we didn't have any connection ... you have to come in here and communicate in English, [it] was difficult. Even the service provider, we didn't know how to do, or who to approach and ask about the area. (COM founder)

The founder related to me the story of his initial activities in Newcastle, working as a volunteer at VOL. One day a refugee had arrived with a letter refusing her status and giving her a deadline to appeal, but due to a lack of English proficiency and access to translation she had not been able to understand the contents of the letter and did not know where to go for support, and the deadline had expired:

> So [on] that day [a worker at VOL] said ... you know it's better for you to have your own community organisation, like African, where people can come and maybe ask you as a first contact, 'I've got this issue, what do you think?'. And then you can look at it ... It's difficult for us to go there to find out what's happening to the community. But ... like this lady if you've got a community she could go and ask someone there who speak Swahili and they would say 'Go and see [the relevant agencies]'.

COM was therefore initiated as a further support to the development of trust and engagement between refugees and VOL, and through VOL the Home Office. Yet the organisation was simultaneously conceived as developing a collective confidence and sense of belonging in the local area among African refugees:

> At the same time as well [we wanted] to think about the social situation, where people can start to feel they are part of this area. Because we felt isolated, even food, everything, was new to us, different to somewhere there are a lot of Africans, where you can go and find African food and everything. (COM founder)

This is part of a broader trend, with extensive evidence suggesting a tendency across a diversity of historical and geographical settings for migrants to form voluntary associations, more frequently compared both to their country of origin and to non-migrants in their destination country, increasing in number particularly rapidly where other institutions are failing to meet social needs such as health-care, leisure and companionship. This suggests an impetus to organise inherent in the migration process itself, related to migration's potential to sharpen collective identities and interests (Moya 2005: 837–40). COM was thus seen by members as both developing trusted links with the state and developing collective confidence and self-reliance.

Previous research has found a general tendency within voluntary organisations for the lack of regularity and/or total time of volunteers' participation to lead to structures involving a core membership, often including paid workers, who interact with a wider periphery of volunteers, but without the individuals in this periphery interacting with each other, creating an informal hierarchy (Pearce 1993: 10). COM appears as a particularly acute form of this, where a single central figure, both the founder and the first paid worker, was reported by multiple participants as a focus of expectations and trust, reinforced by the basing of the organisation in this individual's house in its early stages:

> … for five years I've been with [the manager], he really helped me … he was always with us, advising us. (COM volunteer 4)

> … if people had problems, they could call him any time, people were not bothered, any time when there is a problem, yes [the manager] will help. (COM management committee member 1)

This role of 'ambassador and advocate' has been found to be common among migrant communities, and essential to the development of 'bridging and linking social capital' connecting people to networks and resources outside the migrant group (Zetter et al. 2006: 16). Through this central role, extended and reinforced through the organisation, high levels of trust in this individual by other refugees enabled a stabilisation of engagement with the state, despite individuals' negative experiences of it:

> ... he kept just encouraging us, he said you have to hang on and wait. He's been telling us a story, he didn't want us to go astray ... Sometimes you get tired and you say 'How, how can I be like this? I used to work in my country', but [the manager] said 'You have to wait'. (COM volunteer 4)

COM's leading volunteers are clearly highly motivated and committed to improvements in the wellbeing of both collectives of refugees and their local area, and for some volunteers a much wider area. Their preference for gradual and non-confrontational forms of action does not appear to be a result of direct constraint by the state, but rather it is individuals favouring this approach who the state has chosen to support by financial and other means.

Contradictions and Dilemmas in the Role of Mediating Organisations

For organisations, major pressure to make use of any available voluntary labour is created by the lack of funding and the need to make the best possible use of available resources (WLRI 2005: 58). In the voluntary and community sector more widely, there is a trend towards the replacement of a 'volunteering ethos' by a managerialism favouring work by paid and contracted professionals. This exists in tension with a continued reliance on volunteers, prompted both by a lack of resources and by their importance as a link to the communities organisations seek to engage. Morison (2000) suggests that a dominant approach to resolving this contradiction has been to reconceptualise 'the community' as a mobilising focus for collective action in a way that links 'the sturdy "self-reliance" of the past' (drawing upon nostalgia for traditional working class communities) with the '"active citizenry" of community action in the present' (Morison 2000: 109–10). In the case of the refugee sector, this has contributed to a situation where the wider pressures acting on refugees as clients, volunteers and staff have kept the work as a whole under constant pressure and instability, and have severely limited the potential for support and development (Evelyn Oldfield Unit 2004: 7).

COM provides a case where a lack of preparation by the state prior to dispersal led refugees without status to actively engage with the state in an attempt to deal with hostile elements of the local population:

> ... our phone used to ring even at 2am, someone [who had] just been attacked by their neighbour used to call, we had to do something, we had to go – to force ourselves to be known to the local authorities, I'm talking about the police, especially the police ... prior to the dispersal programme the government did not prepare the region ... it was like how many beds can you prepare, oh a hundred beds, phew, and people were found in an area where there were no connections, the local community were not prepared for that, and so that's why [there were]

those funny stories about asylum seekers, they have nice phones, whatever.
(COM management committee member 1)

Yet even with this trust and willingness to engage with the state, the same project found limits to how far up the state hierarchy they were permitted access, and a lack of trust from the state to the point where Home Office representatives would not set foot in the centre:

> ... we don't deal directly with the government, the government always uses its local representation, its regional representation ... and the regional representation [are] using other services to reach us. It's very rare to have a direct link – I remember one year, I think it was 2005, there were a group of directors from the Home Office, they were touring in the different regions ... they came, but they didn't want to come in, they were just in the bus, so we had to go in the bus! (COM management committee member 1)

This limitation of participants' 'linking' role, to within boundaries set by the 'partner' with greater power, was echoed in reports suggesting the disempowering impact of acting as a 'messenger' for the real decision-makers:

> ... we don't have any power like the government to decide on their behalf ... We have no power. (COM management committee member 2)

> [Being] support workers means that we're not legal representation, and we are not the decision maker ... we're taking the client's enquiry and everything to the Home Office, and we're taking the Home Office decision ... to the client, and basically we explain to the client what ... the Home Office are saying, what's their policy, what's their law. And we're sending the client's everything to the Home Office. (VOL volunteer 4)

> ... you're just here like intermediate help, but you can't really do anything much, it's all up to the Home Office. (VOL volunteer 2)

Yet despite this lack of power on the part of volunteers, participants reported the practical linking roles played by VOL as reaching a point where any distinction between VOL as a voluntary project and the state was absent in the eyes of some users:

> I've found actually the role of [VOL] very, very useful, just like a bridge. You know, it's just like the medium, whatever problem people bring in ... they'll take it on, and they'll try, and they try to link up with anybody, with the Home Office, whatever it is, [VOL] is there to help these people link up and get help for whatever it is ... some people think maybe it's the Home Office. (VOL volunteer 5)

A recurring theme across different projects was the importance of winning trust through dialogue and the example of organisations' actions, in order to overcome divisions and build effective collective action. One participant from COM explained the organisation's initial challenge of winning the trust and understanding of other refugees:

> ... people used to find it strange ... there were some misconceptions among the community ... that [we were] getting the money from the public funds [and were making money from the project], and we had to explain all the time. But the goodness of what we are doing, beside the explanation, we were showing the work. So we were accountable for whatever work we were doing. And that made us to be strong at a certain point. (COM management committee member 1)

Several refugees I interviewed who were engaged in more oppositional forms of action suggested that VOL's close relationship with the state seriously compromised that organisation's relationship to refugees, constituting a weakening of trust between refugees and VOL as the price for the level of engagement between VOL and the state:

> [VOL] isn't really a group that I particularly trust ... because for me it's just another face of the Home Office. (Ivory Coast, arrived 2000)

Several participants, most prominently those volunteering with VOL but extending to volunteers at other projects, reported dilemmas arising from the tension between their position as a refugee and their desire to defend the interests of other refugees, and the requirements in their organisational role to act as a bridge to the state:

> ... sometimes you are put in a very difficult situation that you're reluctant to interpret. For example once I spent the whole day, from 10am till 8pm in a hospital for somebody to interpret, he had an operation, and he was asking me difficult questions, he was asking me to interpret difficult things, like saying 'I know this man is a trainee doctor, he's going to practice on me', I said it's not possible, these doctors are experienced, he said 'No, ask him' ... it was very stressful and I didn't want to upset the doctor, or maybe to upset the client. (Iranian refugee volunteering with a church-based project in Newcastle)

> We can't be more supportive of clients than supportive of the Home Office, we're supposed to be in the middle, but sometimes when you see how the Home Office is trying to make it really hard for people ... it's really hard to stay detached ... knowing how hard it is for people sometimes you just say 'oh, forget it' and you really try to help people ... here people are just in charge of other people's lives, because it's so important, like one wrong move can just wreck someone's life ... you're always under pressure and tension. (VOL volunteer 2)

In the latter account, this tension may be understood as arising from the attempt to 'bridge' simultaneously between interests that stand in objective contradiction to one another, in this case the interests of refugees without status on the one hand and the interests of the British state on the other, and behind it the British ruling class. Thus, by operating through delegated and 'partner' NGOs, the British state has been able to both maintain engagement of many refugees despite their deep mistrust of the state itself, and at the same time to define the acceptable limits within which refugees may organise in defence of their interests (Griffiths et al. 2005: 209–10). One thing that has been distinctive about the development of the refugee relations industry, when compared to earlier elements of the race relations industry, is that it has developed in a context of increasingly direct delegation of tasks by the state to voluntary organisations, enforced through mechanisms such as 'market tendering', 'best value frameworks' and 'contractual compliance', and with a focus on bureaucratic efficiency rather than democratic accountability (Morison 2000: 101–2). There was some evidence among participants that this may have transferred some of the tensions away from the organisational level, where contracts operate, but intensified them at the level of individual volunteers, who, by the nature of their unpaid work, are resistant to reduction of their activity to a contractual basis.

Mediating the Contradictions in the 'Big Society'

There are strong lines of continuity between the structures of governance developed under Labour governments to manage the oppression of refugees and the Coalition government's 'Big Society'. Like recent Labour governments, the Coalition has promoted the transfer of large areas of service provision and governance to the private and voluntary sector. Alongside the sweeping public sector cuts discussed in Chapter 3, which it seems likely will provoke many forms of resistance, the government announced soon after the General Election that it would be training 5,000 'community organisers' and that these would be targeted at areas of 'low social capital' (Cabinet Office 2010a). In February 2011 the government awarded a £15 million contract to the voluntary sector coalition Locality, to begin training community organisers on a curriculum set by the government (Cabinet Office 2010b; Locality 2011; NCIA 2011). At one level, the 'Big Society' may be seen simply as a cynical way to justify public sector cuts by shifting responsibility for provision of services onto local communities. But beyond this, the proposals for community organisers have been explained by some of their proponents in terms of responding to 'disaffection'. Drawing on a case study of community organiser training by the Gamaliel Foundation in North East England, Mills and Robson (2010) argue that contrary to its 'apparently radical pedigree', community organising 'can lend itself to conservative and pluralist purposes and thereby can be used to reinforce, rather than transform economic and social inequalities'. In a post on his blog in September 2010, the 'Big Society' advisor to the government and recently knighted Nat Wei writes under the heading 'Reform or Revolution':

> To turn that anger [at public sector cuts] to constructive reform is to follow a noble tradition which will invariably help lead us out of the crisis which we all face – a crisis which otherwise threatens to turn into a bitter, unforgiving, bloody revolution that will once again set community against community – the opposite of what Big Society is all about. (Wei 2010)

This suggests that management of opposition to government policies to within 'acceptable' limits is central to the government's conception of community organisers, and may represent an extension of the kind of role previously played by the race relations and refugee relations industries to much wider sections of the working class.

Conclusions

The history of modern race relations in Britain and many other imperialist countries has represented a dialectic, wherein racialised exploitation provokes resistance, which, where successful, has forced retreats by dominant institutions to new systems of racialised exploitation, which bring them some of the same benefits while lowering the costs incurred by resistance, but which inevitably provoke new strategies of resistance (Geschwender 1977: 1–2). In the period since 1962, the British state has developed sophisticated interventions through the voluntary and community sectors, alongside the cultivation of a black middle class, to mediate its relation to black sections of the working class. Since the 1990s, this has been expanded, albeit with limited resources, to the endorsement of an array of specifically-targeted refugee organisations.

Griffiths et al. (2005: 201–2) report resistance by some refugees to formalise groups or networks, in a stated attempt to avoid incorporation into official structures and the 'funding driven political economy of refugee organisation'. This may suggest a degree of scepticism on the part of some refugees as to the nature and purpose of the government's strategies. Similar concerns were encountered by Hynes (2009), who found instances of RCOs turning down significant funding for Home Office contracts on the basis that it would lead to a loss of trust by their members and the expectation that they would have to provide information on their members to the Home Office, which could potentially be used to target them for detention or deportation. However, overall the state has to a great extent succeeded in the management of these intensely oppressed sections of the population.

The state interventions outlined above played a role in managing a relationship with refugees, often experienced as intensely hostile at an individual level, and in particular helped to divert more oppositional and overtly political forms of activity by refugees themselves. It may be argued that this gave the state the breathing space it needed to carry out the fundamental reorganisation of the UK asylum system represented by the New Asylum Model. Understanding how this has operated at the level of individual refugees calls for greater attention to Labour governments' interventions under the banner of 'building social capital', which will form the focus of Chapter 5.

Chapter 5

Social Capital and the Management of Refugees' Oppression

While Chapter 4 examined the role of organisations that mediate refugees' relationship to the British state, this chapter explores processes by which refugees are involved in these organisations as volunteers. Exploring the motivations and perspectives of individuals enables us to move beyond simplistic accounts of co-option and explain why refugees engage in unpaid activities which help the state to maintain their objective oppression. A key element of recent Labour governments' attempts to ensure the smooth running of British capitalism has been an array of interventions aimed at building 'social capital' as a means of social control down to the individual level. At its most basic, social capital may be considered as purposive and ongoing forms of voluntary engagement, with implicit norms and values. This chapter interrogates the role and nature of social capital formations connecting refugees to the British state, including their consequences for the different parties engaged in them. Following discussion of Labour governments' interventions in social capital since 1997, I explore incentives for refugees to volunteer, and consider the outcomes of such activities. I conclude by discussing the continuation of the Labour government's attempts to structure social capital in the Coalition government's 'Big Society' initiatives. This discussion draws heavily on refugees' accounts of their own incentives to engage and the roles they have observed organisations to be playing. Although much of the discussion is structured around themes and concepts drawn from the literature on social capital, volunteering and incentives, insights arising from refugees' accounts have problematised and/or transformed the meaning of some of these concepts, grounding the theoretical discussions in refugees' lived experiences. Equally important is the 'step backwards' taken in the last part of the chapter, in order to present a perspective of the impact of particular social capital formations on refugees' wider situation, producing outcomes that include contradictory elements which were not necessarily anticipated, desired, or fully perceived within the individual perspectives of some refugees.

Introduction

Social capital theory is highly contested, with the potential to play a variety of roles. Social capital explanations that view society as 'prior to and causative of the production of the economy' distract attention from material factors influencing social problems, presenting society instead as composed of 'communities and individuals' divorced from a material basis, rather than divided into social categories according to class, racialisation or gender (Franklin 2007: 5–6). For the ruling class, social capital thus serves a role in abstracting the consideration of social relations away from questions of class and power (Fine 2001: 25–8). The suggestion by Robert Putnam, one of the most prominent proponents of social capital, that civic virtue determines economic success has made it attractive to theorists around institutions such as the World Bank, offering a way to explain away economic inequalities between countries, through a racialised discourse of Western superiority:

> Social capital started to play a role in a sort of Western triumphalism towards the East and the South in the sense that Western culture apparently harboured the 'right' kind of social capital, which sustained capitalist development and the creation of democracy. The alleged absence of civic virtue, or having the 'wrong' kind of social capital (the 'amoral familism' type) became emphasised as important developmental explanatory factors. (Schuurman 2003: 993–8)

Some critics of this approach have argued that it is deregulation of transnational capital that has lead directly to the erosion of social capital, in the sense that the imposition of increased labour flexibility has broken up existing social structures and undermined 'traditional' norms (Steger 2002: 266–70). What this omits is the simultaneous increasing need for social control in the period of monopoly capitalism, including the tightening regulation of international labour migration, which has gone hand in hand with loosening regulation of capital. The capitalist state faces contradictions arising from the fundamental relations at the base of capitalist society. These are such that wage-workers are removed from the products of their labour and thereby alienated from one another, interacting through commodities with the result that 'social relationships within communities come to be constructed upon conditions of alienation and thereby upon conditions of distrust' (Roberts 2004: 481). More specifically, for refugees from oppressed countries, the products of their countries' labour have been removed to Britain, adding a national element to their alienation, and this process has been mediated by racism. A spontaneous tendency of such alienation is to provoke confrontation, which may destabilise conditions for capital accumulation. This calls for increased imperialist control of processes of social capital rather than their absolute destruction, with 'linking capital' playing a key role in maintaining social cohesion in conditions of widening inequality, establishing consensual relationships between people with different degrees of power and often contradictory interests.

Against the understanding promoted by Putnam and the World Bank, social capital may instead serve as an intermediary concept in relation to class, connecting individual experience and agency to historical processes in order to concretely situate the individual in relation to questions of class and power. Mutual dependence is continually forced upon people by their needs; as Marx says:

> It is natural necessity, *essential human properties*, however alienated they may seem to be, and *interest* that holds the members of civil society together; *civil, not political* life is their *real* tie. It is therefore not the state that holds the *atoms* of civil society together ... only *political superstition* today imagines that social life must be held together by the state, whereas in reality the state is held together by civil life. (Marx and Engels [1845] 1956: 163, emphasis in the original)

I argue there is potential for social capital to be understood within a Marxist framework, as part of a focus on processes within the class struggle, and the ways that particular forms of engagement interact with social stratification to produce particular outcomes. The question for Marxists, as for many others who share a concern with realities of power and inequality, is not only the strength of networks that individuals or groups are connected to, but what forces and interests are involved, the character of social capital in which they are engaged, and their position within contextualised social capital formations, including differential power relations 'within' as well as 'between' groups (Anthias 2007: 791–2).

Labour's Turn Towards Social Capital as Theory and Practice

As outlined in previous chapters, recent Labour governments have been characterised by strategies of devolved governance. Zetter et al. (2006: 7) identify a tension in Labour's social cohesion policy, between the promotion of a national set of 'shared values' and a diversity of local conditions and approaches. In the absence of an assumed homogeneity, local communities delegated as 'guardians of moral worth' can become instead political battlegrounds over resources (Back et al. 2002: 447–9). Securing the outcome of these processes therefore requires the state to intervene in the way members of working class communities relate to each other and to the state, in order to structure their participation and representation in ways that do not challenge the status quo. Roberts (2004: 483–7) suggests that social capital played a role for recent Labour governments in socialising the worst consequences of neo-liberalism through a 'consumer-led' approach to social policy, where those most excluded were blamed for failing to 'invest in themselves'. This was achieved through extensive intervention by the state to shape normative processes influencing the actions of society's members (Coole 2009: 376–7), with the poorest sections of society assigned the role of nominally political actors within strictly circumscribed limits, not as workers, but as 'social capitalists' (Mayer 2003: 124–5). Prefigured in practice with Labour's 'New Deal for Communities' beginning in 1998, from 2001 then Prime Minister Tony Blair began to make increasing references to Putnam's rosy picture of the potential for formal engagement by different sections of society to encourage a propensity to informally 'help each other out' when needed (Roberts and Devine 2003: 309–11). Strategies were presented within the 'synergy' model of social capital, with an ideal of the state stimulating mutually beneficial cooperation between itself and members of civil society (Brunie 2009: 256).

The particular historical context in which Labour's turn towards social capital took place was one urgently calling for the repair of the 'ideological resources' of liberal states and the reinvention of means of managing their populations (Coole 2009: 376–7). In Britain, this followed a widening gap in 'civic participation' along class lines, with large sections of the working class which had previously been 'incorporated into the political system through a powerful nexus of trade unions, local Labour Party branches, and affiliated associations and clubs', becoming increasingly disengaged (Warren 2009: 100). These had been the classic organisations for maintaining the dominance of a labour aristocracy over the rest of the working class (Clough 1992). The 'New Labour' leadership did not simply remove the famous Clause IV from the party's constitution, with its commitment to nationalisation, but replaced it with a conception of governance through 'partnership', which assigned voluntary sector organisations a significant role. The gap left by a Labour Party active within the working class, as opposed to merely drawing electoral support from it, was filled by a conception of 'the third sector as the organised vanguard of civil society', seen to be playing a role not only in delivering services but shaping the ideas and actions of society (Morison 2000: 105–6). Central to this was the use of organised voluntary activity involving working class people to shape their ideas and relationships; that is, for voluntary activity to play an ideological role. For example, McGhee (2003) discusses interventions in Bradford and Oldham following the uprisings in 2001 that involved central, regional and local government, acting through 'the community' and associated organisations to break up social capital formations that were viewed as problematic, in particular targeting 'the "cultures" of local neighbourhoods and communities, and the affiliations, allegiances and attachments forged within them'. The eventual aim was to make a reconstructed form of 'the community' a '*means* of government'. Implicit in this was the assumption that 'normal' processes of socialisation were insufficiently reliable, and that 'problematic communities' required state-directed reorientation (McGhee 2003: 389–96).

The Role of Nationalism in Labour's Social Capital

The overall framework for Labour's social capital interventions was a form of nationalism drawing heavily on the ideas of Putnam. Putnam (2007) uses findings of a negative association between ethnic diversity and trust to argue for the need to reconstruct a sense of 'we' among immigrants and existing residents, as part of managing migration, 'to encourage permeable, syncretic, "hyphenated" identities; identities that enable previously separate ethnic groups to see themselves, in part, as members of a shared group with a shared identity' (Putnam 2007: 159–65). With increasing coherence from 2002, Labour governments engaged in strategies aimed at the restructuring of just such a 'national consensus', compliant with the needs of British capital and implemented through a romantic nationalist conception of voluntary activity, summed up in a speech by then Chancellor Gordon Brown:

> ... the Britain we admire of thousands of voluntary associations; the Britain of mutual societies, craft unions, insurance and friendly societies and cooperatives; the Britain of churches and faith groups; the Britain of municipal provision from libraries to parks; and the Britain of public service. Mutuality, cooperation, civic associations and social responsibility and a strong civic society ... at the core of British history, the very ideas of 'active citizenship', 'good neighbour', civic pride and the public realm. (Brown 2006: 5)

This was implemented through carefully directed interventions at a micro level, including approaches through the family, such as parenting classes and Sure Start, through religion, with the reframing of faith communities as a means to social inclusion, and in schools, through citizenship education (Coole 2009: 380–81). An array of new roles was created in the local state, from 'street wardens' to 'ward coordinators' to 'participation officers', intervening in multiple arenas to structure particularly working class people's participation and relations with the state. On the basis of a systematic survey of core policy documents between 1997 and 2007, 6 et al. (2010) argue that efforts at behaviour change were central to the domestic policy programme of governments of this period, from Antisocial Behaviour, Curfew, Dispersal and Parenting Orders, to initiatives encouraging community surveillance and reporting of suspected 'benefit fraudsters', to regulation of young people on their way to and from school, to encouraging cycling on the way to work, to energy conservation at home. Through such measures, responsibility was delegated, at the same time as control was increasingly centralised, with a tendency for more coercive measures to be used in interventions with poorer sections of the working class (6 et al. 2010).

Interventions in existing communities have combined with attempts to influence social capital at migrants' points of entry, with 'knowledge about life in the UK' and 'British values' introduced as requirements for citizenship in 2002, and extended to include those applying for settlement or family reunification in 2007. In 2009, this was extended beyond one-off citizenship tests to expectations of ongoing contributions to society over a succession of stages on a 'pathway to citizenship', with engagement in particular forms of voluntary activity a key element. In August 2009, a public consultation was announced to discuss proposals to further extend the 'earned citizenship' approach, including a broader definition of non-criminal actions which could negatively affect applications and result in punitive sanctions (Kostakopoulou 2010: 832–7). As reported in *The Independent* on 4 August 2009:

> According to the Immigration Minister, Phil Woolas, 'migrants who contribute to the democratic life of the country by canvassing for political parties, for example, or who show active citizenship by serving in their communities

may have their applications shortened from three years to one. But those who show an "active disregard for UK values" which could include protesting at homecoming parades of British troops, may find their applications blocked'. (Cited in Kostakopoulou 2010: 832–7)

This represents a clear increase in the social control function of immigration controls, where permission to remain in the country is conditional on not only obeying laws, but conforming to prescribed forms of political and social activity.

Backing up these somewhat unreliable structures of co-option in oppressed communities stand the police, who, since the 1980s, have played an increasingly political and moral role, taking over various roles previously played by the church and medical profession in defining concepts of social sickness and deviance, including the recurring depiction of an unruly 'black underclass' (Cashmore and McLaughlin 1991: 1–3). More recently, the police played a prominent role in lobbying for the extension of the period for which terror suspects can be held without trial, up to ninety days (Home Affairs Committee 2007; Blair 2009). The relation of voluntary activity to the physical enforcement of social control is clear in a further passage from the speech by Gordon Brown cited previously:

> Just as neighbourhood policing – being pioneered here in London as well as elsewhere – is showing, greater local engagement and improved public services can go hand in hand: the police able to respond more quickly to local concerns and local people taking greater responsibility for working with the police to tackle these concerns. (Blair 2006: 11)

This indicates the government's enthusiasm for the potential of social capital formations to not only shape the activity of large sections of the working class, but to consensually incorporate them in intelligence gathering to guide more direct repression of those who refuse to be incorporated.

Labour Targets Refugees

The powerful potential of refugees organising collectively created the context for state intervention under Labour. A recurring theme among refugees I interviewed was the trust and understanding arising from shared experiences of seeking asylum, which gave refugees more confidence that their needs would be understood and respected when an organisation was staffed by refugees:

> I think they trust more a group like [CAMP], where asylum seekers are really present. So it's easier for them to ask for help, because then they don't feel inferior to the person who they're asking for help, they know that the person is not going to feel superior or isn't going to treat them badly. (CAMP 4)

I think sometimes it's better to have at least someone who has been through the process so they can explain to people who haven't been, to say 'no this is actually how they do feel, because I went through that same thing'. (VOL 1)

These accounts, and others that I encountered like them, suggested that the involvement of refugees as volunteers was an important factor in the development of empathy as a basis for trust and sustained engagement in all the organisations in my research. This trust may serve different ends. Where refugees volunteer with organisations delivering state agendas, it may play a role in maintaining refugees' oppression, by gaining their trust and thus weakening resistance. In other cases, social capital formations formed on the basis of shared experience as refugees may form the kind of 'compact social blocs' which Gramsci ([1929–1935] 1982) argues are a necessary prerequisite for the development of social movements. This is particularly likely where shared experiences and material conditions combine with an absence of provision 'from outside' and a collective process of reflection to develop a wider systemic understanding of the roots of individuals' problems, as was evident in my research on the campaigning asylum rights organisation, CAMP. Such blocs have the potential to 'give birth to their own intellectuals, their own commandos, their own vanguard – who in turn will react upon these blocs in order to develop them' (Gramsci [1929–1935] 1982: 204–5). This helps to explain the importance recent governments have placed on participation of refugees in approved voluntary roles, in order to allow the state influence over their activity and so disrupt the formation of blocs capable of forming a basis for resistance.

The accounts of refugees I interviewed indicated that the incorporation of refugees into organisational roles is not passive, but involves an active process, in which individuals assess and test known available opportunities in order to access resources, information and networks they consider to be of benefit in achieving their goals, including material and non-material incentives. A similar degree of agency and critical approach to services has been found in other research that prioritises refugees' perspectives (e.g. Williams 2006; Bowes et al. 2009). This underlines the importance of listening to refugees' accounts of why they enter into particular forms of organised activity, as a way of understanding in the relationship between refugees' experiences and consciousness and their engagement in different forms of activity, with implications for their oppression and resistance.

Refugees' Incentives to Build New Networks and Relationships

Però and Solomos (2010: 14) call for greater attention to 'what migrants seem to get out of mobilising, especially when concrete gains and changes appear clearly out of reach from the outset'. The approach taken here responds to this call, placing overtly political mobilisations in the context of other available forms of voluntary activity. While highlighting the significance of subjective motivations, it is also important to bear in mind that social capital formations may be contradictory and uneven, and may produce outcomes out of line with the intentions and motivations of some parties. For example, Allen (2009) suggests that 'access to co-ethnic social capital that helps refugees find employment could also constrain their labour market activity because of reciprocal obligations and adherence to social norms that accompany the use of social capital' (Allen 2009: 333). It will therefore be necessary to use the analysis of the material basis of relations between refugees and the British state, developed in previous chapters, to problematise refugees' accounts of the processes in which they are engaged. A distinction also needs to be made between refugees engaging with organisations as project users, as grassroots volunteers, or the small number of refugees occupying some of the highest positions in funded organisations, who in the few cases where they do not receive a wage may have firm expectations of a waged position once their status is granted. The latter may be viewed as a kind of 'migrant aristocracy', with a direct material interest in continued cooperation with the state, while the involvement of grassroots members and volunteers is potentially more complex and contradictory, and forms the focus of this chapter.

Understanding 'Volunteering'

In addressing incentives to volunteer, I draw on the resources of two distinct research traditions. Within Marxist studies of socialist societies, considerable attention has been given to the role of 'non-material incentives' and voluntary labour in the transformation of consciousness (e.g. Guevara [1959–1967] 2003; Yaffe 2009). Within organisational studies, wide-ranging discussions have taken place as to the motivations and role of volunteering (e.g. Pearce 1993; Antoni 2009). I engage here with both bodies of work, by extending the Marxist investigation of the relationship between consciousness and voluntary labour into the context of a capitalist society and the formation of social movements. Various typologies have been developed for categorising incentives to volunteer, from material, solidary (including fun) and purposive (Pearce 1993: 20), to 'giving alms', 'giving back', 'getting on' and 'getting by' (Hardill et al. 2007: 400). Although refugees' responses demonstrate that actual incentives rarely, if ever, fall solely into any such category, these typologies provide a useful starting point for considering the range of possible reasons for volunteering among refugees in Newcastle, to be further explored using empirical data.

The meaning of voluntary activity for an individual needs to be understood in relation to their broader biographical trajectory. Volunteering has been conceptualised as having a 'dual character', mixing both altruism and self-interest, with dominant contemporary conceptions differing between volunteers who are 'beyond' the labour market for reasons such as age, disability or care commitments, and those for whom volunteering plays a role in training and retraining for paid work (Hardill et al. 2007: 396). The majority of refugees in VOL's volunteer files in 2007 listed 'asylum seeker' or 'unemployed' as their occupation status at the time of their application to volunteer, while among non-refugees, 'student' was the most frequent response, followed by 'retired' and then 'employed' for women, and 'employed' for men. There were also indications of a broader spread of ages among refugees than non-refugees. This may be linked to the most common positions occupied by volunteering in refugees' and non-refugees life-pathways: for refugees, as a route into paid employment or as the only available option in the context of its legal prohibition, or for non-refugees, as a rewarding activity alongside university studies or retirement.

In general, the amount and range of participation in voluntary activities in Britain has been found to be far greater among those with greater wealth and power (Field 2008: 83). Yet, in the case of refugees who volunteer, most have little wealth or power. Whether providing services or campaigning for change, it may be argued that for all organisations in my research, there was a degree of material incentive to volunteer at a collective level, as refugees volunteering were also part of the target group the organisation aimed to help. Many refugees I interviewed described their original decision to volunteer as the result of having nothing else meaningful that they could legally do with their time, being prohibited from paid work and with limited educational opportunities. This raises questions about the 'voluntary' nature of volunteering for refugees without status:

> [I] had to await my decision from the Home Office ... I had nothing to do, so the only thing [that] could give me value as a human being was to do that work to support others. (COM volunteer 1)

> [Refugees who volunteer] don't get any money, but they are happy that they are useful ... because just to sit at home or just look at the television or something like that, it kills everyone. (CHUR volunteer 4)

Such limited options may carry implications for the kind of social capital generated through refugees 'volunteering'. One study went as far as to exclude volunteering with trade unions and churches from measures of formal social capital, on the basis that in some countries participation was more a matter of necessity or practicality than genuine voluntary choice (Gesthuizen et al. 2008: 126–7). Rather than making such exclusive distinctions, qualitative analysis allows us to explore the complexities of material and non-material aspects of incentives to volunteer, as they operate within the specific context of refugees' lives in imperialist Britain.

Survival as a Starting Point for Engagement

Marx and Engels ([1845] 1965: 87–8) point to the conditioning of social life by the combination of human needs and the means available for their satisfaction in a particular historical context. Reflecting this, the needs of refugees I interviewed and the resources available for their satisfaction influenced their forms of action. At the extremes, refugees without status have been shown to rely heavily on other refugees, themselves impoverished, for basic subsistence (Dwyer 2005: 635–6).

Those arriving in Newcastle early in the dispersal process responded to the gulf in provision by engaging in activities aimed at developing links among refugees, between refugees and local voluntary organisations, and between refugees and aspects of the local state, driven by the need to increase communication and access to services. While some refugees without status set up their own organisation, COM, others contributed to improve the capacity of existing organisations:

> At first I didn't realise it was anything important, but once I went in and I saw some people, very nice people there, and by accident somebody from my country arrived and he couldn't speak English, and one of the people from [CHUR] asked me 'Do you speak English?', I said yes, and he asked me if I could help, and I said no problem, I helped them, and thereafter I volunteered. (Volunteer with CHUR, arrived 2000)

The British state has backed long-running distinctions between white, middle class volunteers, with benevolent motivations and operating largely in the 'mainstream' voluntary sector, and black volunteers within the refugee and wider 'BME' sector, who it is suggested are motivated by community self-interest and associated with 'the undesirable face of political activism' (WLRI 2005: 28–9). Regardless of their non-correspondence with reality, such representations operate as an implicit warning to anyone who might engage in volunteering as anything other than obedient cooption, particularly if they are working class and black.

For many of the refugees I interviewed, volunteering was a means of survival in a position of severely limited social, economic and political power, where existing qualifications, skills and experiences had been delegitimised through a combination of lack of legal recognition and destruction of confidence in a new and hostile environment:

> I realised I wouldn't be able to work in the travel industry [in Britain], it would be too challenging for me. (Former 'travel rep', Kenya)

> I have experience, but I can't use it, physically I'm unable [to do manual work and] to sell things here [would be too different]. (Former skilled non-manual worker, Iran)

Given the background of forced flight followed by a marginal and insecure position, which is characteristic of the contemporary refugee experience in Britain, it is unsurprising that meeting basic needs of survival was a common starting point for diverse forms of engagement. Involvement in volunteering has also been anecdotally reported as an influential factor in securing status in some asylum claims and in the NAM 'Legacy Exercise', and for many refugees, therefore, their physical survival.

All organisations addressed in my research were reported by refugees as playing a role for at least some of their volunteers in facilitating social engagement at a basic level, which in other situations, notably in the absence of forced flight, dispersal and prohibition on paid work, might have been performed primarily through longer-established networks of family and friends:

> ... if you're an asylum seeker and you come to another country it's really different, firstly feeling lonely and every small thing [seems] very big and very difficult, especially for language or something. But this office has helped me a lot, I'm confident here, I feel when I come here things are nearly [like] my country, out of the stress. (Former skilled non-manual worker, Iran)

> I was working with women, people come with their ideas, so you have to share our ideas as Africans to sort things out ... some people have children and they don't know how to cook for their children, and so [we] have to sit down and talk because we are parents ... some people are very stressed, then we can help them and explain look, I [have] been through this. (Former skilled non-manual worker, DRC)

One refugee described 'staying busy' in order to survive mentally as an important factor in their engagement in volunteering:

> I take every bits and pieces [of voluntary work, to stay as] busy as I can, because it's only when I'm at home and I do nothing that I go crazy, and those thoughts dominate my mind, and I ... enter into a vicious circle ... So I usually go home at 10pm, because I go to college even after work, which is great, and I'm hoping to keep going like this until I get status. (Former engineer, Iran)

Refugees in the mixed focus group further emphasised the importance of these non-material aspects of survival, supporting findings by Hynes (2009) of the importance of engaging in social networks to re-establish a 'sense of belonging':

> ... when you've left all your family, your friends, you've been [living] somewhere for maybe twenty years, twenty-five years, and just suddenly change and come somewhere [else], when you need support it's not just in terms of finances, but it's also in terms of mental ... it's not when I come to your place and you give me money, it's the way that you welcome me, if you just smile, and it's a genuine smile. (Former professional, DRC)

The material, social and psychological situation of refugees, shaped in large part by international conditions and state policy, thus create an imperative to engage in bridging capital with someone as a matter of survival, on multiple levels.

Material Incentives for Engagement

Pearce (1993: 59) points out that there is no straightforward distinction between motivations for paid and voluntary work, with some volunteers acting on material incentives such as enhancing their CV, and some paid workers working primarily for love of their job. Despite being prohibited from taking paid work during the asylum process and facing uncertainty over whether their claim would be accepted, many of the refugees without status that I interviewed described their volunteering primarily in terms of improving their CV, for future employment within Britain. One refugee without status discussed the wider implications of volunteering versus undertaking paid work illegally:

> ... a lot of people ... prefer to go and work illegally rather than volunteer, because [they think] 'I'm working voluntering, I won't get anything out of it, whereas I could go and work somewhere else, the same thing I'm doing here but I'm getting paid, who's going to know?' But you do get people who do volunteer, and that's because they know that in the future it's going to get them somewhere. (VOL volunteer 1)

Considering the disproportionate numbers of refugees from more highly-educated backgrounds who volunteer (WLRI 2005: 34), it may be that the decision to work illegally or volunteer as a strategy of personal advancement is closely linked to aspirations and expectations, based on individuals' perception of their long term class trajectory. For those from a more middle class background, who expect to resume a similar position in the future, there may be a strong pull towards volunteering to gain acceptable experience and also to avoid the risk of working illegally, even if this means greater hardship in the short term.

Other refugees, who considered their past career finished, described a role for their volunteering in exploring new options:

> I'm only doing this because I feel it's a line I would want to pursue in future, because I think it's very interesting, and very wide, and I like challenges, that's why I came to volunteer. (Former 'travel rep', Kenya)

Another person indicated the role of her volunteering with other organisations, in gaining experience for future employment:

> The main motivation for me to volunteer in [a charity shop] is ... I get different skills ... If I obtain status I can use the skills. As a cashier there, I can go to work in any supermarket and say that I've been working at [a shop]. So I get motivation because I can also use them as a reference in future. (Volunteer with CAMP, former computer technician)

They drew a contrast between their incentives for volunteering with the charity shop and with CAMP. The material incentive which appeared paramount for CAMP members was the support offered by other members of the organisation in the event of them being threatened with deportation, as described by another member:

> ... if we [have] any problem and we want to demonstrate for it they help you, and they give you advice what to do. (CAMP volunteer 3)

In this respect, CAMP was fundamentally different from the other organisations surveyed. In this sense holding more in common with a trade union than with the other organisations in my research, CAMP provided different kinds and levels of support to members and non-members. In part, this reflected the political ethos of the organisation, and in part the fact that, unlike the other organisations surveyed, CAMP had no external funding or paid workers, and therefore relied on its members as its main resource:

> The good things is that everyone there in [CAMP] is there for everybody, if anybody is snatched we stand up for each other, so it's like a kind of solidarity for all the members of [CAMP]. (CAMP volunteer 2)

Immediate material incentives also featured prominently among volunteers with VOL, in the form of support, information and networks arising from its role administering aspects of the asylum process and its connections with other projects and institutions:

> ... when I was not doing volunteering I didn't know what's Home Office, what's NASS, what's social services, what's council, what's MP, what's the property provider ... they're opening your eyes, and you're seeing if tomorrow you're going and applying for the job ... you'll have that ability that you did the volunteering ... you could work in social services, you could work with the council, you could work with the refugees, you could work with the reintegration. (VOL volunteer 4)

> ... from volunteering you'd be amazed with how many things I'm involved with at the moment. If I hadn't volunteered here, I don't think I'd even be in college, I think I'd just be at home doing nothing. But for volunteering I'm involved in youth groups [and other projects]. Especially at [VOL], it's amazing because they have their hands in everything. (VOL volunteer 1)

Volunteering with CHUR, VOL and COM thus all offered direct material incentives in the form of experience and references for future paid employment. In very different ways, VOL and CAMP both offered individual, purposive, material incentives in improved chances within the asylum system, in VOL through specialist knowledge of official procedures and systems, and in CAMP through specialist knowledge and resources for political mobilisation. They thus both reflect the development of social capital as part of a strategy for personal survival, but in the case of CAMP relying more on collective resources and solidarity, and in the case of VOL relying on access to networks and information among the state and broader 'establishment'.

Non-Material Incentives for Engagement

As volunteers are all paid at the same level – nothing – there is no economic reason to formalise the status of different voluntary workers (Pearce 1993: 10–11). Consequently, status and rewards, and their impact on the structure and results of organisations, operate on an informal level, which qualitative methods are well suited to capture. In Hardill et al.'s (2007: 404) qualitative research with four voluntary projects in a working class area, two distinct themes emerged, 'giving to people they perceived as different (and less fortunate) and supporting others with shared experiences'. This was echoed among refugees in my own research. A primary form of non-material incentive reported by many refugees I interviewed was the ability to put skills and experience to use to help other refugees. For individuals prohibited from engaging in productive work and with few other resources with which to respond to the oppression encountered by those around them, the opportunity volunteering provided to help others through distinctive skills and experience was a powerful non-material reward in its own right. One of the most widespread forms this took was the use of language skills:

> I'm speaking French, I'm speaking Portuguese, I'm speaking Lingala, those are kind of skills I've got, that I can give ... to people, that I can help people through. (COM volunteer 2)

> what I've learned at school, learning how to speak French and English, and this is really helping out ... in [CAMP] sometimes I sit where there's someone who speaks French, a person who asks [me because they] cannot really understand what [other people are] saying, but I just translate. (CAMP volunteer 1)

Temple et al. (2005: 36–9) found English-language competency to be closely linked, for some refugees, to knowing their rights and developing a wider range of connections. Such language support may, therefore, be important for advocacy and mobilisation, particularly given longstanding reports of restrictions on access to language provision. These include inappropriate venues and a lack of flexibility to refugees' employment and childcare situations (Temple et al. 2005: 36–9), compounded more recently by restrictions on ESOL funding for refugees without status for the first six months (Aspinall and Watters 2010: 44–7).

Another aspect of experience that volunteering offered an opportunity to make use of was the understanding of the asylum process developed through refugees' own experience. This was particularly relevant for VOL, where some volunteers' work focused directly on supporting asylum applicants through the process, but was also apparent in some other organisational contexts:

> ... usually I do all our family's letters and everything that goes through the Home Office, so it was like it would be a nice place to come here and do it ... at a working level. (VOL volunteer 2)

> ... after eight years ... I have known a lot of people who have different problems, so when somebody comes with a problem, I would have known somebody in the past who had that and I can direct them to where I think they should go. (CAMP volunteer 4)

Another volunteer described their experience as a refugee without status adding to their motivation and commitment, to develop both empathy with project users and knowledge about the technicalities of the asylum system:

> ... being an asylum seeker maybe [I] have got more interest in learning how the Home Office works, how immigration works, and ... what ... experiences other asylum seekers are going through, or even refugees, or even those who are coming here to work ... I can relate to them, their lifestyle or their problems because of my background, probably if I wasn't an asylum seeker I would maybe look at things differently. (VOL volunteer 5)

Zontini (2010: 818–19) found many people motivated to participate in networks and engage in reciprocal exchange of resources for reasons other than competition or personal gain, but rather because solidarity and cooperation within the group were viewed as important values and a powerfully emotional part of identity. This challenges the rational choice underpinnings of social capital as understood by Putnam (2000) and Coleman (1993). Echoing Zontini's findings, a common form of non-material incentive reported by refugees I interviewed was the inspiration gained from witnessing the support provided by the organisation they had chosen to volunteer with, both to themselves and to others:

> ... they are very helpful and they care about people, so that's why they gave me too much motivation. (CHUR volunteer 3)

> I see [CAMP] like a fighting group and fighting for all refugees without status and immigrants ... I view [CAMP] like a human rights group, because they are protecting our rights. (CAMP volunteer 1)

This may be viewed as a form of emulation, which has been central to the cultivation of non-material incentives in socialist countries, particularly Cuba (Yaffe 2009: 212–13). Some refugees I interviewed related their motivation to help others directly to their experience of being helped themselves to deal with past trauma and their situation as a refugee:

> I had to see lots of bad things in my country ... there's lots of damage to my life ... I just think oh my god, [I] just must be good person, and help [other people] if you can ... because lots of people here help me, and now I ... feel better about things. (CHUR volunteer 2)

> Because I've been like them, I couldn't speak English, so [to] improve their life ... that's one of the things for me, fantastic. (VOL volunteer 3)

Another recurring form of non-material incentive across all organisations was the sense of fulfillment gained from contributing towards concrete and visible benefits for individuals. In some cases, the intensity of this fulfillment was described as closely linked to the desperation of those they felt they were helping:

> ... you'll be proud of that service, the hopeless people coming in the office, the people that they don't have not enough support, they don't have anything ... but the advising service we don't make them hopeless, we'll give them the right advice ... the people are praying to you and saying ... 'god bless you', so that's the things that you want to achieve. (VOL volunteer 4)

For some volunteers, their affective impact on other refugees as users of the project seemed a major part of their motivation:

> ... imagine a person who doesn't speak English at all, I've seen a couple of them, very frightened, very nervous, I found it very rewarding to help them, as much as I could. It's really good, it's [a] nice feeling to see somebody is happy. (CHUR volunteer 1)

This aspect of volunteers' motivations may be captured by what Antoni (2009: 360–64) describes as 'intrinsic motivations', including factors such as ideals and the desire to feel useful to others, and contrasted to extrinsic motivations such as social recognition, improving their 'human capital', or increasing their social network.

The Influence of Previous Forms of Engagement

Turcotte and Silka (2007: 113) suggest that an unproblematised focus on the 'right' norms and values can lead to failure to understand social capital in migrant communities, which may be based on norms other than 'dominant Anglo-European' ones. Despite the state's many interventions, social capital does not take shape simply according to its dictates, but as a result of a combination of its interventions with multiple other influences, lending it an uneven character. In a survey across a wide range of immigrant organisations, Moya (2005: 840–51) found particular ways of organising influenced by a combination of current needs, legacies from migrants' countries of origin, and prevalent forms of organisation in the destination country. An important element apparent in my own research was the legacy of individuals' experience of previous social capital formations, emerging particularly clearly because of the abrupt change in individuals' situations as a result of forced flight. Several refugees I interviewed commented on the difference in the conception of 'volunteering' between their countries of origin and Britain:

> ... it is very, very poor in our country, people do voluntary work, but it is not like organisation and everything here. (CHUR volunteer 4)

Another refugee suggested that a key part of this difference was the approach to volunteering in their country of origin as a collective, but informal, response to human need rather than individual development or advancement:

> ... in my country we do volunteer work, not as it has been emphasised here, you know you follow proper procedures, there it just is maybe if someone has a funeral in your area you go and help ... volunteer to do some work, because you sympathise. But here ... you do volunteer work just to gain experience, to learn new skills. (COM volunteer 1)

This suggests social capital formations involving norms of reciprocity, which encouraged individuals to act without necessarily expecting anything immediate or personal in return, but instead a generalised expectation that others would offer them help if needed in future. The 'carrying over' of such norms from refugees' countries of origin was evident in explicit references to socialisation by parents or experience of effective strategies as influences on their activities in Britain. However, these existed in tension with more individualised conceptions, of volunteering as a route to employment, which are dominant within Britain, and were mediated in particular ways by the refugee experience.

An early member of COM described their experiences of organisational forms in their country of origin, and COM as a new adaptation drawing on these forms but adapted to new and unfamiliar circumstances:

> ... back home, we always have groups, traditionally in villages there are always a council of elders ... and the council and the chief of the village sit there every day, to treat the day-to-day problems of the village ... So people could come with their issues, and everything could be treated and solved in that way ... [With COM] it was almost the similar thing, a mechanism where people had issues, racism, harassment, and they could not access services, they had different needs, so maybe coming together and being easy to address our issues to the relevant authorities, not only individual cases ... if people have to express

concerns or needs it won't be heard, but when you are united you are becoming stronger, that's the philosophy behind it ... We were expecting ... elders in the group ... to organise us, but unfortunately at that time that experience could not be applied in a context where we were, because it was a new place for everyone. So we had to find a different way, but at least ... we had an idea in our heads, but how to put that in place. (DRC, arrived 2002)

Here, there is no direct or formal continuation of the form of social capital previously engaged in, and different material circumstances mean that its direct replication proves unfeasible. Yet, in developing a new form of social capital to enable people to respond more effectively to identified needs in the context of contractual relationships in the modern UK voluntary sector, aspects of the previous form play a role in shaping the response, here based on the principle of collective deliberation informed by pooled expertise.

The Impact of the 'Refugee Experience' on Forms of Activity

The definition of people as refugees includes a history of particular relationships to the state in their country of origin, often involving antagonism, a negative balance of forces and forced flight (McSpadden 1998: 147–9), and this carries implications for social capital formation in the destination country. Crawley (2010: 29–31) found significant changes in refugees' relationships with networks in which they had been engaged in their countries of origin, even where there had been expectations of continued contact once in Britain Some people have raised the question of whether experience of state repression in refugees' country of origin may lead people to 'retreat', from the public sphere of formal social capital into the private sphere of informal social capital, within networks severely limited in numbers and involving only people they know well (Gesthuizen et al. 2008: 125). Backing this up, data from Canada and Australia on self-reported participation in a variety of protest activities suggests that experience of political repression in migrants' country of origin may have a very significant impact, with past experiences of higher levels of repression decreasing the likelihood of migrants engaging in a range of political activity in the receiving country (Bilodeau 2008: 986–91). This was highlighted by participants in the focus group I conducted with refugees from different organisations, as a significant factor deterring even mixing between refugees from different countries in a drop-in waiting room:

> ... every time when I go there, they say that we are asylum seekers and refugees, [but] you will see Arabic people sitting together, Africans in the corner, and even African English speakers in the corner, and French speakers, or some people from the Congo will sit together just talking in Lingala. (DRC, arrived 2005)

> ... it is because most of them came from the countries which is dictatorships, and always they were careful to don't say nothing which will be a problem ...

> the suspicion, it is in their bodies, in their minds, and now they … came here, however, it's pressured them to do the same. (Iran, 45 years old)

Two refugees from different countries who had each been actively engaged in overtly political activities in opposition to the state prior to coming to Britain, and who had experienced state repression as a result, were no longer engaged in these forms of action. One described this primarily in terms of their perspectives and preferred forms of action changing as they got older:

> … my generation, we were young and we thought we could change … not just [our country], that we could change the world … We didn't like this one where a [few] people has a lot of money and they have power and they have freedom to do everything that they want, and the rest of the people, they haven't anything, and they are poor, and they are under pressure of this little group of the people, and police and army, and we saw that … they are aggressive against the people … We wanted to change everything … to have honest society, to have equality in our society. (Iran, 45 years old)

This individual described the change in their expectations as they had grown older and had undergone demoralising experiences:

> … when you become a little older and when you lose every hope, [it is not] like when you are young, it is difficult to change the situation in your life …

Although represented primarily in terms of physical ageing, it seems reasonable to think that the meaning assigned to aging may be influenced by the outcome of actions at previous stages of the person's life. This is reinforced by the same individual's view of the impact of many refugees' previous experience of repression in deterring them from engaging in oppositional activities in Britain, which they thought could change if refugees overcame their fear and experienced the power they could exercise collectively:

> … usually because of [refugees'] bad experience in their last life, in their country [of origin], they don't go to the demonstration … because they are afraid, maybe the same problem … the police … take them to the prison or deport them or something … Because of that asylum seekers don't [get involved in] these activities or show their power. I'm sure that if one day, one time, they saw their power, I'm sure that they would go and go …

Another refugee who described involvement in anti-government activities, both in their country of origin and in Britain, had ended their involvement since securing leave to remain. Their account suggested this was the result of a combination of exhaustion and demoralisation, despite being successful in their most recent struggle:

I got my papers, yeah, with all the chances I got from people, now they have accepted me, to give me leave to remain. Now my life is safe, I'm going to be quiet with my family, and enjoy my life.

... the world is too bleak ... the way my life has gone, what I've seen, the world is too big for me ... too strong for me, I can't lift them up. (CAMP volunteer 5)

This provides an example of the ways in which forms of activity relate to not only understandings of the world and estimated outcomes, but also factors such as emotional exhaustion, trauma, political confidence, and hope. The forms of unpaid activity refugees engage in, and the social capital formations arising from them, may both be influenced by these factors, and impact back on them.

Outcomes of Social Capital Building with the State

The relationship between trust in the state and trust among civil society is presented by Putnam (2000) as a mutually beneficial one, with a greater density of connections outside of the state and market encouraging trust among citizens and having a knock-on effect in increased levels of generalised trust and engagement, including with the state. Within this framework it is assumed both that trusting engagement with the state constitutes a more 'healthy' democracy (Schuurman 2003: 995) and that increased trust and engagement increases the range of 'opportunities' available to people who engage (Franklin 2007: 6). However, Field (2008: 79) points to the potential for social capital to also be mobilised by opposing interests, problematising the conception of social capital as a universal good, neutral in relation to opposing class interests. Different social capital formations may contradict one another, such as where the ability of authorities to enforce norms is 'jeopardized by the existence of tight networks whose function is precisely to facilitate violation of those rules' (Portes 1998: 9–15; also Zetter et al. 2006: 10). Beyond this, there is potential for multiple and potentially contradictory outcomes of the same social capital formation, varying with the position of a given individual within the formation. Allen (2009: 332) offers as a common definition of social capital: 'the ability of an individual who is a part of a social network to access various resources that reside within that social network'. This offers a potential link between individual and collective conceptions of social capital, and raises the question not only of the density and quality of connections within a network, but of the particular position of individuals within the network, and their potentially different levels of access to the network's shared resources. As Anthias (2007) argues, an individual may be connected to networks and resources, but not be in a position to mobilise them towards achieving their goals. This implicitly introduces questions of power into consideration of the outcomes of social capital.

Social Capital and the Asylum Context

Gramsci's ([1929–1935] 1982: 204–5) 'compact social blocs' correspond closely to what others have described as the 'collective' model of social capital, assuming dense networks among small and mutually exclusive groups (Brunie 2009: 255). It is therefore interesting to note the conception, which was central to the approach of recent Labour governments, of socially and normatively 'bad' bonding capital associated with segregation, racism and sectarianism, and opposed to 'good' bridging capital associated with integration and inclusion, and through this also national security. The underlying implications of such a conception are made explicit in a report by Camden council in 2006, which expresses concern that close-knit groups could play a role in uniting individuals 'unwilling to cooperate with the authorities' (Coole 2009: 389–90). As Portes (1998: 7) points out, 'To possess social capital, a person must be related to others, and it is those others, not himself, who are the actual source of his or her advantage.' Dependence is thus fundamental in any social capital formation, and who this dependence is on, and on what terms, has important implications for the nature and outcome of engagement in particular social capital formations. Roberts (2004: 486) points to the way in which formalised collective agreements between trade unions and employers have been replaced under neo-liberalism with individualised and informal relationships of 'trust and reciprocity', contributing to increased job insecurity and the potential for employers to repeatedly change expectations and 'cajole' longer hours of more intensive work from workers. This represents the imposition of class discipline through the restructuring of forms of engagement and their associated norms (Mayer 2003: 124). Likewise, the real question is not whether refugees engage with ruling structures – their oppressed position leaves them little choice – but of whether they do so on a collective and therefore more powerful basis, enabled by 'internal' social capital formation, or whether they do so as atomised individuals, able to offer little resistance to being effectively 'integrated' into oppressive structures on whatever terms the state chooses. It may be argued that neo-liberalism has fundamentally been about breaking up or taking over organisations with an independent politics and class basis. Social capital interventions by the state then represent attempts to reconstruct / include / integrate working class people on an individualised basis, in formations whose politics and class interests are defined by the capitalist state as the dominant 'partner'. This offers the potential to manage refugees' oppression, without the kind of conflict and resistance which may be provoked by more direct repression.

In situations of stable residence of groups of people in the same geographical area, the formation of compact, collective blocs may develop through, or at least be closely tied to, trust and networks arising from extended family relationships. There is evidence to suggest that this is the experience of many refugees-to-be before they left their country of origin. In one study, 63 per cent of refugees had found their most recent job prior to leaving their country of origin through informal kinship or social networks (Bloch 2007: 34). Many refugees I interviewed described family connections and responsibilities as a key factor influencing their activities before they were forced to leave:

> I was working in a shop where we were selling oils … like a family business. (Afghanistan, 23 years old)

> … the guy that owned the company was my father's best friend, so he just told me 'oh come, and I'll teach you' … now I was actually an assistant computer technician to him. (Zimbabwe, 20 years old)

This contrasted with a sense of isolation and dislocation after arriving in Britain:

> I haven't seen my parents for eight years, and if I had money I would have invited them here, but I don't have money. And if I get status the first thing I'm going to do is to work hard and to earn some money and invite them here to see them. (Iran, 38 years old)

> I'm still struggling, although I speak English but I don't really understand … and I struggle to socialize. (Cameroon, arrived 2008)

> I'm alone here; I haven't got any community here in UK. (China, arrived 2002)

For several people, the death of a family member emerged as a decisive point in the decision to leave their country of origin, representing an attack on existing social capital formations around the family as a key element of refugee creation.

As a result of dispersal, opportunities for continuing support from networks linked to refugees' countries of origin were further reduced. In the context of the isolation generated by this and other factors, opportunities to develop links based on points of commonality such as religion and nationality appear to have played a prominent role, particularly for refugees who arrived in Newcastle early in the process of dispersal. This indicates some of the complexity in considerations of different lines of possible formation for social capital, with connections which may appear from one level as within-group, 'bonding' capital also representing between-group, 'bridging' capital, such as connections between different religious groups from the same country of origin, or between generations with the same religion and country of origin:

> I know [the project manager] because he's from the Congo. (COM volunteer 4)

> … as soon as I arrived here, I was at that time in Sunderland, and because personally I was a Christian, I was told there was a Christian community in Newcastle, when I came I met [the project manager]. (COM volunteer 1)

These complexities of bonding and bridging capital have also been identified in research on established Muslim populations in Britain (Jayaweera and Choudhury 2008: 114–15) and among established diasporic refugee communities (Lindley 2009: 1324–5). In the case of COM, shared national, religious and cultural elements of experience and identity formed the basis for the reestablishment of bonding capital, which, through the organisation, also linked refugees to the state and other agencies, representing a distinct social capital formation which drew on existing social resources to respond to new needs, but simultaneously aided the state in its attempts to manage refugees' oppression.

Overall, state policies from 1999 onwards combined with key features of the refugee situation to break up social capital formations involving refugees independently of the state. As refugees struggled to rebuild their lives from the resulting fragments, the state was able to step into the gap, and in many cases played a dominant role in shaping social rebuilding, producing social capital formations whose norms of engagement can be traced in the stories of refugees I interviewed.

Norms and Values in Refugees' Engagement with the State

The potential for volunteering to shape norms and values occupies an important place in social capital theory. Norms and values are not formed purely at an individual level, but also through collective action, as they 'emerge out of joint endeavours' (Devine and Roberts 2003: 98). The forces involved in a particular social capital formation, their relative strengths and material interests, and the overall basis for their engagement, have major implications for the kind of norms and values produced and for the wider impact on an individual's understandings and outcomes. Conversely, observations of the norms and values implicit in a given engagement may offer insights into the basis of the social capital being formed, including its impacts on different interests.

Enforced Engagement and the Demand for Obedience

One refugee's account of their initial arrival in Britain offers a vivid insight into the nature of the norms and expectations involved in social capital formations between refugees without status and the British state as part of the 'asylum process':

> ... when we came we were just put in the waiting room where there were ... a lot of ... people seeking asylum ... Only us and another man ... were ... accepted to go and enter the country ... everybody was ... envying us, and we felt very bad, because they were going to be sent home, and it was like very, very bad, and then it was just people talking to us as if we were like animals. (26 years old, arrived in 2000)

In this situation, there is strong engagement, and the refugees without status are forced into a position of such disempowerment and dependency that they have no choice but to trust in the state and their personnel. The norms of this engagement, set entirely on the terms of the state and repeated for thousands of other refugees, include the expectation that as long as a refugee is 'in the system' and without status, they will obey all instructions from the state and not stand in collective solidarity with other refugees. In exchange, refugees without status are told they can expect a 'fair hearing' of their claim to be allowed to remain in Britain, despite collective experiences that repeatedly suggest that consideration is anything but fair. Even for those refugees I interviewed who had secured leave to remain through such engagement, many found the expectations of then enjoying a situation of equality with British citizens to have proven untrustworthy, which is borne out by the continuing experiences of racism discussed in previous chapters. Another refugee experienced engagement with the state as so oppressive and degrading, when he was accused by a psychiatrist of making up his symptoms in order to gain state support, that he attempted to reject all further engagement, even to the point of endangering his life:

> [Because I was an] asylum seeker, they suspected everything I said, they suspected even my symptoms ... I said I'm not going to stay under your care, and ... I ran, escaped from hospital with a pyjama and tracksuit bottoms, I had nothing on me, nothing, nothing, they had taken away everything ... I had no phone, no money, no keys ... And I slept rough for three days ... I was really, really suffering under the rain and cold, in a skip, in the open air, it was really cold, my teeth were hitting each other, but I prefer to die, but not to go under his care. (Iran, arrived in 2000)

These examples demonstrate the ways in which individual refugees engaging with the state may have little power to shape the terms of their engagement. While these individuals were embedded in networks with considerable resources, they were in no position to mobilise them, but instead were subject to the state mobilising these resources in order to 'manage' and contain them. Participation in these social capital formations was thus a means of power for the state, and disempowerment for refugees. Interestingly, both of these refugees went on from these experiences to engage in collective formations engaged in advocacy work, with a prominent role for members of user-groups to shape priorities. Both types of formation connected them with those in positions of much greater power, but the latter formations were experienced as a far more confident and secure relationship because the engagement was carried out collectively, by organisations with users in control.

Paternalism and the Threat of Self-organisation

Disempowering norms of engagement were also evident in less directly coercive areas. One refugee I interviewed described the central basis for engagement with state services being a response to basic need, but with nothing beyond this, and a weak degree of trust:

> ... there were quite a few services that could support us, but not those services ... where we could feel confident ... to be supported. Yes, there were very few like the housing provider who just came, give you a room, maybe they give you a few information that if you have any problem, this is the place to go, if you have any medical needs, you have to go to such place, and that's it. (COM management committee member 1, arrived 2002)

They described the norms of these engagements as involving a conditional framework of paternalism:

> ... those drop-ins are willing to help, but wow, maybe it's the fact that I'm a grown up, I don't like to be treated like a young boy, a child, yes people want to help, but do they really understand my needs ... are they going to meet what I'm expecting them to do?

While some needs were met within this social capital formation, others were omitted, and the norms of the relationship were experienced as oppressive. This represents an acute form of the general character of reciprocity dominant under capitalism, which Roberts (2004) terms 'isolated reciprocity'; the reciprocity between workers forced to sell their labour to the capitalist in order to survive, and the capitalist forced to buy workers' labour power in order to generate surplus value. The interests of the ruling class and their state drive them to attempt to preserve this form of isolated reciprocity, while the interests of the working class drives it to attempt to disrupt it, with the development of new forms of knowledge and understanding by both sides a crucial aspect of this struggle (Roberts 2004: 476–7). The position of refugees as displaced members of the reserve army of labour results in particularly acute forms of incorporation and resistance.

In the case of the experiences of paternalist services cited above, this gave rise to the development of new social capital formations, where refugees would be in stronger position to set the terms of engagement, combining norms of commonality of refugees' situation and mutual respect, in order to mediate continued engagement with state services:

> ... we thought it could be a good idea for ... a community group like us, who's composed [of] the same people, and [we] came together to say let's have a community group where we can help each other, and to play the bridge between the services. (COM management committee member 1)

This was a spontaneous response to deep-rooted state racism which even permeates many institutions that are supposed to be focused on refugees' welfare. It is in the interests of the British state to intervene and prevent such moves toward self-organisation among refugees from becoming a source of resistance. The retreat from individual engagement with the state to more collective formations with other refugees underlines the importance of the state delegating to voluntary and community organisations to maintain effective governance, and the significance of strategies to influence the social capital formations they produce. That is, it is often unfeasible for the state to consensually manage oppression directly, leading it to delegate some functions to agents who are more trusted by those it oppresses.

Whose Interests Does Social Capital Serve?

Compared to financial exchange, 'transactions involving social capital tend to be characterised by unspecified obligations, uncertain time horizons, and the possible violation of reciprocity expectations' (Portes 1998: 4). This 'fungibility' creates considerable scope for manipulation and shifting of goalposts by the more powerful party in social capital formations. Some conscious consideration of their engagement by all parties, and the relation of their engagement to desired outcomes, is implicit in more focussed conceptions of social capital (e.g. Anthias 2007). The contradictions between the aims of different parties, and the ways in which their intentions interact within a particular balance of forces to produce outcomes which may be beneficial to some parties and detrimental to others, are important factors distinguishing between different social capital formations.

Contradictions between Subjective Motivations and Objective Outcomes

A recurring theme across volunteers from all organisations in my research was the feeling that their actions simultaneously helped them to cope with their situation, in particular their experience of racism and isolation, and advanced the interests of other refugees:

> ... people look at them as a foreign or some other not very enjoyable reaction ... on the inside they are very upset, and they feel they are rubbish. But when they do voluntary work they feel ... they are very beneficial people, they have lots of benefits for society ... It helps to feel better and improve their life. (CHUR volunteer 4)

> ... with [voluntary work in a Black and Minority Ethnic networking organisation] I think it was about meeting people ... you don't actually have to say that you are an asylum seeker, you can just pretend that you are like everybody else, just pretend that you are just a volunteer. And that was quite nice. (CAMP volunteer 4)

Yet projects such as VOL, performing work contracted and funded by the Home Office, are under considerable pressure to act in line with government agendas. While devolving elements of governance may stimulate new forms of participation, where community structures are required to deliver pre-arranged targets or compete for funding, their agency may be severely constrained, and demands originating from within the community may be driven off the agenda (Roberts and Devine 2003: 314–15). One refugee, who was cited in Chapter 4 as being persuaded to 'hang on' and wait by her project manager, expressed the feeling common to many refugees without status of being worn down to a point of desperation where they were more likely to accept whatever the state offered them:

> I waited for five years … they just sent me a form, I filled the form, [some] people … told me not to sign the form because they may send me back, I said I would sign the form, whatever may happen, I'm tired. I didn't know it was for my paper [to be granted leave to remain]. (COM volunteer 4)

Many organisations in the refugee relations industry provide vital services, without which the pressure on the state and the risk of social unrest would be much greater (Griffiths et al. 2005). As outlined above, without the voluntary labour of refugees without status, many such organisations would have substantial gaps in at least some areas of their provision. This could lead to both more desperate forms of resistance, because of reduced access to 'legitimate' routes to pursue their claims, and weaker control by the state, as a result of the absence of a trusted intermediary. Volunteering by some refugees is therefore important for the management of the oppression of all refugees.

The Insecure Position of Refugee Volunteers
Beyond the general features of insecurity characterising the situation of refugees without status, for refugees who volunteer there is the additional uncertainty and ambiguity involved in voluntary positions. Pearce (1993: 29) argues that this frequently includes volunteers' double role, as deliverer and user of services, a lack of specificity in job descriptions, and the impact of the charitable connotations of voluntary work in creating uncertainty as to what can be expected from a volunteer. While refugees make up a large proportion of unpaid labour in many refugee sector organisations, it has been suggested that combinations of roles such as 'woman', 'refugee' and 'newcomer' have the potential to render individuals vulnerable in the context of struggles within organisations, severely limiting their say in the direction of activity (WLRI 2005: 38). There was some evidence of this among some of those I interviewed:

> They're all volunteers, so nobody's really properly experienced … at times we just all of us gather there. And I think that's the only problem really, proper organisation. (VOL volunteer 5)

They also pointed to a lack of recognition for the contribution of volunteers, further contributing to their insecurity:

> I wish [the] effort [of refugees who volunteer] could be recognised ... they play
> a big role, in the community as well, but probably sometimes they go unnoticed.

Alongside such suggestions of a lack of recognition, several refugees volunteering with VOL indicated a huge weight of responsibility, suggesting an absence of clear limits on their organisational role:

> ... people come and they start crying and you see these faces where people just
> give up, there is nothing else for them, and you can't do anything, that's just
> really horrible ... I don't think this job is like any other job ... here people are
> just in charge of other people's lives, because it's so important, like one wrong
> move can just wreck someone's life. (VOL volunteer 2)

The lack of a definite boundary around voluntary roles is not unusual, with research across a range of organisations finding voluntary workers less likely to have clear divides between their voluntary role and the rest of their lives, leading at times to expectations that they should be available and 'on call' at any time and to use personal domestic space to support their work (Pearce 1993: 38–9). Volunteers at VOL also reported pressures of volunteering on the rest of their lives, with a lack of resources leading management to make proactive use of the flexibility of volunteers' availability:

> ... when I came he just specified some days when he's really desperate for
> workers, for some reason, whatever reason, and volunteers can just be available
> on particular days, and the other days they are not there, so he is very short, and
> he is always begging 'I want somebody for this day, please just say you want to
> work on that day'. (VOL 5)

This was reinforced by a survey of VOL records for two December–May six month periods between 2005 and 2007, which showed that where there were fluctuations in demand for VOL's services, most of the extra capacity was provided by an increase in the total hours worked by volunteers.

The vulnerability of refugees as volunteers also leaves them open to abuse. One refugee described experiences of victimisation by a white paid worker at the project where they volunteered:

> ... the secretary, he used ... to make my life miserable ... all the time he used to
> call another lady, a white lady, to [to ask her to replace my shifts without telling
> me] and when I came I would find this other lady ... also because they provide
> childcare and travel expenses ... one day he was ... checking to say maybe I've
> took too much money ... the coordinator knew the problem, but he apologised
> and he [said other people were] having the same problem. [He said] he is doing
> it also to white people, for example ... there was another lady who was from
> Bosnia, she has the same problem ... the coordinator said to [the secretary]

I'm the person who is in charge of [volunteers], and it's my responsibility to organise [the] rota, so if you want to change something you should let me know in advance. (Female refugee without status)

This presents a clear instance of institutional racism, demonstrating the potential for the insecurity of positions of volunteer and refugee without status to act in conjunction to disempower. Instead of taking action, or even acknowledging the racism when brought to the attention of the coordinator, they firstly denied any racial character because the individual had applied the same abusive behaviour to a woman with paler skin from Bosnia, suggesting a serious lack of understanding about the potential for racism to operate on the basis of factors other than skin colour, including but not limited to religion, accent, country of origin or immigration status. Secondly, the response of the organisation is problematic in that the volunteer coordinator employed a bureaucratic measure of asserting their authority over the secretary to set the rota, rather than directly challenge their behaviour. Another instance of the potential for organisations to undermine the agency of volunteers was highlighted in an account of a refugee without status who had gone to an organisation asking for help finding a voluntary job, and expressed a preference for working with animals, but was left with little option other than to volunteer for the organisation itself, with the promise that they may be able to help them find a volunteering post with animals in the future after they had spent some time volunteering there. This seriously undermines the voluntary character of such work, by consciously or unconsciously tying unpaid work to provision of services.

As discussed above and in Chapter 4, many forms of voluntary activity by refugees may serve the interests of the British state, yet no refugee I interviewed expressed this as one of the desired outcomes from their work, even among those who expressed the most positive views about the asylum system or the British state. Engagement in all these social capital formations therefore required some reasonable expectation of benefit to the volunteer themselves and/or other refugees. The degree to which such expectations can be fulfilled in practice, and the forms they take between collective and individual benefit, is determined by the interaction of factors including volunteers' consciousness, the balance of forces, and the degree of independence or critical distance from the state.

Ideology Mediates Contradictions

The apparent contradictions in many refugees' voluntary activity, between a declared aim to defend the interests of refugees and a practical implementation of government policy which damaged those same interests, were mediated in some cases by the adoption of a variety of justifications for the state's actions. This provides an example of the ways in which norms and values implicit in a particular social capital formation may influence change in the norms and values of individuals who engage in that formation. This was most pronounced in the case of VOL, where practical involvement by refugees in delivering services on behalf of the Home Office operated for some people alongside a consciousness which reflected the priorities of the state. There was insufficient evidence to say definitively which came first, whether refugees who were more sympathetic to the government were more inclined to volunteer at VOL, or whether the experience of delivering these services developed perspectives in line with the state, or both, but it is worth noting that these views were expressed most fully in disagreements between a very recent volunteer and longer-standing volunteers in a focus group of VOL volunteers:

> [The government] don't have a choice, [they] have to let [refugees] in, but [they will] do everything possible not to let you stay here, and the things they do is against the actual human rights law. (New volunteer)

> Yeah, but still ... we must always remember this is their country, they want to keep it the way – if you put yourself in their shoes, they're probably thinking they're sick of having foreigners in their country. (Long-standing volunteer)

Another participant in the same focus group expressed the contradiction at the heart of VOL's role, of supporting and helping individual refugees and other migrants at the same time as servicing a system which oppresses them, reflected at the level of consciousness. On the one hand, they recognised Britain's reliance on migrants for their labour and their super-exploited position:

> The cheap job, the shitty job, and they're all [being done by] migrants, I mean the British people would not do that, I mean they need migrants ... England's been built on migrants. (VOL volunteer 4)

Yet immediately following this, they spoke about the majority of those claiming asylum in Britain in extremely derogatory terms, discounting the basis for the majority of refugees' claims in advance and blaming them for the oppression faced by 'genuine' refugees:

> [Refugees are] coming in Sangatte [refugee camp] in France, which is European country, thousands, thousands ... If they want their safety, if they really have a problem in their country, human rights law and the 1951 policy, they say if you're in your third country you have to claim asylum, where the life is safe for you ... 80 per cent of people coming here for work, for the things that they can't do in their countries, to support their family, to do other things, and 20 per cent of people they have problems. If I give you an example, it's a glass of water, if you [put a] bit of dirty water in there it all becomes dirty ... All people are going in one name, and the water, you cannot split it. So that's the reason they want to do their law tougher and harder, to show to the people their rules.

The metaphor of 'dirty water' carries connotations of dirt and disease which have been strong features of racist narratives towards immigrants in Britain for centuries.

Within COM, two refugees I interviewed expressed gratitude for what the British ruling class had 'done for them', both in Africa and in Britain:

> I have a very good memory of the government, you know, it's like you just came in and you don't know anybody, and they welcome you, that is a good memory for me. Because in my house I never welcome somebody you don't know, you have to tell me you are coming. But I didn't tell them I was coming, just flew here and they welcomed me ... I will never forget about that, they welcomed me, they welcomed my son ... It doesn't mean they can't be bad, but they are good as well. (COM volunteer 4)

> I mean British people traditionally are very good people, welcoming, I mean it's not all the countries have done what the British have done for us. (COM management committee member 1)

In the case of the latter person, current attitudes towards Britain paralleled a past job in their country of origin:

> I was given the task to develop what we normally call the resource centre about the modern [former colonial country], to sell [its image] in the country where I used to work.

In some other cases, refugees I interviewed adopted the government's own arguments to justify the state's treatment of refugees, in a narrative suggesting some degree of identification with the British state and its contracting agencies, over and above their identification with other refugees. For example, one refugee argued the reduction of legal aid was because previously:

> ... most of these appointments [with solicitors weren't] very important, and people had a lot of problems [that weren't] even linked to the asylum seeker's claim, but they went to the solicitor [for] some little thing. [With the government reducing legal aid to] five hours limited, maybe [it's to try and make it] more professional, and ... better help. (CHUR volunteer 4)

Another refugee agreed with the removal of the right to legal work, on the implicit basis that allowing refugees to work would encourage more to seek asylum:

> ... the reason why I will say I agree with the Home Office not giving them work permits is because everybody else would just come in as an asylum seeker knowing they're going to get a work permit. (VOL volunteer 1)

The idea of people lying about their reasons for claiming asylum was echoed by another refugee volunteering with CHUR:

> ... this is too difficult situation for this country, because lots of people came here, [who are] not really, really [an] asylum seeker or refugee. (CHUR volunteer 2)

Another refugee repeated the arguments put forward in sections of the British media portraying Britain as 'overcrowded', with services under pressure from migrants:

> As they're always saying in the newspapers, it has a really big impact on the public services, on the pressure on the health services, pressure on – they say that asylum seekers steal their jobs ... for example buses are full, they say it's because of the refugees and asylum seekers, NHS is overloaded. (CHUR 1)

These examples are an important reminder that it is not only British people who are subject to state and media propaganda and the dominant discourse it shapes, of self-serving immigrants seeking to 'sponge' off a hard working British people. Where refugees perform voluntary roles in organisations that are part of state-sponsored structures of governance, this may create an additional pressure to develop a state-led perspective on other refugees without status, which serves to reconcile the outcome of volunteers' actions with their good intentions.

Despite the apparent intentions of all the refugees I interviewed to advance the interests of fellow-refugees, the majority of social capital formations in which they were engaged thus operated within an ideological framework that reflected the interests of the British ruling class, one of 'deserving and undeserving migrants', without any consideration of the source of Britain's wealth or Britain's relationship to the situations refugees were fleeing. Challenging this may require forms of social capital involving a 'critical distance' from the state and a counter-discourse based on the interests of refugees. Using Putnam's categories as defined by Gilchrist (2004: 6), this may include elements of 'bonding' capital, to develop a coherent and confident perspective among those with a strong mutual commitment based on shared experiences and needs as refugees. These might combine with elements of 'bridging' capital in order to gain necessary support and resources from those with overlapping interests and goals, situate their experiences in wider processes, and effectively implement responses.

The Presence of Labour's Social Capital Building in the Coalition's Big Society

In many ways, the Conservative–Liberal Democrat Coalition's conception of the 'big society' is the logical continuation of Labour's 'social capital building'. This includes a prescribed role for voluntary activity on a very locally-focused basis, as both an alternative to state welfare provision and a means to shape the norms and values of social interactions down to the individual level. The imagined decentralisation and grassroots initiative underpinned by central state control of priorities, which was already present in Labour's approach from 1997–2010, has been intensified. Reductions in funding for the third sector, and the expectation that the new 'community organisers' will find their own wages, might give the impression of a distance of these activities from the state, while the organisers' curriculum is set by the government and plans are debated for compulsory 'National Citizen Service' to establish government-approved values and forms of activity among young people (Conservative Party 2010: 39; de St Croix 2011). As the 'age of austerity' squeezes millions of previously comfortable members of society into working class conditions and grinds down those already in poverty even further, the need for such fine-tuned measures of social control seems likely to increase.

Conclusions

Conceptions of social capital promoted by Putnam and recent Labour governments have been based on assumptions of shared interests and intentions across society, leading to a declared expectation that increased trust and engagement between those in different positions of power would be to the benefit of all. The accounts of refugees I interviewed, together with the wider evidence, suggest this may be contradicted by the case of refugees who volunteer, with the development of engagement based on a degree of trust serving to maintain incorporation in the oppressive structures and relationships outlined in previous chapters. In this critique, oppression replaces exclusion as the prime concern of action for change, in order to undermine the claim of 'inclusion' to be an inherent social good, when inclusion may mean effective incorporation into oppressive systems and structures.

Labour's social capital initiatives between 1997 and 2010 represented a less obvious and directly repressive element in a wider strategy, also including increasing physical repression, in an attempt to cope with negative consequences for ruling elites of the destabilisation of international and national orders resulting from neo-liberalism and attendant population movements, which have been rapid and to an extent uncontrollable (Coole 2009: 379–80). Social capital interventions can be understood as a particular approach within longer traditions of cooption and oppression, with conscious strategies to engage refugees in particular social capital formations operating alongside an expanding apparatus of border police, detention and removal centres, reporting regimes and deportation. Dominant social capital discourse may itself be viewed as an exercise in the shaping of social capital by the ruling class (Franklin 2007: 5–6), mobilising a wide range of networks and resources in order to consensually incorporate sections of oppressed groups into oppressive structures, espousing values of 'fairness' and 'tolerance', which are very different to the implicit values and norms encountered by many refugees. Achieving this incorporation involves formal and informal networks, from one-to-one interventions by professionals to large-scale consultations, control of material resources needed to maintain current services and fill gaps, and control of large-scale means of production and dissemination of ideas, such as the mainstream media and research and educational institutions.

As demonstrated above, effective management of the UK asylum system has required the involvement of refugees, including those without status, in delivery of services, particularly at a face-to-face level. This has been carried out through interventions by the state and its 'partners' to shape social formations, conceptualised here as social capital, which Coleman points out will continue to spontaneously reassert themselves as previously existing structures decay or are broken up, but are open to conscious influence (Coleman 1993: 10–14). Social capital is not viewed here as a neutral resource that is possessed in greater or lesser quantities by groups or individuals, but as ongoing formations of engagement that mediate intentions and interests of individuals, within given material conditions, to shape processes and outcomes including social, political and economic aspects. By recruiting individual refugees to voluntary positions as they attempt to establish new networks, relationships and organisations, the state gains influence both over the shape of these individuals' actions, and through them the activity, understandings and forms of engagement of other refugees.

Complex social capital/market hybrids thus take shape: state institutions engage with voluntary organisations on a contractual basis; voluntary organisations engage individual refugees as volunteers in a form of linking capital offering a range of material and non-material incentives and opportunities; and refugees, as volunteers, engage wider refugees as users, drawing on bonding capital based on the shared experience of asylum and simultaneously creating bridging capital across aspects of difference such as nationality, age, religion and gender, as they do their best to help others within the confines of the asylum system. At the level of the whole system, this represents the continued compliance of large numbers of refugees with the asylum system, despite ongoing experiences of its oppressive character and, in many cases, deep mistrust. Maintaining this process necessitates offering direct or indirect benefits, not only to the individuals involved, but to the wider communities that volunteers wish to help. By making limited concessions, which do not threaten the interests of the ruling class, the state has been able to maintain the involvement of refugees in forms of engagement that, in the final analysis, is to their detriment, by managing and sustaining the oppressive structures outlined in previous chapters. This ensures the continuation of a system involving the deportation, incarceration and enforced destitution of thousands of people every year, thereby containing and disciplining the threat that they pose to imperialist divisions of labour.

Chapter 6
Conclusion

The preceding chapters have demonstrated the range of issues, on multiple levels, which social workers need to consider in work with refugees. Briskman and Cemlyn (2005) discuss some of the difficulties in 'realising social work's transformative potential in a hostile policy environment', particularly in arguing for citizenship rights for a group excluded from any kind of 'nationhood', and finding routes to progress in a situation where disparities in power are so great (Briskman and Cemlyn 2005: 720–21). They call for greater clarity by social workers about their position, and the development of greater leadership within the profession based on values of humanity, social justice and human rights. This book has aimed to contribute to such clarity, by examining the material basis for refugees' subordinate relationship with the British state and some of the mechanisms which manage and maintain such an oppressive relationship. By focussing largely on areas beyond the mainstream of professional social work practice, I hope to have offered a new perspective on some of the ways in which social work and related areas of practice may contribute to processes of both social control and transformation.

To recap: Refugees migrate in the context of an imperialist system, driven by factors including exploitation, poverty, war, persecution and environmental destruction. Within this system, the majority of countries from which refugees flee and claim asylum occupy an oppressed position, while Britain occupies a dominant, imperialist position. When citizens of imperialist countries cross borders, they generally do so with a wider range of options and, for 60 years, have rarely had to claim refugee status. This is reflected in the position of refugees within Britain, and in their relation to the British state. Due to its imperialist position, the British economic, political and social system has achieved a degree of stability and 'social peace' within its borders, on the basis of the exploitation of oppressed countries. This has included the exploitation of a reserve army of labour drawn from oppressed countries. Maintaining this situation relies in turn on racialised divisions between workers from Britain and from oppressed countries. The presence of refugees in Britain poses an implicit threat to these arrangements, both by moving under imperatives of human rights rather than labour demand, and by offering the potential to build alliances with British workers and develop collective identities across borders. This offers a response to the long-standing question of why recent governments have not made more constructive use of refugees' skills (e.g. Dumper 2002; Phillimore and Goodson 2006; Bloch 2007). Between 1999 and 2010, Labour governments responded to this situation with policies that restructured dominant forms of engagement and values among refugees by breaking up existing networks, both among refugees and between refugees and other working class people, and by integrating refugees into individualised forms of engagement with the state, even as they continued to experience racism long after securing status. This has been facilitated through delegated voluntary and community sector organisations, staffed and in some cases run by refugees, some with status and some without, in an approach consistent with the development of the 'race relations industry' in Britain since the 1960s. Refugees' motivations for participating in state-backed initiatives are varied, and in most cases have required some visible benefits for themselves, and to a greater or lesser extent, other refugees.

Però and Solomos (2010) propose a typology of factors interacting with one another to shape migrant mobilisations in a context of available opportunities, including 'the political socialisation, background, experience and values of the migrants; the living and working conditions they experienced in the receiving context (e.g. of exploitation, marginalisation, etc); their networks and social capital, ... their migratory project', and feelings and emotions (Però and Solomos 2010: 10). The methodology adopted in the research which informed this book enabled exploration of the connection between processes operating at these multiple levels, from the international to the personal. Qualitative techniques were used to investigate how refugees see the different forms of activity in which they are engaged, and to ask new questions about social capital formations, including the roles they play for different parties and the norms and values embedded and reproduced through them. Biographical surveys enabled the situation of refugees' present forms of activity in both their previous life history and their anticipated future trajectory. The accounts of refugees I interviewed demonstrate that engagement by refugees in volunteering provides a powerful means of building social capital, but that the nature and outcomes of this social capital has varied. In spite of refugees' intentions to benefit other refugees by volunteering, voluntary activity by refugees in the refugee sector has operated in a context of domination by the state, materially and ideologically, which has tended to produce outcomes that favour its own interests, often to the detriment of refugees. This is reflected in contradictions in the consciousness of some refugees, where, despite having their rights systematically denied by the state as part of an oppressed group, some individuals side with the state in backing this denial, particularly in organisations most immediately under the direction of the state.

At an individual level, the interests and group membership of refugees do not directly dictate their actions, but are mediated by their consciousness of these interests and of their relation to the interests of others, and by choices about what response to make on the basis of this understanding. Where voluntary activity is tied to promises of comfortable future employment, this creates pressure for refugees to identify their interests, on an individual basis, with a class trajectory above their current circumstances, and to act in line with this expectation, which for the majority is likely to lead instead to the continuation of a subordinate position. Some refugees make a choice based instead on a programme of collective liberation. This can be supported both by education and organisation by refugees, among refugees, in a range of settings, and by support and resources made available to refugees by non-refugees, such as by making refugee sector organisations more accountable to their users.

At a social level, the scope for different forms of individual activity to influence the course of events will be set both by the wider material conditions and the social structures available to individuals for engagement. The actions of individual refugees are not determined in isolation, but through interaction with other refugees and wider social forces. While individual experiences and forms of action possess a degree of randomness, in the relation between them at the level of the social, mediated by consciousness, the actions and experiences of individuals connect to historical processes, and a quantity of individuals undergo a qualitative change to mass social forces (Lenin [1895–1916] 1972: 123–4). This relationship may become particularly clear in '"transition moments" in migrants' engagements – when their tacit resistance "comes out" and "scales up" into manifest and larger-scale collective action' (Però and Solomos 2010: 11–12). The history of mutual aid societies, which have been prevalent among migrants in the absence of state welfare provision, suggests that even in the absence of direct state interference, the priority of meeting immediate material needs may contribute to a need for migrant organisations to attract the widest possible number of affiliates and consequently 'to shy away from any creed other than the blandest form of patriotism' (Moya 2005: 844). This suggests a need for different kinds of organisations among refugees, both those meeting immediate needs and those organising for longer-term change. Sustaining action for change on a wider scale may require the identification of alternative allies, in order to undermine dependence on the state for resources. Però and Solomos (2010: 14) suggest these may be found in 'civil society', 'especially in those sectors that retain autonomy from government and are not 'bridled' or domesticated as a result of participating in the processes of governance and service provision', and also in areas of the state where there is space to use contradictions to gain a voice or impact on policy. For refugees, allies might be found among sections of society who have more in common with the interests of refugees, such as migrant workers and other oppressed sections of the working class, and among other organisations and activists with shared aims.

Implications for Practice and Policy

Social workers and other practitioners who are not refugees can support the development of links between refugees and other oppressed groups, offer information on both the underlying interests and the technical workings of the British state, and engage with refugees in building collective anti-racist movements. Integral in this must be respect for the right of refugees to determine their own forms of struggle and to organise separately when they consider it necessary. It is important to reassert the political agency and conscious decision-making of refugees and other migrants. This is particularly urgent at a time when policy has shifted to 'victims of trafficking' as a new priority among migrants for state assistance, in a conception that includes requirements of extreme victimhood and 'helplessness' as a condition for state support (Anderson 2010: 72), as part of the wider objectification of migrants. Ahmad (1993) suggests that 'For social workers, it is often an easier option to focus on the symptoms of oppression than on causes of oppression', leading to an approach equating 'disadvantage' with clients and therefore working to 'help disadvantaged blacks', rather than work with clients to challenge the causes of their oppression (Ahmad 1993: 43). Professionals need to decide whether they are on the side of the state or of refugees, and to acknowledge the fundamental conflict at the heart of the state's relation to refugees as a collectively oppressed group, and the consequences that follow from this, including the implication that the effective development of trust and engagement with the state may be to the extreme detriment of refugees. Social workers and other practitioners can also play a role in building awareness and support for the struggles of refugees among other sections of the working class and wider society. This could lessen refugees' isolation, extend their influence and increase the collective resources available to them. In some cases constraints from funders, employers and others may place paid practitioners in a poor position to take the most effective action. This should not be used as an excuse for taking action which is detrimental to refugees' wellbeing, but may mean that sometimes the most effective action social workers can take is to get out of the way and allow others to act.

For their part, refugees can struggle to both assert the validity of their particular experience and integrate this with other people's histories and frameworks, offering the potential to create new understandings. Davies (1996: 2–3) identifies potential for volunteers to provide a politicising and critical voice within organisations and an organic link to users. This potential could be seized on by refugees as volunteers, to use their position in the organisation to extend links with, and between, refugees as users, with the aim of increasing the accountability of the organisation to refugees outside, over and above the priorities of funders or the state. Some refugees could consider more carefully the basis on which they engage with the British state and the relative risks and advantages of different alliances, and, when engaging collectively, whether to accept money from the state, which may be tied to particular forms of activity.

Everyone concerned with the rights of refugees needs to press for an end to the criminalisation of asylum and migration by the state. As argued throughout this book, racialised oppression and exploitation are not the product of arbitrary policy choices, but are fundamental to the imperialist system. Effective action for change in Britain's asylum and immigration policy therefore needs to be combined with action to transform the wider economic, social and political relations, within Britain and between Britain and other countries.

Future Directions: The Role of Refugees, Social Workers and Volunteers in the 'Big Society'

The fine-tuning of attempts at social control on a consensual basis, analysed in this book, have far-reaching implications. It represents the efforts of the ruling class to maintain bourgeois democracy in the context of an intensifying crisis of the system, where the 'crumbs' available to buy people off directly are increasingly scarce. The challenge is not merely to control people by force, but to make them consent to their position. As Coleman (1993) puts it, the natural aspirations of the ruling class are that:

> The opportunities lie in a future in which social control no longer depends principally on coercion, constraint, and negative sanctions, under the oppressive blanket of closed communities, but instead depends principally on positive incentives and rewards performance. (Coleman 1993: 14)

The Labour Party came into being at a time when increased challenges from other imperialist and developing powers forced a restriction on the numbers of the 'labour aristocracy', who had a direct stake in the system, and called for a means for this minority to maintain political dominance over the rest of the working class. Social capital interventions have been developed by Labour governments in a period where a combination of deepening economic crisis and the political estrangement of the Labour Party from the majority of the working class has called for new mechanisms for control. By devolving responsibility for social divisions and poverty onto oppressed communities themselves, Labour's use of 'social capital' has distracted from the economic or structural causes of inequalities (Temple et al. 2005: 8–9).

As long as imperialism continues, giving rise to the kinds of contradictions, divisions and crises which marked the majority of the twentieth century and the first decade of the twenty-first, then the ruling class will continue to need strategies with which to manage oppressed populations. This is regardless of whether oppressed populations are resisting at a given point in time. As Marx and Engels put it in 1845:

> It is not a question of what this or that proletarian, or even the whole proletariat, at this moment *considers* as its aim. It is a question of *what* the proletariat is, and what, in accordance with this *being*, it will historically be compelled to do. Its aim and historical action is irrevocably and clearly foreshadowed in its own life situation as well as in the whole organisation of bourgeois society today. (Marx and Engels [1845] 1956: chapter 4, emphasis in the original).

This book has demonstrated the insights that can be gained from an empirically informed Marxist analysis. Direct repression will continue to provoke resistance, and it is therefore likely that the ruling class will continue to need approaches such as the social capital interventions of recent Labour governments. Signs indicate that the British state is continuing down the same road under the Conservative– Liberal Democrat Coalition, with David Cameron's 'Big Society' shaped through an army of 'community organisers'. Developing a greater understanding of the dynamics of social control within these processes may enable those engaged in struggle to influence events from a more informed and conscious position, thereby increasing their active role as subjects of history. If new movements are to develop, which can genuinely express the interests of the mass of the working class and fulfill their historical role, they will need to be alert to indirect means of social control and relearn an old motto: 'Beware false friends'.

Appendix
Methodology and Research Background to the Book

A Qualitative Marxist Methodology

The Marxist analytical method is at present largely marginal and discredited within Britain. Sharing similar concerns with social justice, many recent critiques of Marxism have adopted some variety of post-modernist approach emphasising the complex and contingent construction of identities and roles, in apparent opposition to a focus on class. Such critiques may carry weight against cruder understandings of Marxism, which view class structures as simple and homogenous, but they may be amply answered by a rediscovery and critical application of the Leninist framework. Furthermore, the fractured, individualised understanding of the world offered by many post-modernist accounts denies the possibility of conscious, organised action for change in a particular direction. As with various elitist and pluralist conceptions of power, prevalent post-modernist conceptions ignore the fact that social fragmentation, and lack of correspondence between any individual's or group's intentions and outcomes, does not imply an absence of discernible patterns of coherence in social development (Therborn 1980: 135–6), which, if understood, can be used to influence the direction of change.

Ager (2003) views the role of social science as offering a potential bridge, between participant-centred accounts of individuals' 'lived experience' and macro-analyses which address 'political, social and cultural forces' (Ager 2003: 3). Marxism has much to offer in achieving this goal. The Leninist approach, that 'Theory is tested by reality and its truth is measured in its contribution to human control of nature and society' (Rayne undated), is deeply contextual, recognising that we all operate in sets of relations, which exist independently of, and prior to, our will (Marx [1859] 1971: 20–21). This offers a way out from the anti-positivist reaction, which has led many to engage in a total delinking of language and meaning from the objective and natural world (Hughes and Sharrock 1997: 143–68). Marxism offers the potential to overcome the dualism of subject and object, ideal and material, via a theoretical bridge between the actual and the ideal – or the future actual – including the necessary role of human action as part of this historical development (Plekhanov [1898] 1940: 17–19).

The Marxist analytic method involves an iterative movement from holistic and concrete living phenomena to a 'number of determinant, abstract, general relations' and from there back to a more complex understanding of the living whole. Throughout this process, sight must be maintained of the primacy of the material whole, avoiding confusing the analytic process with the actual formation of concrete phenomena through the action of pre-existing and independent abstractions (Marx [1857] 1973: 100–102). In his *Philosophical Notebooks,* Lenin ([1895–1916] 1972) gives a more detailed explanation of this approach, in which science is conceived as an extension of the critique of immediate experience which 'begins as soon as attention, thought is applied to it':

> If the immediate given is represented by a point then, in order to obtain a picture of the real given, one has to imagine that this point is merely a projection of the straight line extending beyond it. This straight line can be broken up into several segments, each of which will embrace, without there being any impenetrable partitions between them, families of relations on which the immediate given depends. (Lenin [1895–1916] 1972: 474)

This indicates the attention to complexity and interrelations which is central to the Marxist method I aim to apply here.

Marxism does not operate on the basis of 'economic man', with each individual assumed to be motivated purely by his own perceived material interest, but recognises that human beings operate on the basis of 'diverse psychological motives', yet are 'unable to transcend the laws imposed by the economic substructure of their society'. While motives may be diverse, outcomes are rarely as individuals intend, and the driving force of history does not necessarily coincide with what individuals perceive as the driving force of their motives (Kemp 1967: 14–15). Common misrepresentations of the materialist conception of history in the hands of social scientists have included the acknowledgement of 'material factors', but also their isolation, such as into social, political, economic and philosophical aspects, without viewing them in their totality. For example, Hardt and Negri refer to Marxism (e.g. Hardt and Negri 2001: 325–6), but separate economics and politics into principles of 'capital and sovereignty', a dislocation completely contradictory to Marxist practice. In other cases, distortions of the Marxist approach have taken the form of crude economic materialism, which lacks a dialectical view and seeks and expects to find a direct economic motive or interest behind every phenomenon (Kemp 1967: 9–10). Marx argued that in order to understand a given society it is necessary to not only examine its subjects or structure, but also to analyse its processes of reproduction (Therborn 1980: 137), and this calls for a systemic view. 'Everything is ... mediated, bound into One, connected by transitions [in a] law-governed connection of the *whole (process)* of the world' (Lenin [1895–1916] 1972: 103, emphasis in the original).

Ethics and Politics in Marxist Social Research

Ethical questions of what researchers should do and political questions of researchers' relationship to others cannot be separated. As producers of knowledge, researchers have the potential to codify myths into 'unquestionable certitudes', thus defending the status quo and sections of society that it privileges, or instead to 'criticise' and 'imagine other possibilities', presenting critical spaces for change (Guanche 2007: Parts V–VI). It is therefore impossible to separate knowledge from power and politics from culture (Guanche 2007: Part II). No particular method can be relied upon to navigate this minefield and arrive safely at empowering or emancipatory outcomes (Wood et al. 1999: 164–5), and the utility of 'ethical canons', embodied in codes of ethics, in solving concrete questions has been subject to debate (Sjoberg 1967: xi–xii). What is needed is a research practice driven by broader values and an epistemology which informs how methods are employed and is not 'purely technical', but reflects back on the purposes of knowledge and who it is produced for (Althusser 1969: 171).

Reflexive and Committed Research

The methodology of the research that informs this book was driven by the political and ethical objective to increase the potential for human freedom by contributing to a complex understanding of the world. Lenin ([1909] 1970: 156–7) suggests that the difference between nature and human society lies not in the absence of causal laws in the latter, but in the potential for human beings to become conscious of human society's laws and therefore able to use them to transform the world. This is based on an ontological view of a succession of levels of causes, from the general cause of the development of the productive forces, to the particular causes of historical circumstances, to the 'accidental' causes of individual actions, each impacting within a scope of different degree. To the extent that we understand the relationship between these spheres, we are able to influence the course of history:

> If I know in what direction social relations are changing owing to given changes in the social-economic process of production, I also know in what direction social mentality is changing; consequently, I am able to influence it. Influencing social mentality means influencing historical events. Hence, in a certain sense, I *can make history*, and there is no need for me to wait while 'it is being made. (Plekhanov [1898] 1940: 58–61, emphasis in original)

As workers engaged in the critique, development and propagation of knowledge, researchers have a responsibility to reflect on the implications and impact of their work.

There is a tendency to regard as 'objective' that which fits dominant vocabulary and values, such as Eurocentric accounts in apartheid South Africa (Van den Berghe 1967: 194). The liberal Weberian ideal of the objective and autonomous researcher (Weber [1904] 1949) has been given additional credence by Cold War demonisations of the 'committed intellectual' as a 'child of collectivist totalitarianism' (Guanche 2007: Part VI). Similar tendencies have been noted within social work, where a liberal commitment to individual freedom has frequently operated in the absence of any consideration of 'societal flaws that are fundamental barriers to individual freedom' (Ahmad 1993: 44). Yet, by necessity of their existence as part of society, researchers are embedded in particular sets of relations and struggles, and will inevitably identify more with the perspectives and interests of some sections of society than others (Colvard 1967: 338–40). Therefore, I make no claims to the objective or neutral nature of this research, but aim to offer an honest and reflexive approach, which will support the reader in contextualising the research and engaging critically with my analysis.

The Marxist understanding of the relationship between material social divisions and ideas makes clear that there is no such thing as 'objective' knowledge, but rather different kinds of knowledge beneficial or dangerous to the interests of different classes, whose members possess different capacities to propagate their kind of knowledge (Marx and Engels [1845] 1991: 64; Bukharin [1921] 1969: 9–10). This highlights the danger of uncritically accepting the account of any individual. Yet, in reflecting on Hegel's *Science of Logic*, Lenin ([1895–1916] 1972) points out that individual perceptions are also objective, in that they comprise an aspect of the objective world, overcoming artificial divisions of subjective and objective: 'the movement of a river – the foam above and the deep currents below. *But even the foam* is an expression of essence!' (Lenin [1895–1916] 1972: 130). By openly articulating a perspective based on the experiences and interests of an oppressed and often 'silenced' – or more accurately ignored – section of society such as refugees, I aim to contribute to a fuller and more collective understanding of the world, in what Sandra Harding describes as a 'strong objectivity', which, to be fully realised, must be accompanied by a 'strong reflexivity' and a 'strong method' (Hirsh and Olson 1995).

The Newcastle Research

This book has drawn data and insights from three pieces of research I conducted in Newcastle upon Tyne from 2004–2010.

2005: 'The Role of Racial Harassment in Processes of Racialisation and Racism in Newcastle upon Tyne', Case Study of a Local Authority Project

This study, conducted from October 2004–April 2005, examined the role of racial harassment in constructing and sustaining 'whiteness' as a political discourse and drew lessons for practice from the work of a local authority project. This included in-depth semi-structured interviews with nine professionals, including two former workers with the project, three current workers with the project, one former manager of the project, and three professionals from other organisations who had experience of partnership working with the case study organisation.

2007: 'Unpaid Refugee Labour in the Asylum System', Refugee Relations Industry Pilot Study

This study, conducted from June–August 2007, examined the role of unpaid labour by refugees in the asylum system, using VOL as a case study. Five volunteers and two managers were interviewed, and this data also contributed to the study which followed:

2007–2010: 'The Management of Oppression', Refugee Relations Industry Full Study

This study took place from October 2007–September 2010. It involved extensive empirical research, including interviews with a further four professionals, each with decades of experience working with issues of migration and racism in the city in a range of roles, historical research using archives and local press records, and examination of four case study organisations which worked with refugees as both users and volunteers. The main criteria in selecting these 'case organisations' were that between them they represented a range of relationships to the state but were all formally independent, that between them they covered a range of activities, and that they had all existed for more than two years and were still in existence in 2008. Cases were also sought on the basis that they were representative of a more general trend. The selection of projects occupying a range of positions along a continuum from heavily state-influenced to overt opposition to the state opened the possibility both for points of replication and contrast between cases (Yin 2003: 46–53). Case organisations are indicated by anonymised acronyms: VOL, CHUR, COM and CAMP (see below for a summary of each organisation). Contextual interviews about the organisations were conducted with five individuals in management roles across the four projects, three of whom were also refugees. Organisational literature, such as annual reports and, in some cases, volunteer records, was sought from these individuals.

Significant differences among refugees have been found to include relationships to countries of origin, employment and educational backgrounds, family support within Britain, gender, and age (Cowen 2003: 25; Centrepoint 2004; Griffiths et al. 2005: 17–18; WLRI 2005). Unpaid practitioners from each case organisation were selected for the first round of interviews, in discussion with managers, in an attempt to cover where possible a range of ages, genders and regions of origin (see below for a breakdown of participants' attributes). The range of occupational and educational backgrounds was limited by the predominance of individuals from professional backgrounds among refugees who volunteer (WLRI 2005: 34), and the range of all factors was limited at some projects by the small number of refugees volunteering there. This imposed limits on the extent of generalisation from the findings to all refugees in Newcastle, as those engaged in organised voluntary activity are, by definition, among less isolated refugees. The strength of the sample is that it offered insights into experiences and views among a cross-section of refugees engaged in public activity, who may thereby exert greater influence on the wider situation of refugees than less engaged individuals, including playing key roles in the management of oppression and resistance.

Following preliminary analysis of the first round of interviews, including production of a case summary for each participant, a second round of interviews was conducted with the intention of enabling a more in-depth understanding of a sub-sample of participants across all case organisations. This was possible with participants from all of the organisations except for VOL, where, owing to the greater length of time since the original interviews, it was not possible to make contact with any of the original participants. However, an additional focus group had been conducted with this group at the time of the first interviews, and this was used to supplement the data from the individual interviews. Two of the original participants from each of the other organisations were interviewed a second time, producing a total sample of 18 refugee volunteers, six of whom were interviewed twice, four of whom took part in a focus group including volunteers from VOL, and four of whom took part in a mixed focus group including volunteers from CHUR, CAMP and COM.

Summary of Contemporary Case Studies

VOL: A large, regional voluntary sector organisation, delivering substantial front-line contracts for the Home Office since 1999, as part of a wider portfolio of service delivery and integration work. At the time of the research the organisation had premises in several cities and a large number of paid workers, alongside an even larger number of volunteers, mostly in front-line roles but with some in administrative roles including a management committee.

COM: A community advice and signposting organisation, established by refugees mostly from the same country of origin but providing services to refugees on a regional basis and non-refugees in the geographical neighbourhood. At the time of the research the organisation had funding for one full time worker and a building, supported by an active management committee and a small number of formal volunteers, and was in the process of securing funding for a second paid worker.

CHUR: A church-based voluntary sector project delivering signposting, advice and a hardship fund, mainly to refugees without status resident in a particular geographical neighbourhood. At the time of the research the organisation had funding for several full time workers and a building, and also engaged a small number of volunteers, mostly refugees on a sporadic basis as interpreters.

CAMP: An asylum rights and anti-racist campaign group, established by refugee and non-refugee activists, mainly focused on a city-wide basis but with periodic activity in the wider region. At the time of the research the organisation had a large but loose membership, around a core of regular voluntary activists, with very limited funding from individuals and no paid workers or premises.

Characteristics of individual refugee volunteers interviewed:

Gender:
Men (x9), Women (x9)

Accessed through volunteering with:
VOL (x5), COM (x3), CHUR (x4), CAMP (x6)
(Although some participants had volunteered with more than one of the case organisations, their work with this organisation was the starting point for discussion.)

Year of arrival in Newcastle:
2000 (x4), 2001 (x3), 2002 (x5), 2004 (x2), 2005 (x2), 2006 (x1), 2008 (x1)

Country of origin:
Afghanistan (x1), Angola (x1), Cameroon (x1), Chad (x1), China (x1), Côte d'Ivoire (x1), DRC (x3), Iran (x3), Kenya (x2), Togo (x1), Ukraine (x1), Zimbabwe (x2)

Age:
20–25 (x3), 26–30 (x3), 31–35 (x1), 36–40 (x4), 41–45 (x2), unknown (x5)

Immigration status at time of interviews:
At first round (2007–2008): 5 with status, 13 without
At second round (2009–2010): 4 with status (of whom 2 had gained status since the first round), 2 without
At mixed focus group (2010): 4 with status (of whom 1 had gained status since the second round), 0 without

References

6, P., C. Fletcher-Morgan and K. Leyland 2010. Making people more responsible: The Blair governments' programme for changing citizens' behaviour. *Political Studies*, 58(3), 427–49.

Adamson, O., C. Brown, J. Harrison and J. Price 1976. Women's oppression under capitalism. *Revolutionary Communist*, (5), 1–48.

Adar, S. 2010. What are Israeli flags and Jewish activists doing at demonstrations sponsored by the English Defence League? *Haaretz*, 13 August.

Ager, A., Ed. 2003. *Refugees: Perspectives on the Experience of Forced Migration*. London: Continuum.

Ahmad, A. N. 2008. The labour market consequences of human smuggling: 'Illegal' employment in London's migrant economy. *Journal of Ethnic and Migration Studies*, 34(6), 853–74.

Ahmad, B. 1993. *Black Perspectives in Social Work*. Birmingham: Venture Press.

Ahmad, W. I. U. and K. Atkin 1996. *'Race' and Community Care*. Buckingham: Open University Press.

Ahmad, W. I. U. and H. Bradby 2007. Locating ethnicity and health: Exploring concepts and contexts. *Sociology of Health & Illness*, 29(6), 795–810.

Allen, R. 2009. Benefit or burden? social capital, gender, and the economic adaptation of refugees. *International Migration Review*, 43(2), 332–65.

Allen, T. W. 1995. *The Invention of the White Race: Volume one, racial oppression and social control*. London: Verso.

Althusser, L. 1969. *For Marx*. Harmondsworth: Penguin.

Amin, A. 2003. Unruly strangers? The 2001 urban riots in Britain. *International Journal of Urban and Regional Research*, 27(2), 460–63.

Anderson, B. 2010. Mobilizing migrants, making citizens: Migrant domestic workers as political agents. *Ethnic and Racial Studies*, 33(1), 60–74.

Andrews, E. 1998. Racist hell that is a sad fact of everyday life. *Evening Chronicle*, 3 April.

Anthias, F. 2007. Ethnic ties: Social capital and the question of mobilisability. *The Sociological Review*, 55(4), 788–805.

Antoni, G. D. 2009. Intrinsic vs. extrinsic motivations to volunteer and social capital formation. *Kyklos*, 62(3), 359–70.

Archive Mapping and Research Project 2007. *Remembering Slavery 2007: A brief guide to the Archive Mapping and Research Project*. Newcastle upon Tyne.

Armstrong, S. 2004. Racists forced us to flee our home. *Evening Chronicle*, 29 April.

Aspinall, P. and C. Watters. 2010. *Refugees and Asylum Seekers: A review from an equality and human rights perspective*. London: Equality and Human Rights Commission.

Atkinson, A. M. 1972. Coloured immigrants and their families: A study of assimilation in an inner urban area of Newcastle upon Tyne. Newcastle upon Tyne: Newcastle University.

Back, L., M. Keith, A. Khan, K. Shukra and J. Solomos 2002. New Labour's white heart: Politics, multiculturalism and the return of assimilation. *Political Quarterly*, 73(4), 445–54.

Banks, S. 2004. *Ethics, Accountability and the Social Professions*. Basingstoke: Palgrave MacMillan.

Barber, P. G. and W. Lem 2008. Introduction: Migrants, mobility, and mobilization. *Focaal: European Journal of Anthropology*, 51, 3–12.

Barmaki, R. 2009. Criminals/refugees in the age of welfareless states: Zygmunt Bauman on ethnicity, asylum and the new 'criminal'. *International Journal of Criminology and Sociological Theory*, 2(1), 251–66.

Barzun, J. 1965. *Race: A study in superstition*. New York: Harper and Row Publishers.

Bauman, Z. 1999. *Globalization: The human consequences*. Cambridge: Polity Press.

Ben-Tovim, G., J. Gabriel, I. Law and K. Stredder 1986. *The Local Politics of Race*. Basingstoke: MacMillan Education.

Ben-Tovim, G., J. Gabriel, I. Law and K. Stredder 1993. A political analysis of local struggles for racial equality, in *Racism and Antiracism: Inequalities, opportunities and policies*, edited by P. Braham et al. London: Sage Publications, 131–52.

Berger, J. and J. Mohr 1975. *A Seventh Man: The story of a migrant worker in Europe*. Harmondsworth: Penguin.

Berthoud, R. and M. Blekesaune. 2007. *Persistent Employment Disadvantage*. London: Department of Work and Pensions.

BID. 2009. *Out of Sight, Out of Mind: Experiences of immigration detention in the UK*. London: Bail for Immigration Detainees.

Bilodeau, A. 2008. Immigrants' voice through protest politics in Canada and Australia: Assessing the impact of pre-migration political repression. *Journal of Ethnic and Migration Studies*, 34(6), 975–1002.

Black Youth Movement. 1987. *Application for Grant Aid 1987/88*. Newcastle upon Tyne: Steering Group.

Blair, I. 2009. The police are right not to remain silent on civil liberties. *The Guardian*, 8 December.

Blair, T. 2006. *The Duty to Integrate: Shared British Values*. London: The National Archives.

Bloch, A. 1999. Refugees in the job market: A case of unused skills in the British economy, in *Refugees, Citizenship and Social Policy in Europe*, edited by A. Bloch and C. Levy. Basingstoke: MacMillan Press.

Bloch, A. 2007. Refugees in the UK labour market: The conflict between economic integration and policy-led labour market restriction. *Journal of Social Policy*, 37(1), 21–36.

Bloch, A. and L. Schuster 2005. Asylum policy under New Labour. *Benefits: The journal of poverty and social justice*, 13(2), 115–18.

Borjas, G. J. and J. Crisp, Eds. 2005. *Poverty, International Migration and Asylum*. Basingstoke: Palgrave MacMillan.

Boswell, C. 2003. Burden-sharing in the European Union: Lessons from the German and UK experience. *Journal of Refugee Studies*, 16(3), 316–35.

Bowes, A., I. Ferguson and D. Sim 2009. Asylum policy and asylum experiences: Interactions in a Scottish context. *Ethnic and Racial Studies*, 32(1), 23–43.

Brickley, C. 2005. Shoot-to-kill in London. *Fight Racism! Fight Imperialism!* (187 October / November).

Briskman, L. and S. Cemlyn 2005. Reclaiming humanity for asylum-seekers: A social work response. *International Social Work*, 48(6), 714–24.

British Red Cross. 2010. *Not Gone, but Forgotten: The urgent need for a more humane asylum system*. London.

Brown, G. 2006. *The Future of Britishness*. Fabian Society New Year Conference, 14 January, London.

Brown, G. 2009. *Speech on Immigration: A transcript of a speech on immigration given by the Prime Minister in Ealing, west London, on 12 November 2009*. [Online]. Available at: http://www.number10.gov.uk/Page21298 [accessed: 17 November 2009].

Brunie, A. 2009. Meaningful distinctions within a concept: Relational, collective, and generalized social capital. *Social Science Research*, 38(2), 251–65.

Bryan, B., S. Dadzie and S. Scafe 1988. *The Heart of the Race: Black women's lives in Britain*. London: Virago.

Bukharin, N. [1921] 1969. *Historical Materialism: A system of sociology*. Michigan: University of Michigan Press.

Bulpitt, J. 1986. Continuity, autonomy and peripheralisation: The anatomy of the centre's race statecraft in England, in *Race, Government and Politics in Britain*, edited by Z. Layton-Henry and P. B. Rich. Basingstoke: The MacMillan Press, 129–47.

Bunyan, P. 2010. Broad-based organizing in the UK: Reasserting the centrality of political activity in community development. *Community Development Journal*, 45(1), 111–27.

Burkett, I. 2007. Globalised microfinance: Empowerment or just debt?, in *Revitalising Communities in a Globalising World*, edited by L. Dominelli. London: Ashgate, 151–60.

Burnett, J. 2011. Public spending cuts savage dispersal system. *IRR News*. Available at: http://www.irr.org.uk/2011/january/ha000029.html [accessed: 11 April 2011].

Butt, J. 2006. *Are We There Yet? Identifying the characteristics of social care organisations that successfully promote diversity*. London.

BVSC. 2011. *Report: Voluntary Sector Funding Cuts Survey*. Birmingham: The Centre for Voluntary Action.

Byrne, B. 2002. *How English Am I?* London: Goldsmiths College, University of London Critical Urban Studies Occassional Papers.

Byrne, D. 2001. Partnership – participation – power: The meaning of empowerment in post-industrial society, in *Partnership Working: Policy and practice*, edited by S. Balloch and M. Taylor. Bristol: Policy.

Cabinet Office. 2010a. *Building the Big Society*. London.

Cabinet Office. 2010b. *Business Plan 2011–2015*. London.

Callinicos, A., J. Rees, C. Harman and M. Haynes 1994. *Marxism and the New Imperialism*. London: Bookmarks.

Cameron, D. 2011. *PM's speech on Welfare Reform Bill*, Toynbee Hall, 17 February, London.

Cashmore, E. and E. McLaughlin, eds. 1991. *Out of Order? Policing black people*. London: Routledge.

Cashmore, E. and B. Troyna 1990. *Introduction to Race Relations*. Basingstoke: The Falmer Press.

Cassirer, E. 1967. *The Myth of the State*. New Haven: Yale University Press.

Castells, M. [1975] 2002. Immigrant Workers and Class Struggles in Advanced Capitalism: The Western European experience, in *The Castells Reader on Cities and Social Theory*, edited by I. Susser. Malden, MA: Blackwell.

CEBS. 2010. *2010 EU Wide Stress Test Exercise, 23 July*. Committee of European Banking Supervisors.

Centrepoint. 2004. *Waiting in Line: Young refugees in the labour market*. London.

Cerni, P. 2006. Imperialism in the twenty-first century. *Theory and Science* 8. Available at: http://theoryandscience.icaap.org/content/vol8.1/cerni.html [accessed: 27 March 2007].

Chahal, K. 2003. *Racist Harassment Support Projects: Their role, impact and potential*. York: Joseph Rowntree Foundation.

Chahal, K. 2004. *Experiencing Ethnicity: Discrimination and service provision*. York: Joseph Rowntree Foundation.

Chahal, K. and L. Julienne 1999. *'We can't all be white!': Racist victimisation in the UK*. York: York Publishing Services.

Chantler, K. 2010. Women seeking asylum in the UK: Contesting conventions, in *Gender and Migration: Feminist interventions*, edited by I. Palmary et al. London: Zed Books, 86–103.

Charlton, H. 2001. Police called out to refugee hostel. *The Journal*, 18 January.

Cheong, P. H., R. Edwards, H. Goulbourne and J. Solomos 2007. Immigration, social cohesion and social capital: A critical review. *Critical Social Policy*, 27(1), 24–49.

Chinweizu, C. 2006. Asylum and immigration: Maximising Britain's economy. *Fight Racism! Fight Imperialism!* (190 June/July).

Chinweizu, C. 2007. Nigeria: Imperialist plunder impeded. *Fight Racism! Fight Imperialism!* (199 October / November).

Chinweizu, C. and N. Jameson 2008. Immigration and the reserve army of labour in Britain. *Fight Racism! Fight Imperialism!* (201 February / March).

CIPD. 2009a. *Labour Market Outlook: Quarterly survey report summer 2009*: Chartered Institute of Personnel and Development.

CIPD. 2009b, 13 October. *1 in 10 UK men unemployed by 2010 as male employment rate heads toward record low*. [Online]. Available at: http://www.cipd.co.uk/pressoffice/_articles/mennotatwork131009.htm?IsSrchRes=1 [accessed: 29 October].

CIPD. 2009c. *Jobs: The Impact of Recession and Prospects for Recovery*: Chartered Institute of Personnel and Development.

Clancy, G. 2008. Employment of foreign workers in the United Kingdom: 1997 to 2008. *Economic and Labour Market Review*, 2(7), 18–30.

Clark, K. and S. Drinkwater 1998. Ethnicity and self-employment in Britain. *Oxford Bulletin of Economics and Statistics*, 60(3), 383–407.

Clough, R. 1992. *Labour: A party fit for imperialism*. London: Larkin Publications.

Cohen, R. 2006. *Migration and its Enemies: Global capital, migrant labour and the nation-state*. Aldershot: Ashgate.

Coleman, J. S. 1993. The rational reconstruction of society: 1992 presidential address. *American Sociological Review*, 58(1), 1–15.

Colvard, R. 1967. Interaction and Identification in Reporting Field Research: A critical reconsideration of protective procedures, in *Ethics, Politics and Social Research*, edited by G. Sjoberg. Cambridge: Schenkman Publishing Company.

Commission on Weak States and US National Security. 2004. *On the Brink: Weak States and US National Security*. Washington, DC.

Commonwealth Immigrants Working Group. 1968a. *Minutes 1st April 1968*. Newcastle upon Tyne City Council.

Commonwealth Immigrants Working Group. 1968b. *Minutes 6th May 1968*. Newcastle upon Tyne City Council.

Community Relations Council Newcastle upon Tyne. 1968. *Minutes of inaugral meeting held in the civic centre on 26th November, 1968*. Newcastle upon Tyne City Council.

Community Relations Council Newcastle upon Tyne. 1969. The Race Relations Board. *News Bulletin*(2).

Community Relations Council Newcastle upon Tyne. 1970. *Conference: Community relations on Tyneside*. Newcastle upon Tyne.

Community Relations Council Newcastle upon Tyne. 1971. *Minutes of the extra-ordinary council meeting of the Community Relations Council, held at Connaught Hall, YMCA, on 18th August, 1971*. Newcastle.

Community Relations Council Newcastle upon Tyne. 1972. *Minutes of council meeting held on Wednesday 26th April, 1972 at 7pm*. Newcastle.

Community Relations Council Tyne and Wear. 1973a. *Minutes of meeting held on Thursday 31st May 1973*. Newcastle.

Community Relations Council Tyne and Wear. 1973b. *Minutes of council meeting held on Thursday 26th July 1973*. Newcastle.

Conservative Party. 2010. *Invitation to Join the Government of Britain: The Conservative Manifesto 2010*. London.

Conte-Helm, M. 1989. *Japan and the North East of England: From 1862 to the present day*. London: Althone Press Ltd.

Coole, D. 2009. Repairing civil society and experimenting with power: A genealogy of social capital. *Political Studies*, 57(6), 374–96.

Cordesman, A. H. and A. A. Burke. 2010. *The Uncertain Security Situation in Iraq: Trends in violence, casualties, and Iraqi perceptions*. Washington, DC: Centre for Strategic and International Studies.

Coulter, J., S. Miller and M. Walker 1984. *State of Siege: Miners' strike 1984*. London: Canary Press.

Cowen, T. 2003. *Exiled from Work: Promoting Refugee Employment in the NHS*. London: Lambeth NHS Primary Care Trust.

Craig, G. 2007a. 'Cunning, unprincipled, loathsome': The racist tail wags the welfare dog. *Journal of Social Policy*, 36(4), 605–23.

Craig, G. 2007b. They come over here…and boost our economy: The impact of migrant workers on Yorkshire and Humber region. *Yorkshire and Humber Regional Review*, 17(1), 33–5.

Craig, G., A. Gaus, M. Wilkinson, K. Skrivankova and A. McQuade. 2007. *Contemporary Slavery in the UK*. York: Joseph Rowntree Foundation.

Craig, G. with S. Kaur, S. Mumtaz and M. Elliott-White. 2000. *Giving Voice: Mapping older people's needs in Kirklees*. Kirklees: Age Concern.

Craven, J. and T. Rayne 2008. Iraq: 'Surge success' unravels. *Fight Racism! Fight Imperialism!* (202 April / May).

Crawley, H. 2006. Forced migration and the politics of asylum: The missing pieces of the international migration puzzle? *International Migration*, 44(1), 21–6.

Crawley, H. 2010. *Chance or Choice? Understanding why asylum seekers come to the UK*. London: Refugee Council.

CRE. 1985. *Annual Report 1984: The commission's work in the North of England*. London: Commission for Racial Equality.

Datta, K., C. McIlwaine, J. Wills, Y. Evans, J. Herbert and J. May 2007. The new development finance or exploiting migrant labour? Remittance sending among low-paid migrant workers in London. *International Development Planning Review*, 29(1), 43–67.

Davidson, S. 2006. Lifting the veil on racism. *Fight Racism! Fight Imperialism!* (194 December 2006 / January 2007).

Davidson, S. 2011. Jayaben Desai 1933–2010. *Fight Racism! Fight Imperialism!* (219 Feb / March).

Davies, B. 1996. *Volunteering versus Professionalism*. Leicester: National Youth Agency.

de St Croix, T. 2011. Struggles and silences: Policy, youth work and the National Citizen Service. *Youth and Policy* (106), 43–59.

Devine, F. and J. M. Roberts 2003. Alternative approaches to researching social capital: A comment on van Deth's measuring social capital. *International Journal of Social Research Methodology*, 6(1), 93–100.

Dickinson, P. 1999. We're looking for firm friends. *Evening Chronicle*, 21 January.

Director of Education. 1987. *Black Youth Movement*. Newcastle upon Tyne: Newcastle City Council.

Dominelli, L. 1997. *Anti-Racist Social Work: A challenge for white practitioners and educators*. Basingstoke: MacMillan.

Dominelli, L. 1999. Neo-liberalism, social exclusion and welfare clients in a global economy. *International Journal of Social Welfare*, 8(1), 14–22.

Dominelli, L. 2005. Community development across borders: Avoiding dangerous practices in a globalizing world. *International Social Work*, 48(6), 702–13.

Dominelli, L., Ed. 2007. *Revitalising Communities in a Globalising World*. London: Ashgate.

Dumper, H. 2002. *Missed Opportunities: A Skills Audit of Refugee Women in the Teaching, Nursing and Medical Professions*. London: Greater London Authority.

Dwyer, P. 2004. Creeping conditionality in the UK: From welfare rights to conditional entitlements? *The Canadian Journal of Sociology*, 29(2), 265–87.

Dwyer, P. 2005. Governance, Forced Migration and Welfare. *Social Policy and Administration*, 39(6), 622–39.

Dwyer, P. and D. Brown 2008. Accommodating 'others'?: Housing dispersed, forced migrants in the UK. *Journal of Social Welfare and Family Law*, 30(3), 203–18.

Dyer, R. 1999. *White*. London: Routledge.

EHRC. 2009. *Monitoring the Impact of the Recession on Various Demographic Groups*. London: Equality and Human Rights Commission.

Engels, F. [1884] 1981. *The Origin of the Family, Private Property and the State*. London: Lawrence and Wishart.

Eskovitchl, J. 2005. Gate Gourmet at Heathrow union undermines workers' solidarity. *Fight Racism! Fight Imperialism!* (187 October / November).

Eskovitchl, J. 2006. Asylum seekers organise in Scotland. *Fight Racism! Fight Imperialism!* (190 April / May).

Evelyn Oldfield Unit. 2004. *Refugee Volunteering: Integration in Action. Report of a National Conference*. London.

Evening Chronicle. 1972. Asians: Liberals lash 'appalling homes'. *Evening Chronicle*, 14 October, 1.

Evening Chronicle. 1982a. Race hate fire attack. *Evening Chronicle*, 30 June, 1.

Evening Chronicle. 1982b. Chippie arson probe. *Evening Chronicle*, 24 April, 3.

Evening Chronicle. 1983. Cultural feast for Geordies. *Evening Chronicle*, 7 October, 17.

Evening Chronicle. 1984a. The fear of being forced to go home. *Evening Chronicle*, 12 April 1984, 16.

Evening Chronicle. 1984b. Scheme needs more helpers. *Evening Chronicle*, 10 October, 9.

Evening Chronicle. 1989. Protest over refugee's plight. *Evening Chronicle*, 19th January.

Evening Chronicle. 2000. Jail ship plan for migrants. *Evening Chronicle*, 28 February.

Evening Chronicle. 2002. Support for a new start. *Evening Chronicle*, 14 August.

Evening Chronicle. 2004. Family wins right to stay. *Evening Chronicle*, 23 June.

Fanshawe, S. and D. Sriskandarajah. 2010. *You Can't Put Me in a Box: Super-diversity and the end of identity politics in Britain*. London: IPPR.

Fekete, L. 2004. Anti-Muslim racism and the European security state. *Race and Class*, 46(2), 3–29.

Felices, G., G. Hoggarth and V. Madouros 2008. Capital inflows into EMEs since the millennium: Risks and the potential impact of a reversal. *Bank of England Quarterly Bulletin*(Q1), 26–36.

Fell, P. 2004. And now it has started to rain: Support and advocacy with adult asylum seekers in the voluntary sector, in *Social Work, Immigration and Asylum*, edited by D. Hayes and B. Humphries. London: Jennifer Kingsley Publishers, 111–31.

Field, J. 2008. *Social Capital*. Abingdon: Routledge.

Fine, B. 2001. *Social Capital versus Social Theory: Political economy and social science at the turn of the millenium*. Abingdon: Routledge.

Flint, J. 2007. Faith schools, multiculturalism and community cohesion: Muslim and Roman Catholic state schools in England and Scotland. *Policy and Politics*, 35(2), 251–68.

Ford, C. 1998. Deportation flight switch. *The Journal*, 30 June.

Frankenberg, R. 1994. *White Women, Race Matters: The Social Construction of Whiteness*. Minneapolis: University of Minnesota Press.

Franklin, J. 2007. *Social Capital: Between harmony and dissonance*. Families & Social Capital ESRC Research Group Working Paper No. 22. London: Southbank University.

Freeman, G. P. 1986. Migration and the political economy of the welfare state. *Annals of the American Academy of Political and Social Science* (485), 51–63.

FRFI 2001. Support youth uprisings against racism and poverty. *Fight Racism! Fight Imperialism!* (162 August/September).

FRFI 2004. Imperialist coup d'etat in Haiti. *Fight Racism! Fight Imperialism!* (178 April / May).

FRFI 2010. Who are the English Defence League? *Fight Racism! Fight Imperialism!* (215 June/July).

Frisch, H. and M. Hofnung 1997. State formation and international aid: The emergence of the Palestinian Authority. *World Development*, 25(8), 1243–55.

Fryer, P. 1984. *Staying Power – The History of Black People in Britain*. London: Pluto Press.

Fukuyama, F. 2004. *State-Building: Governance and world order in the 21st century*. New York: Cornell University Press.

Geschwender, J. A. 1977. *Class, Race and Worker Insurgency*. Cambridge: Cambridge University Press.

Gesthuizen, M., T. van de Meer and P. Scheepers 2008. Ethnic diversity and social capital in Europe: Tests of Putnam's thesis in European countries. *Scandinavian Political Studies*, 32(2), 121–42.

Gibney, M. J. and R. Hansen 2005. Asylum policy in the West: Past trends, future possibilities, in *Poverty, International Migration and Asylum*, edited by G. J. Borjas and J. Crisp. Basingstoke: Palgrave MacMillan,

Gilchrist, A. 2004. *The Well-Connected Community: A networking approach to community development*. Bristol: Policy Press.

Gill, N. 2009. Governmental mobility: The power effects of the movement of detained asylum seekers around Britain's detention estate. *Political Geography*, 28(3), 186–96.

Gilroy, P. 2000. *Between Camps – Race, Identity and Nationalism at the End of the Colour Line*. London: Penguin.

Gilroy, P. 2001. *Against Race: Imagining political culture beyond the color line*. Cambridge: The Belknap Press of Harvard University Press.

Gledhill, V. 2004. Family's joy at return to the UK. *Evening Chronicle*, 8 December.

GMB Press Release. 2010. *Independent Audit Confirms Underpayment of Overseas Workers on Staythorpe Sit by Italian Contractor Somi.*

Godfrey, D. 1982. A little piece of Belgium in the heart of Durham. *The Journal*, 7.

Godfrey, D. 1989. Settling a question of local colour. *The Journal*, 24 January,

Goldberg, D. T. 1994. *Racist Culture – Philosophy and the Politics of Meaning*. Cambridge: Blackwell Publishers.

Goodman, A. and V. Ruggiero 2008. Crime, punishment, and ethnic minorities in England and Wales. *Race/Ethnicity*, 2(1), 53–68.

Gordon, P. and A. Newnham 1985. *Passport to Benefits? Racism in social security.* London: Child Poverty Action Group and the Runnymede Trust.

Gorodzeisky, A. and M. Semyonov 2009. Terms of exclusion: Public views towards admission and allocation of rights to immigrants in European countries. *Journal of Ethnic and Racial Studies*, 32(3), 401–23.

Gould, C. 2010. The problem of trafficking, in *Gender and Migration: Feminist interventions*, edited by I. Palmary et al. London: Zed Books, 31–49.

Grady, P. 2004. Social work responses to accompanied asylum-seeking children, in *Social Work, Immigration and Asylum*, edited by D. Hayes and B. Humphries. London: Jennifer Kingsley Publishers, 132–50.

Gramsci, A. [1929–1935] 1982. *Selections from the Prison Notebooks*. London: Lawrence and Wishart.

Griffiths, D., N. Sigona and R. Zetter 2005. *Refugee Community Organisations and Dispersal: Networks, resources and social capital*. Bristol: The Policy Press.

Grossman, H. [1929] 1992. *The Law of Accumulation and Breakdown of the Capitalist System*. London: Pluto Press.

Guanche, J. C. 2007. Against Heresy. *Progreso Weekly*. Available at: http://cuba-l. unnm.edu/?nid=32618&cat=cu [accessed: 14 September 2010].

Guevara, E. C. [1959–1967] 2003. *Che Guevara Reader: Writings on Politics and Revolution*. Melbourne: Ocean Press.

Hardill, I., S. Baines and P. 6 2007. Volunteering for all? explaining patterns of volunteering and identifying strategies to promote it. *Policy and Politics*, 35(3), 395–412.

Hardt, M. and A. Negri 2001. *Empire*. Cambridge: Harvard University Press.

Harlan, K. 2007. Voices of the Iraqi Resistance: Leaders of the Iraqi National Resistance Speak at an International Solidarity Conference. *Fight Back! News*, 28 March,

Harling, P. 2001. *The Modern British State: An Historical Introduction*. Cambridge: Polity Press.

Hart-Landsberg, M. and P. Burkett 2005. China and socialism: Engaging the issues. *Critical Asian Studies*, 37(4), 597–628.

Hayes, D. 2005. Social Work with Asylum Seekers and Others Subject to Immigration Control, in *Social Work Futures: Crossing Boundaries, Transforming Practice*, edited by R. Adams et al. Basingstoke: Palgrave MacMillan.

Head of Policy Services. 1987. *Local Authority Action Against Apartheid Conference Report*. Newcastle upon Tyne: Newcastle City Council.

Heath, A. and S. Y. Cheung. 2006. *Ethnic Penalties in the Labour Market: Employers and Discrimination*. London: Department of Work and Pensions.

Hesse, B., D. K. Rai, C. Bennett and P. McGilchrist 1992. *Beneath the Surface: Racial harassment*. Aldershot: Avebury.

Hessle, S. 2007. Globalisation: Implications for International Development Work, Social Work and the Integration of Immigrants in Sweden, in *Revitalising Communities in a Globalising World*, edited by L. Dominelli. London: Ashgate, 231–42.

Hewitt, R. L. 2002. *Asylum-seeker Dispersal and Community Relations – An Analysis of Developmental Strategies*. London: Centre for Urban and Community Research Goldsmiths College.

Heywood, S. 2000. Asylum seekers in hostel protest. *The Journal*, 11 May.

Hickman, B. 2002. Police hunt four illegal immigrants: Asylum seekers go on the run. *Evening Chronicle*, 26 November.

Hickman, M. J. 1996. *Religion, Class and Identity – The State, the Catholic Church and the Education of the Irish in Britain*. Aldershot: Ashgate.

Hirsh, D. 2003. *Law Against Genocide: Cosmopolitan trials*. London: The Glasshouse Press.

Hirsh, E. and G. A. Olson 1995. Starting from marginalized lives: A conversation with Sandra Harding. *JAC* 15. Available at: http://jacweb.org/Archived_volumes/

Text_articles/V15_I2_Hirsh_Olsen_Harding.htm [accessed: 14 September 2010].

HM Treasury. 2010a. *Budget 2010*. London.HM Treasury. 2010b. *Spending Review 2010*. London.

Hobson, C., J. Cox and N. Sagovsky. 2008. *Deserving Dignity: How to improve the way we treat people seeking sanctuary*. London: Independent Asylum Commission.

Home Affairs Committee. 2007. *The Government's Counter-Terrorism Proposals: First Report of Session 2007–08*. London: House of Commons.

Home Affairs Committee. 2009. *Managing Migration: The Points Based System*. London: House of Commons.

Home Office. 2002. *Secure Borders, Safe Haven*. London.

Home Office. 2005. *Controlling Our Borders: Making migration work for Britain*. London.

Home Office. 2010. *Control of Immigration: Quarterly Statistical Summary, United Kingdom January–March 2010*. London.

Homeless Link. 2009. *Central and Eastern European Rough Sleepers in London: Repeat Survey*. London.

Hoogvelt, A. 2007. Globalisation and imperialism: Wars and humanitarian intervention, in *Revitalising Communities in a Globalising World*, edited by L. Dominelli. London: Ashgate, 17–42.

Hughes, J. and W. Sharrock 1997. *The Philosophy of Social Research*. Harlow: Pearson Education.

Humphries, B. 2004. An unacceptable role for social work: Implementing immigration policy. *British Journal of Social Work*, 34(1), 93–107.

Hutchinson, L. and P. Dickinson. 2000. Refugees riot after cash cut. *Evening Chronicle*, 11 May.

Hynes, P. 2009. Contemporary compulsory dispersal and the absence of space for the restoration of trust. *Journal of Refugee Studies*, 22(1), 97–121.

IRR. 2001. *Counting the Cost: Racial violence since Macpherson*. London: Institute of Race Relations.

Irving, S. 2010. UK's discriminatory criminalization of dissent. *Electronic Intifada*. Available at: http://electronicintifada.net/v2/article11199.shtml [accessed: 24 June 2010].

Isacson, A. and A. Poe. 2009. *After Plan Colombia: Evaluating 'Integrated Action,' the next phase of U.S. assistance*. Washington, DC: Centre for International Policy.

Islington Local Authority 2007. Guidance for local authorities: Accessing and supporting destitute people from abroad with no recourse to public funds (NRPF). London: Islington Local Authority.

Jameson, N. 2005. The reality of capitalism's immigration policy. *Fight Racism! Fight Imperialism!* (185 June / July).

Jameson, N. 2006. Labour's racist immigration policy. *Fight Racism! Fight Imperialism!* (193 October/November).

Jameson, N. 2010. Close Yarl's Wood! Close Harmondsworth! Close all immigration prisons! *Fight Racism! Fight Imperialism!* (214 April / May).

Jameson, N. and E. Allison, Eds. 1995. *Strangeways: A serious disturbance*. London: Larkin Publications.

Jayaweera, H. and T. Choudhury. 2008. *Immigration, faith and cohesion: Evidence from local areas with significant Muslim populations*. York: Joseph Rowntree Foundation.

Jefferson, T. 1991. Discrimination, disadvantage and police work, in *Out of Order? Policing black people*, edited by E. Cashmore and E. McLaughlin. London: Routledge.

Jones, B. and M. Keating 1985. *Labour and the British State*. Oxford: Oxford University Press.

Kahani-Hopkins, V. and N. Hopkins 2002. 'Representing' British Muslims: The strategic dimension to identity construction. *Ethnic and Racial Studies*, 25(2), 288–309.

Karlsen, S. and J. Y. Nazroo 2006. Defining and measuring ethnicity and 'race': Theoretical and conceptual issues for health and social care research, in *Health and Social Research in Multiethnic Societies*, edited by J. Y. Nazroo. Abingdon: Routledge.

Kay, D. and R. Miles 1992. *Refugees or Migrant Workers? European volunteer workers in Britain 1946–1951*. London: Routledge.

Kayembe, I. 2006. DR Congo: Imperialists organise war and plunder. *Fight Racism! Fight Imperialism!* (192 August / September).

Kayembe, I. 2007. Congo: Nothing changes after DRC elections. *Fight Racism! Fight Imperialism!* (197 June / July).

Kemp, T. 1967. *Theories of Imperialism*. London: Dobson Books.

Kennedy, S. 2000. Refugees want a humane deal. *Evening Chronicle*, 2 October.

Kennedy, S. 2002. Asylum group to set up base in the North East. *Evening Chronicle*, 24 October.

Khan, K. 2008. *Employment of Foreign Workers: Male and Female Labour Market Participation*. London: Office for National Statistics.

Kiwanuka, M. 2010. For love or survival: Migrant women's narratives of survival and intimate partner violence in Johannesburg, in *Gender and Migration: Feminist interventions*, edited by I. Palmary et al. London: Zed Books, 163–79.

Kostakopoulou, D. 2010. Matters of control: Integration tests, naturalisation reform and probationary citizenship in the United Kingdom. *Journal of Ethnic and Migration Studies*, 36(5), 829–46.

Kundnani, A. 2007. *The End of Tolerance: Racism in 21st Century Britain*. London: Pluto Press.

Kundnani, A. 2009. *Spooked! How not to prevent violent extremism*. London: Institute of Race Relations.

Kynaston, C. 1996. The everyday exploitation of women: Housework and the patriarchal mode of production. *Women's Studies International Forum*, 19(3), 221–37.

Kyriakides, C. and S. Virdee 2003. Migrant labour, racism and the British National Health Service. *Ethnicity and Health*, 8(4), 283–305.

Lawless, R. I. 1995. *From Taizz to Tyneside: An Arab community in the North-Easr of England during the early twentieth century*. Exeter: University of Exeter Press.

Lawrence, F. 2009. Union takes migrant worker fight to Tesco AGM. *Guardian*, 30 June.

Lenin, V. I. [1895–1916] 1972. *Philosophical Notebooks*. London: Lawrence and Wishart.

Lenin, V. I. [1909] 1970. *Materialism and Empirio-Criticism*. New York: International Publishers.

Lenin, V. I. [1916] 1975. *Imperialism, the Highest Stage of Capitalism*. Moscow: Progress Publishers.

Lenin, V. I. [1917] 1972. *The State and Revolution*. Moscow: Progress Publishers.

Lentin, A. 2004. *Racism and Anti-Racism in Europe*. London: Pluto Press.

Lepper, J. 2011. Barnardo's to run welfare services at centre for failed asylum seekers. *Children & Young People Now*. Available at: http://www.cypnow.co.uk/news/1059411/?DCMP=EMC-DailyBulletin [accessed: 29 March 2011].

Lewis, H. 2009. *Still Destitute: A Worsening Problem for Refused Asylum Seekers*. York: Joseph Rowntree Charitable Trust.

LEWRG London Edinburgh Weekend Return Group 1980. *In and Against the State*. London: Pluto Press.

Lindley, A. 2009. The early-morning phonecall: Remittances from a refugee diaspora perspective. *Journal of Ethnic and Migration Studies*, 35(8), 1315–34.

Local Government and Racial Equality Subcommittee. 1987. *Minutes 15th July 1987*. Newcastle upon Tyne: Newcastle City Council.

Locality. 2011. *Community Organisers*. [Online]. Available at: http://locality.org.uk/projects/community-organisers-2/ [accessed: 7 April 2011].

Lockley, H. 1975. New plan to help shy City immigrants. *Evening Chronicle*, 13 March, 13.

Loebl, H. 1978. Government-Financed Factories and the Establishment of Industries by Refugees in the Special Areas of the North of England 1937–1961, University of Durham. M.Phil.

Londra Gazette. 2011. Homerton Hospital cuts crisis. *London Turkish Gazzette*, 10 February.

Loraine, P. 2008. Protest in support of asylum seeker Rose. *The Journal*, 10 April.

Lorde, A. 1996. *The Audre Lorde Conpendium*. London: Harper Collins.

MacDermott, T. P. 1977. The Irish Workers on Tyneside, in *Essays in Tyneside Labour History*, edited by N. McCord. Newcastle upon Tyne: Department of Humanities, Newcastle upon Tyne Polytechnic.

Madden, K. 2009. Coordinated Portfolio Investment Survey, 2002 to 2007. *Economic and Labour Market Review*, 3(11), 16–23.

Manthorpe, J., J. Harris and S. Lakey. 2008. *Strategic Approaches for Older People from Black and Minority Ethnic Groups*. London: Better Government for Older People.

Marley, J. 2002. Race hatred fears are triggered by mosque. *Evening Chronicle*, 6 May.

Marley, J. 2003. Refugee groups fear a backlash. *Evening Chronicle*, 8 May.

Marx, K. [1857] 1973. *Grundrisse*. London: Penguin.

Marx, K. [1859] 1971. *A Contribution to the Critique of Political Economy*. London: Lawrence and Wishart.

Marx, K. [1894] 2006. *Capital, Volume 3*. London: Penguin.

Marx, K. and F. Engels [1845] 1956. *The Holy Family*. Moscow: Progress Publishers.

Marx, K. and F. Engels [1845] 1965. *The German Ideology*. London: Lawrence & Wishart.

Marx, K. and F. Engels [1845] 1991. *The German Ideology*. London: Lawrence & Wishart.

Mayer, M. 2003. The onward sweep of social capital: Causes and consequences for understanding cities, communities and urban movements. *International Journal of Urban and Regional Research*, 27(1), 110–32.

McDowell, C. 2005. Global displacement: The state and the refugee. *Open Democracy*, http://opendemocracy.net/globalization-institutions_government/refugee_2624.jsp. Available at: [accessed: 4 July 2007].

McGhee, D. 2003. Moving to 'our' common ground: A critical examination of community cohesion discourse in twenty-first century Britain. *The Sociological Review*, 51(3), 377–404.

McKegney, A. 1998. Probe into PC's race abuse claims. *Evening Chronicle*, 13 February.

McSpadden, L. A. 1998. 'I must have my rights!' The presence of state power in the resettlement of Ethiopian and Eritrean refugees, in *Power, Ethics and Human Rights: Anthropological Studies of Refugee Research and Action.*, edited by R. M. Krulfeld and J. L. MacDonald. Lanham: Rowman and Littlefield Publishers.

Miles, R. 1987. *Capitalism and Unfree Labour: Anomaly or necessity?* London: Tavistock Publications.

Miles, R. and M. Brown 2003. *Racism*. London: Routledge.

Miles, R. and A. Phizacklea 1980. *Labour and Racism*. London: Routledge and Kegan Paul.

Miles, R. and A. Phizacklea 1987. *White Man's Country: Racism in British politics*. London: Pluto Press.

Mills, J. and S. Robson 2010. Does Community Organising empower or oppress? *cdx magazine* (Winter 2010), 12–14.

Ministry of Health. 1940. *Memo. W.R.1. War Refugees*. London.

Mir, G. and P. Tovey 2003. Asian carers' experiences of medical and social care: The case of cerebral palsy. *British Journal of Social Work*, 33(4), 465–79.

Morison, J. 2000. The government-voluntary sector compacts: Governance, governmentality, and civil society. *Journal of Law and Society*, 27(1), 98–132.

Morris, L. 2007. New Labour's community of rights: Welfare, immigration and asylum. *Journal of Social Policy*, 36(1), 39–57.

Morrissens, A. and D. Sainsbury 2005. Migrants' social rights, ethnicity and welfare regimes. *Journal of Social Policy*, 34(4), 637–60.

Moya, J. C. 2005. Immigrants and associations: A global and historical perspective. *Ethnic and Migration Studies*, 31(5), 833–64.

Muhr, T. 2010. Counter-hegemonic regionalism and higher education for all: Venezuela and the ALBA. *Globalisation, Societies and Education*, 8(1), 39–57.

Mullard, C. 1973. *Black Britain*. London: George Allen and Unwin.

Nazroo, J. Y. 2006. Demography of multicultural Britain, in *Health and Social Research in Multiethnic Societies*, edited by J. Y. Nazroo. Abingdon: Routledge,

NBCWN National Black Carers and Workers Network. 2008. *Beyond We Care Too: Putting Black Carers in the Picture*. London: Afiya Trust.

NCIA. 2011. *Newsletter No. 20 March 2011*: National Coalition for Independent Action.

Neil, B. 2004. Backing for PC over race hate claims. *Evening Chronicle*, 13 February.

NERS. 2007. *North of England Refugee Service Annual Report 2005/2006*. Newcastle.

Newbigging, K., M. McKeown, E. A. Hunkins-Hutchinson, D. B. French, with Z. Habte-Mariam, L. Coleman-Hill, D. Mullings, A. Stephens and K. Holt. 2007. *Mtetezi: Developing mental health advocacy with African and Caribbean men*. London: Social Care Institute for Excellence.

Newcastle City Council. 1985. *Notes of Meeting Re: Vietnamese Community*. Newcastle upon Tyne.

Newcastle City Council. 1990. *Minority Ethnic Communities Survey 1990*. Newcastle upon Tyne.

Newcastle General Hospital. 1940–1962. *Student registers*. Newcastle upon Tyne.

Northern Echo. 1976. Black and white 'happy' along Tyne. *Northern Echo*, 7 August, 3.

ONS. 2006a. *Focus on Ethnicity and Identity: Labour Market*. Office for National Statistics. [Online]. Available at: http://www.statistics.gov.uk/cci/nugget.asp?id=462 [accessed: 28 October].

ONS. 2006b. *Focus on Ethnicity and Identity: Employment Patterns*. Office for National Statistics. [Online]. Available at: http://www.statistics.gov.uk/cci/nugget.asp?id=463 [accessed: 28 October].

ONS. 2008. *Employment of Foreign Workers: Focus on Earnings*. Office for National Statistics. London: Office for National Statistics.

ONS. 2009. *United Kingdom National Accounts: The Blue Book 2009*. Office for National Statistics. London.

OU. 1978a. *Professional and Non-Professional Roles 1*. Milton Keynes: Open University Press.

OU. 1978b. *Social Work in Practice 2*. Milton Keynes: Open University Press.

Palmary, I. 2010. Sex, choice and exploitation: Reflections on anti-trafficking discourse, in *Gender and Migration: Feminist interventions*, edited by I. Palmary et al. London: Zed Books, 50–63.

Palmer, S. 2008. Time to face the music. *Fight Racism! Fight Imperialism!* (201 February / March).

Parker, D. 2000. The Chinese takeaway and the diasporic habitus: Space, time and power geometries, in *Un/Settled Multiculturalisms – Diasporas, Entanglements, Transruptions*, edited by B. Hesse. London: Zed Books, 73–95.

Patel, B. and N. Kelley. 2006. *The Social Care Needs of Refugees and Asylum Seekers*. London: Social Care Institute for Excellence.

Pearce, J. L. 1993. *The Organizational Behaviour of Unpaid Workers*. London: Routledge.

Però, D. 2008. Political engagement of Latin Americans in the UK: Issues, strategies, and the public debate. *Focaal: European Journal of Anthropology*, 51, 73–90.

Però, D. and J. Solomos 2010. Introduction: Migrant politics and mobilization: Exclusion, engagements, incorporation. *Ethnic and Racial Studies*, 33(1), 1–18.

Petras, J. 2001. The geopolitics of Plan Colombia. *Monthly Review*, 53(1), 30–48.

Phillimore, J. and L. Goodson 2006. Problem or opportunity? Asylum seekers, refugees, employment and social exclusion in deprived urban areas. *Urban Studies*, 43(10), 1715–36.

Phillips, D. 2006. Moving towards integration: The housing of asylum seekers and refugees in Britain. *Housing Studies*, 21(4), 539–53.

Pina, K. 2007. Haiti and Latin America: It is as it always was. *Race and Class*, 49(2), 100–108.

Piper, N. 2010. Temporary economic migration and rights activism: An organizational perspective. *Ethnic and Racial Studies*, 33(1), 108–25.

Platt, L. 2007. *Poverty and Ethnicity in the UK*. Bristol: Policy Press.

Platt, L. 2009. Social activity, social isolation and ethnicity. *The Sociological Review*, 57(4), 670–702.

Plekhanov, G. V. [1898] 1940. *The Role of the Individual in History*. London: Lawrence and Wishart.

Policy and Research Services. 2002. *Towards a Fair Distribution of Asylum Seekers Across the Regions of the United Kingdom*. Newcastle upon Tyne: Strategic Support Directorate, Newcastle City Council.

Portes, A. 1998. Social capital: Its origins and applications in modern sociology. *Annual Review of Sociology*, 24, 1–24.

Prior, J. 2006. *Destitute and Desperate: A report on the numbers of 'failed' asylum seekers in Newcastle upon Tyne and the services available to them*. Newcastle upon Tyne: Open Door.

Psaroudakis, S. N. 2010. An arm hanging in mid-air: A discussion on immigrant men and impossible relationships in Greece, in *Gender and Migration: Feminist interventions*, edited by I. Palmary et al. London: Zed Books, 196–214.

Putnam, R. D. 2000. *Bowling Alone*. New York: Simon and Schuster.

Putnam, R. D. 2007. E Pluribus Unum: Diversity and community in the twenty-first century: The 2006 Johan Skytte Prize Lecture. *Scandinavian Political Studies*, 30(2), 137–74.

Rai-Atkins, A., with A. A. Jama, N. Wright, V. Scott, C. Perring, G. Craig and S. Katbamna. 2002. *Best practice in mental health: Advocacy for African, Caribbean and South Asian communities*. York: Policy Press.

Ramamurthy, A. 2006. The politics of Britain's Asian Youth Movements. *Race and Class*, 48(2), 38–60.

Rayne, T. 2003. Inter-imperialist rivalry: A fight of hostile brothers. *Fight Racism! Fight Imperialism!* (172 April / May).

Rayne, T. 2010. The Spending Review: The refined cruelty of the British bourgeoisie. *Revolutionary Communist Group*. Available at: http://www.revolutionarycommunist.org/index.php/fight-the-cuts/1945-the-spending-review-the-refined-cruelty-of-the-british-bourgeoisie- [accessed: 1 April 2011].

RCG, Revolutionary Communist Group. 1979. *The Anti-Nazi League and the Struggle Against Racism*. London: RCG Publications.

Redvers, L. 2003. Race-hate soaring in the North East. *Evening Chronicle*, 16 July.

Renton, D. 2007. *Colour Blind? Race and migration in North East England since 1945*. Sunderland: University of Sunderland Press.

Renton, D. 2008. Newcastle; city of migration. Available at: http://www.dkrenton.co.uk/newcastle.html [accessed: 15 April 2012].

Research and Information Services. 1999. *Rehousing of Minority Ethnic Communities*. Newcastle upon Tyne: Newcastle City Council.

Richmond, A. H. 2002. Globalization: Implications for immigrants and refugees. *Ethnic and Racial Studies*, 25(5), 707–27.

Roberts, C., S. Campbell and Y. Robinson. 2008. *Talking like a manager: Promotion interviews, language and ethnicity*. London: Department of Work and Pensions.

Roberts, D., Ed. 2011. *Reading the Riots: Investigating England's summer of disorder*. London, The Guardian.

Roberts, J. M. 2004. What's 'social' about 'social capital'? *British Journal of Politics and International Relations*, 6(4), 471–93.

Roberts, J. M. and F. Devine 2003. The hollowing out of the welfare state and social capital. *Social Policy and Society*, 2(3), 309–18.

Robinson, F. 1988. *Post-Industrial Tyneside: An economic and social survey of Tyneside in the 1980s*. Newcastle upon Tyne: Newcastle upon Tyne City Libraries and Arts.

RRF 2011. *Finding routes for Refugees to use their skills and experience and contribute to the North East region's economic future.* Gateshead: Regional Refugee Forum North East.

Sales, R. 2002. The deserving and the undeserving? Refugees, asylum seekers and welfare in Britain. *Critical Social Policy*, 22(3), 456–78.

Sassen, S. 1988. *The Mobility of Labour and Capital.* Cambridge: Press Syndicate of the University of Cambridge.

Sawbridge, M. and J. Spence 1991. *The Dominance of the Male Agenda – In community and youth work: The work experience of 42 women full-time community and youth workers in nine local authorities in the Northern Region.* Durham: University of Durham Department of Adult and Continuing Education.

Sawer, P. 2008. Black and Asian police line up race bias claims. *The Telegraph*, 13 July.

Saxton, A. 1990. *The Rise and Fall of the White Republic.* London: Verso.

Schuster, L. 2002. Asylum and the lessons of history. *Race and Class*, 44(2), 40–56.

Schuster, L. 2003. *The Use and Abuse of Political Asylum.* London: Frank Cass Publishers.

Schuster, L. and J. Solomos 1999. The politics of refugee and asylum policies in Britain: Historical patterns and contemporary realities, in *Refugees, Citizenship and Social Policy in Europe*, edited by A. Bloch and C. Levy. Basingstoke: MacMillan Press, 51–75.

Schuurman, F. J. 2003. Social capital: The politico-emancipatory potential of a disputed concept. *Third World Quarterly*, 24(6), 991–1010.

Shaw, M. and I. Martin 2000. Community work, citizenship and democracy: Re-making the connection. *Community Development Journal*, 35(4), 401–13.

Shukra, K. 1995. From black power to black perspectives. *Youth and Policy* (49), 6–18.

Silverman, S. J. 2011. *Immigration Detention in the UK.* Oxford: The Migration Observatory.

Sivanandan, A. 1974. *Race and Resistance – The IRR Story.* London: Race Today Publications.

Sivanandan, A. 1991. *A Different Hunger – Writings on Black Resistance.* London: Pluto Press.

Sjoberg, G. 1967. *Ethics, Politics and Social Research.* Cambridge: Schenkman Publishing Company.

Skellington, R. 1996. *Race in Britain Today.* London: Sage Publications.

Small, J. 2007. Rethinking and unravelling the interlocking dynamics of caribbean emigration and return, in *Revitalising Communities in a Globalising World*, edited by L. Dominelli. London: Ashgate.

Smith, E. and M. Marmo 2011. Uncovering the 'Virginity Testing' Controversy in the National Archives: The Intersectionality of Discrimination in British Immigration History. *Gender and History*, 23(1), 147–65.

Solomos, J. 1993. *Race and Racism in Britain*. Basingstoke: The MacMillan Press.

Solomos, J. and T. Rackett 1991. Policing and urban unrest: Problem constitution and policy response, in *Out of Order? Policing black people*, edited by E. Cashmore and E. McLaughlin. London: Routledge.

Sorensen, N. N. and K. F. Olwig, Eds. 2002. *Work and Migration: Life and livelihoods in a globalizing world*. London, Routledge.

Spalek, B. 2007. *Knowledgeable consumers? Corporate fraud and its devastating impacts*. London: Centre for Crime and Justice Studies, King's College London.

Special Committee as to Commonwealth Immigrants. 1966. *Minutes 19th September*. Newcastle upon Tyne: Newcastle City Council.

Steger, M. B. 2002. Social capital: Critical perspectives on community and 'Bowling Alone', edited by L. McLean et al. New York: New York University Press.

Stewart, E. 2008. Exploring the asylum-migration nexus in the context of health professional migration. *Geoforum*, 39, 223–35.

Stewart, H. and K. Hopkins. 2009. One in five black men out of a job figures reveal, and worse to come. *The Guardian*, 13 October.

Surman, W. 2008, 13 June. Government silent as food rots across the UK. [Online]. Available at: http://www.farmersguardian.com/government-silent-as-food-rots-across-uk/18435.article [accessed: 30 December 2009].

Tasse, A. 2007. Ethiopian Migration: Challenging Traditional Explanatory Theories, in *Revitalising Communities in a Globalising World*, edited by L. Dominelli. London: Ashgate.

Taylor, M. 2010. English Defence League: Inside the violent world of Britain's new far right. *The Guardian*, 28 May 2010.

Telang, S. D. 1967. *The Coloured Immigrant in Newcastle upon Tyne*. Newcastle upon Tyne: Newcastle City Council City Planning Department.

Temple, B., R. Moran, with, N. Fayas, S. Haboninana, F. McCabe, Z. Mohamed, A. Noori and N. Rahman. 2005. *Learning to Live Together: Developing communities with dispersed refugee people seeking asylum*. York: Joseph Rowntree Foundation.

The Journal. 1971. Immigrant checks tightened at airport. *The Journal*, 26 October.

The Journal. 1973. Coloured people 'must have say'. *The Journal*, 10 April.

The Journal. 1977. Five illegal migrants held. *The Journal*, 8 December.

The Journal. 1982. Tenants 'flee race attacks'. *The Journal*, 2 April, 3.

The Journal. 1986. Groups split in race row. *The Journal*, 15 April, 3.

The Journal. 1987. Groups call for citizenship cash. *The Journal*, 30 November.

The Shipyard 1936. Obituary: Charles Johnstone. *The Shipyard – The Works Magazine of Swan, Hunter, & Wigham Richardson, Ltd and Barclay, Curle & Co., Ltd*, 18(150), 10.

The Telegraph. 2009. How the Telegraph investigation exposed the MPs' expenses scandal day by day. *The Telegraph*, 15 May.

Therborn, G. 1980. *What Does the Ruling Class Do When It Rules? State apparatuses and state power under feudalism, capitalism and socialism.* London: Verso.

Townsend, M., M. Bright and T. Thompson. 2003. Inside the ranks of police racism. *The Observer*, 26 October.

Tran, M. 2008. Miliband admits US rendition flights stopped on UK soil. *The Guardian*, 21 February.

Turcotte, D. and L. Silka 2007. Social capital in refugee and immigrant communities, in *Race, Neighbourhoods and the Misuse of Social Capital*, edited by J. Jennings. New York: Palgrave MacMillan.

Tyne and Wear Archives 1939. Correspondence regarding Polish refugees arrived in the Tyne on the MS Piludski. Newcastle upon Tyne.

UKBA. 2005. *Contact management policy, process and implementation (CMPPI).* London: United Kingdom Borders Agency.

UN Security Council. 2002. *Final report of the Panel of Experts on the Illegal Exploitation of Natural Resources and Other Forms of Wealth of the Democratic Republic of the Congo.* New York: United Nations.

UN Statistics Division. *National Accounts Main Aggregates Database.* [Online]. Available at: http://unstats.un.org/unsd/snaama/dnllist.asp [accessed: 7 August].

UNCTAD. 2001. *World Investment Report.* United Nations Conference on Trade and Development.

UNCTAD. 2007. *World Investment Report.* United Nations Conference on Trade and Development.

UNCTAD. 2009. *World Investment Report.* United Nations Conference on Trade and Development.

Valtonen, K. 2008. *Social Work and Migration: Immigrant and refugee settlement and integration.* Farnham: Ashgate.

Van den Berghe, P. L. 1967. Research in South Africa: The story of my experiences with tyranny, in *Ethics, Politics and Social Research*, edited by G. Sjoberg. Cambridge: Schenkman Publishing Company,

Vertigans, S. 2010. British Muslims and the UK government's 'war on terror' within: Evidence of a clash of civilizations or emergent de-civilizing processes? *British Journal of Sociology*, 61(1), 26–44.

Vertovec, S. 2007. Super-diversity and its implications. *Ethnic and Racial Studies*, 30(6), 1024–54.

Vickers, T., G. Craig and K. Atkin 2012. *Research with black and minority ethnic people using social care services.* London: NIHR School for Social Care Research.

Vincent, T. 2005. GE: Imperialism at work. *Fight Racism! Fight Imperialism!* (188 December 2005 / January 2006).

VMDC Viraj Mendis Defence Campaign 1986. *Viraj Mendis Must Stay.* London: Larkin Publications.

VMDC Viraj Mendis Defence Campaign 1988. *Viraj Mendis Life or Death*. London: Larkin Publications.

Warren, M. R. 2009. Community organizing in Britain: The political engagement of faith-based social capital. *City and Community*, 8(2), 99–127.

Weber, M. [1904] 1949. Objectivity in Social Science and Social Policy, in *The Methodology of the Social Sciences*, edited by M. Weber. London: Free Press.

Wei, N. 2010. *Nat Wei's Blog: Observations on Social Reform, Big Society, and Shoreditch*. [Online]. Available at: http://natwei.wordpress.com/ [accessed: 16 September].

Welbourne, P., G. Harrison and D. Ford 2007. Social work in the UK and the global labour market: Recruitment, practice and ethical considerations. *International Social Work*, 50(1), 27–40.

Welford, G. 1988. Father wins battle to stay with his family. *The Journal*, 17 November, 9.

Whitaker, M. P. 2007. *Learning Politics from Sivaram: The life and death of a revolutionary Tamil journalist in Sri Lanka*. London: Pluto Press.

Whitaker, S. 2006. The UK international investment position. *Bank of England Quarterly Bulletin* (Q3), 290–96.

Wilkinson, M., G. Craig and A. Gaus. 2009. *Turning the Tide: How to best protect workers employed by gangmasters, five years after Morecambe Bay*. Oxford: Oxfam.

Williams, C. J. 2005. In defence of materialism: A critique of Afrocentric Ontology. *Race and Class*, 47(1), 35–48.

Williams, F. 1992. *Social Policy: A Critical Introduction*. Cambridge: Polity.

Williams, F. 1995. Race/ethnicity, gender, and class in welfare states: A framework for comparative analysis. *Social Politics*, 2(2), 127–59.

Williams, L. 2006. Social networks of refugees in the United Kingdom: Tradition, tactics and new community spaces. *Ethnic and Migration Studies*, 32(5), 865–79.

Williams, L. 2007. 'Home Alone', in *Revitalising Communities in a Globalising World*, edited by L. Dominelli. London: Ashgate, 255–70.

Williams, M., S. Palmer and G. Clapton 1979. Racism, imperialism and the working class. *Revolutionary Communist*, (9), 8–43.

Wilpert, G. 2007. *Changing Venezuela by Taking Power: The history and policies of the Chavez Government*. New York: Verso.

Wilson, R. and H. Lewis. 2006. *A Part of Society: Refugees and asylum seekers volunteering in the UK*. Leeds: Tandem Communcations and Research.

WLRI. 2005. *Women Refugees – From volunteers to employees: A research project on paid and unpaid work in the voluntary sector and volunteering as a pathway into employment*. London: Working Lives Research Institute.

Wood, S., B. Mayall and S. Oliver, Eds. 1999. *Critical Issues in Social Research: Power and prejudice*. Buckingham: Open University Press.

World dataBank. *World Development Indicators and Global Development Finance*. [Online]. Available at: http://databank.worldbank.org [accessed: 7 August 2010].

Yaffe, D. 2000. Globalisation: Parasitic and decaying capitalism. *Fight Racism! Fight Imperialism!*(158 December 2000 / January 2001).

Yaffe, D. 2006. Britain: Parasitic and decaying capitalism. *Fight Racism! Fight Imperialism!* (194 December 2006 / January 2007).

Yaffe, D. 2009a. Years and years of austerity ahead. *Fight Racism! Fight Imperialism!* (209 June / July).

Yaffe, D. 2009b. Britain's crisis: Public services under attack. *Fight Racism! Fight Imperialism!* (211 October / November).

Yaffe, D. 2010. Paying for the Crisis. *Fight Racism! Fight Imperialism!* (217 October / November 2010).

Yaffe, H. 2009. *Che Guevara: The Economics of Revolution*. Basingstoke: Palgrave MacMillan.

Yaffe, H. 2011. The Bolivarian Alliance for the Americas: An alternative development strategy. *International Journal of Cuban Studies*, 3(2 & 3), 128–44.

Yin, R. K. 2003. *Case Study Research: Design and Methods*. Thousand Oaks: Sage Publications.

Young, P. 1986. Race row blows up. *Evening Chronicle*, 18 September, 7.

Young, P. 1989. No – it's not all depressing. *Evening Chronicle*, 19 September, 10.

Young, P. 1999. We must be kept informed. *Evening Chronicle*, 8 December.

Zanotti, J. 2010. *U.S. Security Assistance to the Palestinian Authority*. Washington, DC.

Zetter, R., D. Griffiths, N. Sigona, D. Flynn, T. Pasha and R. Beynon. 2006. *Immigration, Social Cohesion and Social Capital: What are the links?* York: Joseph Rowntree Foundation.

Zontini, E. 2010. Enabling and constraining aspects of social capital in migrant families: Ethnicity, gender and generation. *Ethnic and Racial Studies*, 33(5), 816–31.

Author Index

Subject Index